MW01089190

DARING
TO SUCCEED

Editor: Agnès Saint-Laurent
Translator: Matthew Brown
Graphic Artist: Andréa Joseph [pagexpress@videotron.ca]
Reviser: Robert Ronald
Proofreader: Reilley Bishop-Stall

EXCLUSIVE DISTRIBUTOR:

For Canada and the United States:
Simon & Schuster Canada
166 King Street East, Suite 300
Toronto, ON M5A 1J3
Phone: (647) 427-8882
      1-800-387-0446
Fax: (647) 430-9446
simonandschuster.ca

Catalogue data available from Bibliothèque
et Archives nationales du Québec

10-16

Legal deposit: 2016
National Library of Québec
National Library of Canada

ISBN 978-1-988002-63-7

Conseil des Arts   Canada Council
du Canada   for the Arts

We gratefully acknowledge the support of the Canada
Council for the Arts for its publishing program.

We acknowledge the financial support of the
Government of Canada through the Canada Book
Fund for our publishing activities.

GUY GENDRON

DARING
TO SUCCEED

HOW **ALAIN BOUCHARD** BUILT THE
COUCHE-TARD & **CIRCLE K** CONVENIENCE STORE EMPIRE

JUNIPER
PUBLISHING
A Quebecor Media Corporation

Preface

It might seem strange to begin the preface of a book on Couche-Tard/Circle K by talking about Desjardins Group, which I chaired from 2008 to 2016. However, in 2013, the financial cooperative was about to carry out its largest acquisition in history by purchasing the Canadian activities of American mutual insurance leader, State Farm. At the time, I recommended that my management team meet the founders of Couche-Tard to benefit from their advice. Why would Desjardins—ranked by the Bloomberg agency as the second most solid financial institution in the world—have needed advice from convenience store owners before carrying out a transaction that would make it the third largest general insurer in Canada?

This book answers that question in a convincing and captivating way, by tracing the unlikely path of a man, Alain Bouchard, who had the audacity to succeed where nobody thought it possible. There is more involved in the international success of Couche-Tard/Circle K, an empire of 12,000 convenience stores and 100,000 employees, than work and determination. You will discover Bouchard's vision, method, discipline and, above all, perseverance, along with a capacity to face adversity, the intelligence to call himself into question and the courage to continuously reinvent himself. A healthy dose of these qualities was necessary from the get-go for Alain

Bouchard and his incredible partners Jacques D'Amours, Richard Fortin and Réal Plourde to build this constellation of convenience stores from scratch with a business model that made it one of the most innovative and efficient corporations in the world.

Their fascinating entrepreneurial story, told here by journalist Guy Gendron, demonstrates how a company is not merely a business plan. It is a living organism that represents the sum of the personal qualities, talents and values of the individuals who comprise it. They show their colours through the successes but especially the failures that cross their paths. Couche-Tard's life, as you will see, is not a long, slow-moving river. It is rather a series of rapids like the rushing waters of the Quebec North Shore that Quebecois ingenuity successfully mastered to become a world leader in clean energy.

No matter where their interests lie, whether in science, sports, culture or business, I am convinced that every reader will find in this captivating book a source of inspiration and motivation to take charge of their own life. They will feel the boldness to succeed, a boldness to go beyond borders and differences, to see the rest of the world as an opportunity to be seized instead of a threat to be feared, which is desperately needed in Quebec and the rest of the world.

Monique F. Leroux,
Chair of the Board, President and CEO
of Desjardins Group, 2008-2016
President of the International Co-operative Alliance
Chair of the Board of Investissement Québec

Foreword

In June of 2015, a new word appeared in the Oxford English Dictionary, the world's foremost reference for English vocabulary for more than 130 years. It told readers that the term "depanneur"—deprived of its acute accent (*dépanneur*)—was borrowed from Canadian French, and designated a "convenience store," also known as a "corner store."

It's no accident that the word originated in Quebec. The predominantly Francophone province has eight million inhabitants: it's an island in an ocean of 350 million Anglophones. The Quebecois descendants of the first European colonists— the French settlers of North America in the early 17th century— were forced to adopt defensive legislation in order to preserve their language and culture. One such law, aimed at promoting the presence of French, concerns the language of commercial signage. Even in predominantly Anglophone neighbourhoods, the use of English terms like "convenience store" is prohibited; the word *dépanneur* must be used in their place. And so, surrounded by *Dépanneur Sherbrooke* and *Dépanneur Drummond*, Anglophone Quebecers integrated the word into their contemporary language. They even created a diminutive: "the dep."

But of course, before English could borrow the word from French, the commerce it designated had to be invented. Combining a smoke shop, newspaper kiosk, grocery store, beer store, general store and takeout restaurant counter, the depanneur has had many incarnations over the last 35 years—ever since one man decided to make it his business and his life's work.

That man is Alain Bouchard. Strangely, his name isn't well known—even in Quebec, where he has always lived. He is, however, one of the wealthiest entrepreneurs in Canada, and one of the most celebrated by his peers on the planet. His multinational enterprise has more than 100,000 employees and tops close to CAD $50 billion (USD $35 billion) in sales. His story is that of the *self-made man*, someone who was driven by an idea that others thought was foolish: to reinvent the *second* oldest profession in the world—that of the local merchant—and then to create an industry made of a constellation of entrepreneurs. "At the time," says Réal Raymond, formerly a banker for Bouchard's company, "everyone around the table just laughed at him. The guy wanted to build a global empire of depanneurs. Think about it!"

The company he founded is called Alimentation Couche-Tard,[1] and it has its headquarters in…actually, it has no headquarters. The concept is verboten at Couche-Tard, because it suggests hierarchical superiority, a vertical line of decision-making authority that the founders reject. At Couche-Tard, says Alain Bouchard, "we are egoless." The company's administrative offices are "service centres," a term meant to reflect the organizational philosophy of the group. The staff working there is at the service of the stores, and not vice versa.

Alain Bouchard's personal office is on the ground floor, overlooking the building's parking lot. The panelled wood walls and ceilings that are typical of headquarters for directors

---

1. For brevity, we will simply use the name "Couche-Tard."

of businesses of this size are nowhere to be found. In their place are plasterboard walls and drywall panels. The only extravagant touch is a Bang & Olufsen sound system, a model from the last century. It's all explained by a point that Bouchard insists upon constantly: "We don't make a cent in these offices. The money is made in the stores." Having started from the bottom—working as a volunteer clerk in his brother's store—and having occupied every role, at least briefly, in that often thankless business, Bouchard repeatedly ended up frustrated at having to apply procedures—procedures that Bouchard saw as inadequate or even inhumane—handed down by a company's headquarters. Having spent so much time in the convenience store environment, he began to see that the clearest insights can sometimes come from the bottom rather than the top. Eventually, this would become a fundamental for his business: Each individual has to learn how to make their role meaningful. And another central tenet: May the best idea win.

Bouchard's disinterest in ego also means that many of the chains he has acquired around the world don't display the "Couche-Tard" banner. They've kept their original identity, or adopted that of other local chains, but they're nonetheless part of the Couche-Tard family. The company understood early on that its name would be hard to export. When Couche-Tard made its first foray outside Quebec, the legendary firm Berlitz was asked to translate the company's flyers. Couche-Tard's executives were later astonished to find that they had been transformed into...a towing company. The word "depanneur" still hadn't appeared in the *Oxford English Dictionary*, but the translators had found a definition in the *Larousse* French dictionary: An individual whose job was operating tow trucks. Thus, for a short time, *les dépanneurs Couche-Tard* became "Couche-Tard Towing."

*   *   *

Where did the neologism *"dépanneur"* originate? It comes from the verb *dépanner,* meaning "to repair." This word also has a metaphorical sense: "to *dépanner* someone" means "to render a service"—hence *dépanneur.* According to Bouchard, the neologism originated with Paul-Émile Maheu,[2] owner of a small grocery store in a popular Montreal neighbourhood in the 1970s. With his customer base dwindling due to the booming popularity of supermarkets—a trend that was spreading across the continent—Maheu decided to cut his staff, expand his range of products and extend his business hours, which were severely regulated for grocery stores at the time. This formula, later adopted by Bouchard and others, was such a success that today Quebec has the world's highest number of convenience stores per capita: one store per 1,200 inhabitants—three times more than the average in California, for example.

The main cause of this phenomenon is connected to the history of prohibition. Quebec was the only region in North America that never completely banned the sale of alcohol. Such a ban almost came to be, when in 1918 the provincial government passed a bill that would introduce full prohibition the following year. The outcry that ensued from this proposed measure forced the government to hold a referendum. The majority of Quebecers objected to the ban being applied to beer, wine and cider. Beer sales were thus relegated to independent grocers, giving these stores a powerful source of revenue—as shown by their proliferation, which reached far beyond what could be justified by food sale alone.

---

2.   His first store was in Montreal's Rosemont neighbourhood, at 2601 Saint-Zotique East.

* * *

Couche-Tard doesn't hold the title of largest convenience store chain in the world in terms of number of establishments—first place belongs to 7-Eleven, which is controlled by Japanese interests—but it's number one in terms of quality and profitability.

How did Alain Bouchard get where he is today? What's the recipe for his success? What are the values that propel this entrepreneur, who started from the bottom and who sees himself as guardian of the company's culture? These are the questions that this book will try to answer, by tracing the extraordinary and winding journey of a man who is inseparable from the company he built from the ground up with a small group of loyal associates.

CHAPTER 1

Biting into the Big Apple

September 25, 2003, New York

The city had just finished commemorating the second anniversary of the attack on the World Trade Center, the towers that had long symbolized the global dominance of American capitalism. The scars of the towers' destruction were far from being healed, as the clean-up work continued.

At 1 Liberty Plaza, a block away from the immense site, universally known as Ground Zero, life went on. Business did the same—even though the 54-storey building had suffered significant damage that raised doubts about the structure's integrity. In a vast room at the top of the skyscraper, the future of Couche-Tard was being decided. On either side of the table sat attorneys, young and old, all more or less interchangeable in appearance: impeccably dressed for their role as the gatekeepers of business acquisitions and mergers. They were the distinguished representatives of the ConocoPhillips oil company. The army of attorneys was flanked by clerks, stenographers and secretaries—at certain moments the team numbered more than 30. Their guests, given their limited number, occupied only the far end of the table. They consisted of one attorney, Michel Pelletier,[3] and his clients, two Canadian entrepreneurs who spoke English with a strong French accent:

---

3. Of the firm Davies Ward Phillips & Vineberg S.E.N.C.R.L LLP. A second attorney, Philippe Johnson, assisted, mainly behind the scenes.

Alain Bouchard, founder of Couche-Tard, and one of his partners, Richard Fortin, financial officer for the group.

It was common then for Quebecers, during the Labour Day long weekend at the beginning of September, to drive down to New York, a mere five- or six-hour jaunt from Montreal, to go shopping. Bouchard himself had never had the time for that kind of thing. Nearing his mid-fifties, this was his first time setting foot in New York City. The purchase he was attempting to negotiate, there in the very heart of Manhattan, was entirely different from a purchase the average Quebecer might have made. He was aiming to buy the Circle K chain, owned by ConocoPhillips; the bill would come out to more than a billion Canadian dollars. With this single deal, he would double the size of the company he had founded 25 years earlier, thereby creating one of the largest networks of convenience stores in North America, ahead of the oil giants Exxon and Texaco.

The trip had gotten off to a bad start the previous day. As soon as the trio arrived in New York, they went to their hotel at the south end of Central Park, where they planned to settle in until they closed the deal. At best, the process would take just a few days; more often than not, however, these negotiations dragged on for several weeks.

But there was a problem with the reservations. The standard rooms that the three men had planned to take were no longer available. As a courtesy, the establishment offered Richard Fortin, the first to arrive at the counter, a large deluxe room with a magnificent view of Central Park, for the price of a standard room. Then, Michel Pelletier was offered the same. "We were pretty happy about it," he recalls. "But when Alain Bouchard arrived—the president, the most important person in the group—there were no upgrades left!" In fact, he recalls, there was no reservation under his name. The receptionist offered the main shareholder and head of Couche-Tard an alternative. "We still have a small room, a tiny one, at the very back of the hotel," he said. "Otherwise, there is one lovely room still available—but it costs extra." Bouchard could enjoy the same luxury that his colleagues were offered, if he coughed up $600.

"Alain chose to take the broom closet," says Pelletier, who, feeling that the situation was awkward, insisted he trade rooms with Couche-Tard's president. "He refused. He said his room was good enough. He also pointed out that Richard and I would be the ones negotiating the next day, and he wanted us to be well-rested for our mission. He also told me, 'I would never pay that much for a room. It's the shareholders who would have to foot the bill.'"

Bouchard was worth hundreds of millions at the time, and was the main shareholder in Couche-Tard by a wide margin. But his principles hadn't changed. He was aware of the value of money—as is often the case for those who have faced a severe lack of it.

* * *

This trip to New York was the culmination of a project that had begun two years earlier. In 2001, Couche-Tard had devised a plan to buy a significant piece of the retail arm of American oil company Phillips Petroleum, whose acquisition game had been aimed at driving its growth in the Southern American states. But the approach had drawn attention from the United States Competition Bureau; the company had been ordered to divest itself of some of its assets. These included a number of gas stations coupled with convenience stores, but from Couche-

Tard's perspective, their number was insufficient. What was the point of extending so far, in geographical terms, from its Canadian base of operations, for a mere a handful of stores, with no chance of forming a significant network there?

This time around, however, things were looking brighter. Phillips Petroleum had merged with Conoco, another oil company, in 2002. The new entity, ConocoPhillips, encompassed close to 5,000 gas stations with convenience stores, from the Atlantic to the Pacific. These businesses were proving to be too much of a distraction for the company. Wanting to put its focus on production activities in which it saw more profit, ConocoPhillips intended to sell half of its stores: 2,200, scattered across the southern United States. Of these stores, 1,650 were wholly owned by the oil company, which operated them under the Circle K banner. The value of the Circle K buildings alone was huge—too huge. As a result, ConocoPhillips would offer the network for sale, piecemeal, hoping to end up with a better price at the end.

On Friday May 9, 2003, the oil company provided potential buyers with a booklet containing information about the company, its assets and liabilities, its sales and profits. Couche-Tard found itself in competition with some very big players, including huge investment funds—financial predators looking for opportunities to invest their fortunes, often in the short term. Couche-Tard's four partners and shareholders—president and founder Alain Bouchard, vice-president of administration Jacques D'Amours, financial officer Richard Fortin, and operating officer Réal Plourde—were very different, both in terms of their resources and in terms of their goal.

The four of them spent the weekend dissecting the confidential document to determine their best opportunity to pursue their expansion into the American market, with the goal of one day pulling off what they had already achieved in Canada: becoming the biggest. Should they buy the eastern portion, with Florida, Georgia and the two Carolinas? Or go for the prize jewel, Arizona, which alone had more than 500 stores? Or should they be California dreaming, aiming for that state, where real estate is expensive, but the economy is vibrant and the climate so inviting?

The following Sunday, the four arrived in Tempe, Arizona, a suburb of Phoenix and home of the Circle K headquarters. The next day they would be attending the formal presentation of the offer. That didn't leave them much time; but it was enough for them to do what they knew best. They went in person, incognito, and visited as many of the stores as possible. They wanted to gauge how the stores operated, to get a sense of their effectiveness and to form an idea of their performance potential if they were being run by the best around: the group themselves, the four leaders of Couche-Tard. Having arrived in Arizona on the eve of the presentation, the group spent all of Sunday on their project—a punishing day for the travellers from the north, with the temperature pushing 47 degrees Celsius (117°F), vastly hotter than the Quebec summer heat they were used to. At the end of their whirlwind tour, they concluded that Circle K had some serious problems. Excessive centralization, a significant technology gap, lack of maintenance, deficient training for staff, and much too high management costs. It was, in a word: perfect!

The next morning, the four partners agreed quickly. "We should take all of it," said Plourde—meaning all 2,200 stores—on one condition, of course. They had to be able to finance the acquisition. "I asked Richard, 'Can you find the money?' He simply answered, 'Can you run the business?'"

The answer to that was most certainly yes. The company's success had grown in leaps and bounds: More than once, Couche-Tard had doubled and even quadrupled in size, overnight. Its acquisitions both in Canada and in the United States had allowed it to develop a unique mode of operation that was simultaneously decentralized and integrated. The business had also thrived because its management team consisted of four men who had built it with their own hands—quite literally—and they had personally experienced what it's like to run a small store, with the successes and failures that this entailed. Each setback had brought their group closer together. Each challenge had made them stronger, more efficient, more impressive. Some competitors made the mistake of underestimating them due to their imperfect English despite the fact their families had been North Americans for generations. But these four men knew where they were going because they also knew where they were coming from.

CHAPTER 2

Life Before

The story of Alain Bouchard's life can be divided into two parts. "There was life before and life after," he says; a clear and precise divide between two distinct periods in his existence. You might think that the defining event would be the founding of his company, or that company being listed on the stock exchange, or one of his multi-million dollar acquisitions. But the change that affected him most deeply—essentially a kind of wound—took place much earlier, when he was only nine years old. Then, his father—Alain's idol—a tireless worker and a proud entrepreneur, was forced into bankruptcy; his wife, Rachel, and children were thrust into poverty.

Jean-Paul Bouchard's life hadn't been easy prior to that dark event. He was a man of his time and place: a Quebec that was largely rural. Public education was rudimentary, teaching the basics of reading and math. After finishing three years of elementary school, many—Jean-Paul included—would find themselves on the job market, ending up stuck working manual labour in the fields, forests, mines and factories of the province. Such was the state of things in that enormous northern country, which had so much geography and so little history, it was said.

Jean-Paul Bouchard, however, was ambitious. Through sheer perseverance and resourcefulness, he founded an excavation company specializing in the construction of logging roads in Chicoutimi, a town 200 kilometres (125 mi) north of the provincial capital of Quebec City.[4] The word "Chicoutimi" was taken from the language of the Montagnais, an Indigenous people who originally occupied the region and whose descendants live there still. The word means "end of the deep water," and designates the point where various tributaries of the mighty Saguenay River meet.[5] The region known as Saguenay–Lac-Saint-Jean, opened to colonization by French Jesuits in 1652, quickly became the hub of the fur trade in New France. Before long, more furs were being exchanged in Chicoutimi than at all the other Canadian trading posts combined—furs that would cover the shoulders of nobility and the elites of politics, business and the clergy throughout Europe. No other region of Quebec has such deep roots with the descendants of the first French colonists: French remains the mother tongue of 97 percent of the population of Saguenay–Lac-Saint-Jean.

After the British conquest of Canada in 1760, the region's economy came into the hands of Anglophone merchants, who took control of the fur trade and, later, the main resource: wood. Lac-Saint-Jean was surrounded by 100,000 square kilometres (38,600 mi^2) of virgin boreal forest at the time. The first sawmill was built there by Peter McLeod in 1810, powered by hydraulic energy from the Moulin River, whose name was taken from the mill (*moulin* is French for "mill").

It was in the Rivière-du-Moulin district, east of Chicoutimi, that Alain Bouchard was born, in the middle of winter in 1949.

---

4.   While the town of Chicoutimi is located at the same latitude as Paris—the 48th parallel north—the climate is resoundingly different. Winter precipitation often exceeds three metres (120") of snow, and temperatures can sometimes drop below -40 degrees Celsius (-40°F). The average annual temperature barely reaches 2.3 degrees Celsius (36°F).

5.   Saguenay is another name borrowed from the Montagnais, in 1535. The word, which means "water source," was used by the French explorer Jacques Cartier. For the Montagnais, the river, lined with steep cliffs, led to a mythical kingdom. The expression "Kingdom of Saguenay" has survived to this day, and is sometimes used to designate the region.

Alain Bouchard was the younger of two sons; his older brother was named Gilles. Two more children, Christiane and Nicole, were born to the family in the two years after Alain's birth. In that era, Quebec society was deeply imbued with Catholic values. Many aspects of life that are typically government responsibility—education, health and social services—were then controlled by the clergy. Until Quebec acquired a ministry of education in 1964, education in the province was provided exclusively by religious communities. Anyone who aspired to learn had a major advantage if their plan was to eventually join the religious orders—or if they had considerable financial resources at their disposal. Hospitals as well belonged to religious congregations, as did orphanages and asylums.

Under these circumstances, the practice of faith became a social obligation that was difficult to escape. "People, kneel down, await your deliverance," proclaims the song *Minuit chrétien*, a staple of Quebec's Christmas mass. The injunction was in line with the rigorous approach to Roman Catholicism preached by the Quebec clergy, particularly with respect to birth control: "Preventing family" was strictly prohibited, and teaching methods of birth control was even more emphatically forbidden. Seeing families with a dozen children was all-too common as a result. Some "lucky" families even had more than 20. This astonishing fecundity—Quebec was able to boast having the world's highest birth rate—also served a nationalistic purpose. The 60,000 French Canadians present at the time of the Conquest—citizens of the British Empire, now cut off from centuries of economic and cultural ties with France and inundated with waves of immigration that were primarily Anglophone—were engaged in a battle to keep their culture and their language alive. And the site of French Canadians' redemption, after the defeat of the French army to General Wolfe's British troops on the Plains of Abraham, would be in the bedroom. The phenomenon came to be known as *la Revanche des berceaux*—the revenge of the cradle.

* * *

Alain Bouchard remembers his early childhood as idyllic. His father's business ran smoothly: his career centred on the extraction of sand and gravel to build roads to support the forestry companies in the region.

With his family expanding, Jean-Paul Bouchard was able to buy his first home in the Bassin neighbourhood of Chicoutimi, an area near downtown that would be almost entirely destroyed in a flood 40 years later.[6] Jean-Paul's wife, Rachel Gagnon, whose seventh-grade education was higher than her husband's, helped out by taking care of the business books.

The 1950s was a period of great transformation in the region. At the beginning of the decade, Chicoutimi finally became connected to the rest of the world via a road that reached as far as Quebec City. Until that time, a boat was needed to leave the area. With that, 300 years of relative isolation for the residents of the "Kingdom of Saguenay" came to an end. But the intense forced isolation had instilled a strong sense of regional belonging, and had fostered a certain singularity.

---

6.   This extreme weather event, dubbed "the Saguenay flood," occurred from July 19 to 21, 1996. In some spots, 48 hours of rainfall were recorded, with 275 millimetres (11″) of rain, at a time when the reservoirs of the region's dams were already full. Overflowing rivers carried away houses, roads and bridges. The torrent eventually reached the downtown, destroying the Bassin neighbourhood, located at the confluence of the Chicoutimi and Saguenay rivers. Only a church and a small white house, later transformed into a museum, were spared. The flood killed 10, and resulted in the evacuation of 16,000 people and caused an estimated $1.5 billion in damages.

The Saguenay accent had its own particular intonations, and residents had the reputation of being a proud people—even arrogant, at times.

The success of Jean-Paul Bouchard's business was directly related to post-war economic growth in the United States and the voracious appetite of American newspapers for paper from Quebec's forests. Roads had to be built, post-haste, to access trees in increasingly remote places. This imperative eventually led a certain entrepreneur to grant Jean-Paul a lucrative contract, one that would finally make him prosperous. The agreement was finalized with a simple handshake: an honour-based agreement, as per a local custom whose traces are still present in the region where everyone seems to know one another.

To do the job, Jean-Paul acquired heavy new equipment that would allow him to clear trees. He got to work quickly, spending an entire winter carving out pathways through the dense forest. He did the same the following winter. But the entrepreneur continued to avoid paying for the work. "The entrepreneur declared bankruptcy, and so my father did as well. He lost everything," says Alain Bouchard. "I was nine when it happened. That was a turning point for me. From my perspective, as a child, there was life before and life after. The life when my father was an entrepreneur was a happy time. After my father lost everything, the happy time was over."

Eventually, Alain Bouchard would come to invent his own life. But at nine years old, he was dragged into his father's disappointments and frustrations. Dispossessed of his business and his home, Jean-Paul Bouchard was forced to take refuge near Baie-Comeau, on Quebec's North Shore, with his wife and their five children. A third son, Serge, had just been added to the family. Together they squeezed into a mobile home, the last refuge of the poorest workers.

His father had been scammed. He had been un-equipped to run his own business, and lacked the necessary counsel. He had poorly managed the debts owed to him, and he had been overconfident.

The young Alain would never forget the lesson he learned from the events that split his life in two.

It is said that the survival of humankind rests on two pillars—a mother's love and a father's protection. But it is equally true that it depends on a powerful lever to propel it forward (or, in some cases, to drag it backward): a son's desire to restore his parents' honour.

CHAPTER 3

The Price of Failure

If only Jean-Paul Bouchard could have started his life over, he might well have been able to succeed. The bankruptcy laws in that period, however, were merciless. He was chained to debts that would take him 10 years to repay. The entire family suffered the punishment. "Before, we would drink whole milk, with cream on the top," says Alain Bouchard. "After, it was powdered milk, and our meat was baloney. They were very hard years."

Uprooted from the city in which they'd grown up, the children found themselves living in a cramped mobile home far from their friends. Their father was gone from the morning till late at night, seven days a week, forced to work two mechanic jobs, in garages in Baie-Comeau and Haute-Rive. He found a better job later on, with higher pay, in the remote mines of Wabush and Labrador City. He would leave for two or three months at a time, abandoning his wife and children. It was all too much; their mother was unable to cope. Not long after her sixth child, Suzanne, was born, Rachel suffered a serious depression and lost touch with reality. The crash had been too brutal; everything they had built was crumbling. In Chicoutimi, she had had her own car, a Cadillac. Now the family drove an old wreck, as ragged as their lives—her life—had become. The only solution was to commit her to a psychiatric institution. The closest option, Saint-Michel-Archange de Québec hospital (better known under its previous name, l'Asile, meaning "the Asylum"), was a few hundred kilometres from the family home.

How long would it take for her to heal? When would she be returning home? No one could answer these questions, to which the children constantly pleaded for answers. Another question was more pressing: How could the family endure her absence when the father was away working from morning until night, and there were six children in the home, including a newborn baby? The oldest daughter, Christiane, was barely 10 years old. Nevertheless, she had no choice but to sacrifice her own education, quitting school to become the surrogate mother for that lost tribe, stranded in the snow-covered woods.

* * *

In the spring of 1960, a wind of change was blowing across Quebec; a hope for renewal. The province had been governed for almost 15 years by Premier Maurice Duplessis, leader of the Union Nationale. Duplessis could be simultaneously charming, authoritative and demagogic. His conservative and somewhat regressive ideas had made him a close ally of the industrialists and the Catholic clergy. Indeed, his death, in 1959, marked the end of a period that had taken on a sinister descriptor: the "Great Darkness." The election on June 22, 1960, gave promise of a new era. The electoral slogan of the main opposition party, the Liberal Party, captured the general feeling of the time: *C'est le temps que ça change* ("Time for a change").

Alain Bouchard had just turned 11 when he was hired to distribute election flyers door to door for the *"l'équipe de tonnerre"* ("the terrific team") led by the Liberals' Jean Lesage, who promised to lead Quebec on the road to modernity. The Liberal Party's campaign headquarters were near Alain Bouchard's home, and the boy was invited to participate in the historic moment, being offered a Coca-Cola in exchange for his services. It would be the only political activism he ever engaged in; undoubtedly it was more a result of circumstances than of his personal beliefs.

Alain Bouchard had no idea at the time, but the Liberal victory to which he had modestly contributed would have significant consequences for his and his family's future. As soon as they were elected, the Lesage government began to push for extensive social and economic reforms. One of the most ambitious reforms, spearheaded by the fiery René Lévesque, a former star journalist with CBC who then became minister of Natural Resources, proposed to nationalize the power generation companies, which were exploiting Quebec's immense wealth of water power and dividing the province's market geographically. With the increasing demand for energy due to rapid industrial development, Quebecers, René Lévesque argued, should use this abundant and renewable natural resource, which belonged to everyone, to gain a competitive advantage. The state-owned corporation Hydro-Québec would produce and sell affordable electricity, drawing new business to the province. The organization would certainly be capable of accomplishing this task: It was already building the biggest dams on Earth, on the North Shore (Côte-Nord) near Baie-Comeau.

However, no consensus had yet been reached on the project of nationalizing the existing hydroelectric power stations. The business community was strongly opposed. The banks, acting as a syndicate—the group was essentially a private club for Montreal Anglophones—formed a united front to block the economic venture that was sailing toward them on a wave of hope for national autonomy.

"Maîtres chez nous" ("Masters of our own house") proclaimed Quebec Premier Jean Lesage, as he proposed his plan to Quebec voters during an early election in 1962. This rallying cry served as a wake-up call, jolting Francophone Quebecers

into standing up for their national identity. With little education and a sizeable population, French-speaking Quebecers
represented a pool of cheap labour for Anglo-Saxon industrialists in North America and their ever-increasing textile and
shoe manufacturing plants. The work, repetitive and poorly
paid, is relegated today to so-called developing countries, the
world's new repositories of poverty. It was Quebec that had the
dubious honour of filling the role in North America during
that time.

The average salary of Francophone men—that of women
was so low it isn't even worth mentioning—was just 52 percent
of the average for Anglophone men, regardless of whether the
latter were bilingual or spoke only English. Francophone
Quebecers earned merely half the income of their Anglophone
neighbours. In this province of then four million inhabitants,
more than 85 percent were Francophone[7], but 83 percent of
the managers and administrators were Anglophone. These
Anglophones were able to live in the province without speaking the language of the majority. Incredibly, in fact, a federal
investigation commission[8] showed that unilingual Anglophones
even had a higher income than bilingual Anglophones. Thus
the highest rank on the scale of income went to citizens of
British origin; French Canadians came in a miserable 12th.
Only Canadians of Italian origin and Indigenous peoples
were worse off in terms of average income. It would be tempt-
ing to attribute this to the lag Francophones suffered in terms
of education. But no: The commission showed that even at an
equal level of education, French Canadians had a lower income

---

7.   Half a century later, in 2015, Quebec has 8 million inhabitants, 78 percent of
      whom are native French-speakers.
8.   The Royal Commission on Bilingualism and Biculturalism was instituted in 1963
      by the government of Canada. It was also known as the Laurendeau-Dunton
      Commission, after its two co-chairs, André Laurendeau and Davidson Dunton.

than any other linguistic group, a situation that had only worsened after the 1930s.

* * *

Alain Bouchard was just entering adolescence when the *Maîtres chez nous* battle was shaking Quebec. He was facing more pressing problems in his own life. He still has heartbreaking memories of visits to the Saint-Michel-Archange psychiatric hospital in Quebec City, where his mother was held for two years, and where she was given "care" in the form of ice baths. When that treatment failed to cure her depression, the doctors considered giving her a lobotomy; she barely escaped the treatment. Each of Alain's visits were the same, and ended with her pleading. "She would say, 'Alain, get me out of here.'" He had to explain that there was nothing he could do, that he would love to bring her home with him but that he didn't have the authority to discharge her from the hospital. When he returned home, he would beg his father, trying to convince him that the children could take care of her far better than the so-called doctors at Saint-Michel-Archange.

But it was impossible. The father knew full well that he couldn't bring his wife into their mobile home, pushing their number to eight, only to abandon her for months when he went off to a work site. It would just pull them all back into the nightmare they had lived through before.

The lives of the Bouchard children were structured as well as could be with a mother in the hospital and an absent father. During his brief stays back home, Jean-Paul Bouchard would take them on an activity that left a deep impression. After they piled into his old car, the family embarked on driving tours of businesses of the region: garages, hardware stores, restaurants, trailer parks. Jean-Paul nurtured a single dream in his heart: to enter the business world once again. His children, brought along on these strange adventures, would see first-hand his yearning to find his way back to that road, that pathway to restoring his dignity.

The unusual team would disembark, arrive unannounced abruptly and begin to examine the premises and question the owner about his or her revenue, traffic levels, the price of rent, inventory, employees and their wages, profit margins and sales prices. Then their father, who had only a third-grade education and had trouble with basic math, would turn to his son Alain. "He would say, 'Alain, do the totals,'" Alain Bouchard recalls. Though the boy was just 12 years old, his father was conferring on him, symbolically at least, the responsibility of understanding the workings of a business, of identifying ways to alter the variables and increase profits. The task became deeply connected with having enough food on the table, restoring his father's honour and lifting his mother's spirits. It was the dream of returning to the life they had led before the tragedy. It would be hard to overstate the invisible weight carried by this exercise of mental calculation or the profound impression it would make on him.

Jean-Paul Bouchard wanted to get his life back on track; what he ended up doing instead was laying a path for his children: "He put it into our heads that it was better to work for yourself. We all took that in." Each of them would later become an entrepreneur, his or her own boss. But none would match the success of Alain Bouchard, who, 50 years later, would be one of the richest businessman in Quebec. His father, however, had predicted a different destiny for him. "He told me, 'You're going to be my engineer.' He wanted me to become an engineer because he had always worked on construction sites."

In Jean-Paul Bouchard's world, engineers were the most educated people; the ones who gave the orders. Moreover, their future was secure, thanks to the great increase of hydroelectric, mining and industrial sites on Quebec's North Shore.

*　*　*

Jean-Paul Bouchard hadn't taken mechanical courses. He had learned his trade by himself while repairing the fleet of vehicles for his road construction company. He may have lacked a diploma, but he had made a name for himself and built a reputation as a dedicated and tireless worker. It allowed him to obtain a good position at Hydro-Québec, doing maintenance and repairs on hydraulic machinery at various "Manic" work sites.[9]

The new job forced the family to move even farther north, to Micoua, a temporary work camp established in the middle of the forest along highway 138, which connected Manic-2 and Manic-5. The improvised village, doomed to vanish when work was finished, housed several hundred workers who stayed in basic trailers, often with their families.

Micoua had no main road, and its only commerce was a grocery store that resembled a general store. Nonetheless, Alain Bouchard says it was a pleasant place to stay. Life was simple, and carried a sense of freedom. "I loved it. I discovered

---

9.　Several hydroelectric plants were built along the Manicouagan River. Construction on Manic-5 (later renamed Daniel-Johnson Dam), which long remained the largest multiple-arch dam in the world, began in 1959 and ended in 1970. Its enormous 2,000-square-kilometre (772 mi^2) reservoir is visible from space, and was dubbed "the eye of Quebec" due to its unique shape. Indeed, it spans a depression made by one of the biggest meteors to hit the Earth; hence its spherical appearance. Other major dams built on that turbulent river include Manic-2, whose power station was commissioned in 1965. It was named Centrale Jean-Lesage in honour of the man who served as premier of Quebec from 1960 to 1966.

fishing and nature," he says. It was while the family was living there that his mother's long exile finally came to an end and she was able to return to the fold.

Conversely, this was also the moment when the oldest children had to leave for months at a time to study away from home, since there were no high schools nearby. And so, at the age of 15, Alain Bouchard went to study at Monseigneur-Taché school in Rivière-du-Loup, on the South shore of the St. Lawrence River, a few hundred kilometres from Micoua. He stayed in Foyer-Patro, a boarding school run by priests. Still, these were good years for him; he enjoyed the curriculum. When classes ended in June, he returned to Micoua, where he took his first steps into the depanneur trade.

His mother had found an ingenious way to help make ends meet: Every morning she made sandwiches that her son, Alain, would sell to the workers at nearby sites. They also offered sodas, which they bought at wholesale prices so they could maximize profits. Alain's first two summers in Micoua were therefore divided between this work in the morning, and spending the afternoons fishing with his friends in the well-stocked rivers of the region.

Although they lived at a distance from the modern world, the boys were not cut off entirely. Chubby Checker brought the world the twist. Elvis Presley brought rock 'n' roll. The Beatles arrived in North America and brought their pop songs. Their driving beat was propelled by the group's drummer Ringo Starr. Envisioning himself in the same role, Alain Bouchard bought a drum kit. He also dipped further into his savings to fund his friends so they, too, could buy instruments. Alas, the musical endeavour proved to be short-lived.

At the age of 16, he took a more stable summer job at a general store at one of the hydroelectric sites. It sold everything, from groceries to clothes to guns. It was an enviable position for a student, but Alain Bouchard felt it couldn't last. He still hadn't completed his preparatory courses for post-high school studies; but what was the point of taking them? His father wanted him to become an engineer, but he didn't have the money to enrol in university. As for his own wishes, Alain Bouchard would have liked to study management or business—but that seemed like just another crazy idea. So what, then? A job working on construction sites? Everyone in his social group dreamed of working for Hydro-Québec. He didn't share their dream. "I knew there was no future for me on the North Shore. Above all, I wanted to start my own business. That was the only thing on my mind. I told myself, I'm going to go to Montreal, I'm going to make a lot of money and I'm going to start my own business." In short: all he had to do was invent his life.

CHAPTER 4

Discovering a Career

Alain Bouchard arrived in Montreal in 1967.[10] The city was set to be the site of the International and Universal Exposition or World's Fair Expo 67, which would attract more than 50 million curious visitors, eager to discover the world, tantalizingly displayed in pavilions from 60 countries. But the young man of 18 was not among these visitors. For him, exploring Montreal, admiring its skyscrapers (the tallest in any Commonwealth country) and taking in the vibrant life of the city was enough of a dazzling spectacle. How would this young man—wandering through the streets with his nose in the air, looking like the country-born tourist that he indeed was—find his place in a city that seemed inconceivably vast, a city he knew absolutely nothing about?

Alain Bouchard had never read a newspaper before he set foot in Montreal. There simply hadn't been any around the home when he was growing up. Some of the biggest upheavals of the century had therefore totally passed him by. The world was churning, unmoored by national independence movements, and by a struggle between East and West, which was playing out both in space and on Earth, particularly in Vietnam. In the United States, revolution was brewing among African-Americans, and the baby boomers dreamed of changing the

---

10. Montreal is the second largest city in Canada, and the most vibrant. Toronto, capital of the province of Ontario and the country's financial hub, was and remains the city with the largest population in Canada.

world. In Quebec, the social and political transformation taking place since the dawn of the 1960s became known as the Quiet Revolution. The name referred to the rapidity with which old customs and institutions were being overturned, released from the tutelage of the Catholic Church, to make way for the building of a modern secular state.

The "revolution," however, was not always quiet. In 1963, a number of desperate young idealists, supporters of political independence for Quebec, began to take action. Inspired by national liberation movements in Africa and South America, they adopted the same methods: bombings and other sensationalistic actions. The Front de Libération du Québec (FLQ) borrowed part of its name from the National Liberation Front (NLF), the organization which had allowed Algeria, formerly a French colony, to seize its independence in 1960.

Paying little attention to these larger debates, Alain Bouchard's personal independence was an urgent priority: He needed to find lodging, and a job to support himself. He took a small apartment on Saint-Germain Street, in a working class neighbourhood east of downtown Montreal, and quickly found a job in a cookie factory nearby. Montreal had the peculiarity of being geographically and demographically divided—almost surgically at the time—by a line of demarcation. To the east were Francophones; to the west, Anglophones. And caught in the middle, as though unable to choose one side or the other, was the long straight artery of Saint Lawrence Boulevard, also known as The Main, home to Chinese, Portuguese, Greek, Jewish and Italian neighbourhoods.

Having no knowledge of English, incapable of holding the briefest conversation in that language—the mastery of which was required by many Montreal employers, mainly for roles involving administration, finance, services and commerce—

Alain Bouchard was limited to menial work that held little interest for him: transporting cookie trays to the employees responsible for packaging the treats.

The task didn't require much in the way of thought, but it had one great advantage for a single young man: The workers in charge of packaging were all female, and most of them were young. Thus it was a matter of some consternation for him when he found out he was being promoted to the shipping department, cutting off his contact with the young ladies. Despite the salary boost the position provided, he decided to quit the factory for another with a predominately female staff: a clothing manufacturer. Once again, his intellectual abilities were not what led to him being hired. During the job interview, the supervisor selected him after comparing the size of his biceps against that of another candidate. They were looking for a man capable of lifting heavy spools with his arms, to feed the noisy mechanical weavers.

*　*　*

Alain Bouchard wasn't distanced from his family for long. A few months after he arrived in Montreal, his father decided to try his luck in the city as well, bringing his wife and children along. "He hitched the trailer to his delivery truck and found a spot to park it in Laval, on some land a farmer was renting." Laval, long described as Montreal's bedroom community, is now the third largest city in Quebec. At the time, it was a vast enclosure of agricultural land intended for residential and commercial development, while the city of Montreal attracted office towers and factories. Jean-Paul Bouchard's skills in mechanical hydraulics would be in high demand there.

Gilles, the eldest son of the Bouchard family, decided to go into business, and bought a franchise located near Laval: a grocery store attached to a dairy. The formula had been created 15 years earlier in Ontario with the Becker's chain. Becker's was a network of convenience stores specializing in the sale of homemade dairy products. The dairy, owned by a Canadian businessman of Greek origin, Frank Bazos, essentially created its own distribution network. The idea was based on the vertical integration model used by major oil companies, which have their own gas stations.

In Quebec, Robert Bazos, another member of the family, had undertaken to reproduce this concept starting with a dairy located in Laval. In a stroke of marketing genius, he named the chain, Perrette.[11] At that time, all Quebec Francophones had grown up hearing the 17th-century fable by Jean de La Fontaine *The Milkmaid and her Pail*. Many had had to memorize it in school, an exercise that had little use in itself, but that had the advantage of occupying students for hours. The story begins like this: "Perrette, having a pot of milk on her head…" thus Francophone Quebecers naturally associated the name Perrette with milk products.

Robert Bazos also had the idea to sell milk in reusable plastic containers. Rather than throwing them out after using them and losing the value for the deposit, clients had a reason to return their milk jugs to Perrette—the only distributor of the brand—and buy a new one. With this tactic, Bazos secured the loyalty of his customers, while hoping that they would also buy other products, like cigarettes or newspapers.

Perrette stores also took advantage of an exception in the law regulating opening hours for stores. Most, including grocery

---

11. The first Perrette store in Quebec opened its door in 1961. Four years later, the chain had some 40 establishments.

store chains, had to close their doors at 6 p.m., Monday through Saturday. On Sunday—the Lord's day—the general rule was that all commercial activity must cease. Some, such as gas stations, were exempt from these restrictions because they provided a basic necessity. The same principle allowed small independent grocery stores to continue to serve their clients late into the evenings and on Sundays, but only for the sale of bread, milk, butter and eggs—fresh ingredients that families could easily end up needing at the last minute. Strangely, cigarettes were on the list of products authorized for sale in the evening, no doubt in early recognition of the addiction they create.

To stay within the constraints, grocery stores that wanted to keep their business open after 6 p.m. had to have a curtain that blocked access to part of their establishment where the other items were found—those deemed non-essential and prohibited for sale in the evening. Many grocery stores chose to abstain; others had opening schedules that varied. Perrette stores were among the first to adopt the strategy to distinguish themselves from traditional grocery stores. Customers knew that they were open seven days a week, late into the evening— that they would be there when one needed them. These grocery stores laid the foundation for the depanneur concept.

* * *

Paradoxically, La Fontaine's fable, which inspired Robert Bazos, is a moral lesson on the illusions of entrepreneurship. It depicts a milkmaid, Perrette, who goes to market to sell her milk, daydreaming about how much money she will make there. She dreams of investing in the family farm, and sees herself raising many animals. Carried away by these great ambitions, she neglects to watch where she's going, stumbles and spills her bucket of milk. "Good-bye calf, cow, pig... Her fortune spread out before her." La Fontaine closes by observing that all humans, rich or poor, tend to build "castles in Spain," to dream that "All the riches of the world are ours." But each of us should be aware that an accident could come about, leaving us "Gros-Jean as before."[12]

Alain Bouchard didn't exactly spill the milk, but he wasn't that far off. The clothing factory where he worked had been rather negligent in terms of employee training. He was required to handle equipment that he didn't know how to operate correctly. Thus, unsurprisingly, he was injured one day while loading one of the machines as it was running. The needles pierced his hand and stitched into one of his fingers; the injury forced him to miss work for a few days. With his sore hand covered in bandages, it was impossible for him to carry the heavy spools of thread. Another painful lesson awaited him when he returned. "When I came back to work, I had been fired," he says.

Without an income, without a job, Alain Bouchard had no choice but to leave his apartment and go back to live in his parents' trailer. His new status: *Gros-Jean comme devant.*

*   *   *

Jean-Paul Bouchard managed to get his son Alain taken on as an apprentice in the construction company he worked for, which specialized in concrete foundations for industrial and

---

12. In French, Gros-Jean; in Old French, the expression "être Gros-Jean" means "to be an idiot." The phrase "Gros-Jean comme devant" ("Gros-Jean as before"), made famous by La Fontaine, means that after her adventure, Perrette would find herself back at square one.

commercial buildings. It didn't take long for the young man to discover that working in the mud and the cold at construction sites early in the morning wasn't for him. "I was careless, I had bad relationships with the other workers. I hated it." Jean-Paul Bouchard saw clearly that his son, for whom he held such high hopes, was not in his element. He told him again and again that the important thing in life is to "make a name for yourself," and that there was only one way to do this: through hard work. Alain should follow his older brother's example, he said. Gilles and his wife devoted themselves utterly to their Perrette store, taking care of all the necessities morning until night, seven days a week.

The couple desperately needed a helping hand to give them some breathing room. "That's where my adventure really started," says Alain Bouchard. He was 19 when he decided to help his older brother out and started replacing him behind the counter at the store, without pay, a few evenings a week or on the weekend. "I did it to help my brother, but I really enjoyed it!" he says. He savoured the direct contact with customers, and above all, discovered a natural talent for interior design. He thought the store should be attractive, clean, and should display the products effectively. He took advantage of the evenings, when there were fewer customers, to reorganize the shelves.

Bouchard also took liberties with the strict rules set out by the owner, Robert Bazos. Perrette stores basically acted on the dealership principle. His brother Gilles didn't own any of it: neither the building nor the store nor even the merchandise for sale. It was all the property of Perrette. The storekeeper had merely the right to run the store and was responsible for hiring and paying employees. In exchange, Perrette gave the dealership a percentage of the sales. It was thus prohibited for the storekeeper to sell any products in the store that were not provided by Perrette management. But Alain Bouchard had an entrepreneurial spirit, and he took advantage of his shifts behind the counter to offer customers snacks that he had bought wholesale, as he had done with soda at Manic construction sites. It was a way to make his volunteering profitable—but it was completely contrary to the company's rules.

In July of 1969, while he was on his annual vacation, Alain Bouchard had taken over the store for his brother so that the storekeeper could take some vacation time for himself. A Perrette supervisor came in just as the young man was reorganizing the shelves. "So you're the one who makes the store look so good?" the supervisor asked him, and promptly offered him the responsibility of organizing the interior of new stores. It was an attractive offer—but salaries in the construction industry were also attractive. Alain Bouchard was earning $3.30 an hour on the construction sites. Perrette was offering $1.50 an hour, which was less than half that. "However, I asked him, 'Can I work as many hours as I want?'" says Bouchard. "No problem," was the supervisor's response.

Having a 20-year-old's energy made all the difference, he says. To make the equivalent wages, he would simply have to work twice as many hours per week; but he would be doing something he actually enjoyed. It would finally allow him to fulfill what his father had taught him: The important thing in a man's life is to make a name for himself through work. Alain Bouchard threw himself into the job with an extraordinary ardour. "I really clocked some hours. It was ridiculous. I was working 80 hours a week," he says.

* * *

His arrival at Perrette coincided with a change to the law concerning opening hours for stores. Small independent grocers would be allowed to stay open later in the evening, with no restrictions on the products they could sell to their clients. That would give them a competitive advantage over major grocery chains, whose doors had to close at 6 p.m. For small independent grocery stores, selling milk and cigarettes, which had sometimes justified their staying open in the evening, was one thing; the new opportunity to sell all the products in their grocery store in the evening—especially beer, which Quebecers consumed, and still consume, in vast quantities—was a big step forward.

"It was a gold rush," says Alain Bouchard.

During the years that followed, Alain Bouchard opened Perrette stores at lightning speed. As soon as a suitable location was found for a franchise, he was given two weeks to design the store, paint it, install coolers, shelves and counters and arrange merchandise. Nothing could get in the way of him attending opening day for each store, which always took place on a weekend. "I loved that moment. You could feel the excitement of everyone waiting outside before the doors opened." The energy was that much higher when Perrette promised a complimentary milk jug to the first 500 clients and granted specials on other products, to promote the full range of their offerings.

The company grew so quickly that Perrette often opened new stores before it had even found managers to run them. It was Alain who was given the job in the interim, but never for long, since he was the sole specialist when it came to openings. The supermarkets watched the growth of the blue-and-white-signed stores with a mixture of astonishment and amusement. "Everyone was laughing at them," said Gaétan Frigon, who headed a number of grocery store chains in Quebec over the decades. "It was a company that wanted to sell milk, period." To his mind, Perrette stores were marginally more menacing than the small corner grocers that had developed anarchically, transforming the living rooms of their apartments into stores.

When the rate at which new stores were opening finally started to slow down after two years of frantic rush, Alain Bouchard was asked to become an occasional replacement manager, sometimes following a hasty departure or to fill an unexpected absence. He agreed, on one condition: that he would be assigned replacement positions outside the Montreal region, since that would allow him to make more money. He planned to marry the following year, and even though he was still living in his parent's trailer, he wasn't succeeding in saving money as quickly as he had hoped. No one could accuse him of not working hard enough, however. He worked 84 hours a week, in seven 12-hour shifts. When he ended up going out-side of Montreal he was given a lump sum, on top of his hourly wage, to cover his daily expenses for food and lodging. He had negotiated the amount: $35 for a hotel and meals. But he actu-ally sometimes spent as little as $8 per day. "I was living in a hole, basically, a rat hole. I would buy a can of tuna to make a sandwich, and that would do me."

Using this strategy, he doubled his salary. But it came at quite a cost. He had been one of the key players in the growth of a dynamic company that had made a fortune for Robert Bazos and provided the latter with a home in the swanky Town of Mount Royal neighbourhood. And still Alain Bouchard had to divide his time between his parents' trailer and the "rat hole," while working 84 hours a week, all just to try to make a decent income. Something was wrong with the equation. He felt like one of Pierre Vallières' "White Niggers of America."

Vallières, a founding member of the FLQ, wrote the book of the same title while he was in prison in New York. The book drew a parallel between the socio-economic situation of African-Americans and that of Francophone Quebecers. "There was a lot of truth in it," says Bouchard.

Not speaking English, Bouchard instinctively shared the feeling of injustice that inspired his French-speaking compatriots, their desire to defend the use of their language at work and on commercial signage. While he was troubled by the social turmoil of the time, he also felt inspired by the winds of revolution that were blowing. Working conditions at Perrette, the lack of respect given to employees, were a daily reminder of the injustice he wanted to rebel against. It reached the point where he dreamed of quitting his job to "help others"—maybe become a social worker, get involved in fighting for justice. But in what capacity? And to do what exactly? He had no particular training in that sphere.

Bouchard finally convinced himself that the best way to contribute lay elsewhere. He had to harness the talents he had been blessed with to help move society forward. "I'm an entrepreneur at heart, in everything I do," he says. He couldn't overcome the instinct, which at times seemed to verge on compulsion. The tours of businesses with his father long ago, with the hope of climbing back to a state of dignity and happiness, had left a deep mark. It was like an unquenchable thirst. His mind was constantly working, doing calculations, everywhere he went. "When I go into a restaurant, I count the number of seats and I can say whether it's profitable or not, based on the traffic. It's like an innate reflex." His relatives thought his behaviour was conditioned by the family trauma that followed his father's bankruptcy—trauma that Bouchard was always subconsciously trying to overcome. It was by creating his own business, by making it ever bigger, stronger and more independent, that he would leave his mark and make a difference.

*   *   *

In 1972, Alain Bouchard married Diane Rioux, whom he had met two years earlier when she was not yet 18. Born in the Montreal region, Rioux had finished school early, as he had, and had become stuck in different entry-level jobs, working as a cashier, first in a department store, then in a grocery store, and finally in a bank, where she began to climb the ladder.

As a sign of appreciation for Bouchard's hard work, overseeing the opening of more than half the Perrette stores in Quebec, Robert Bazos offered him a car as a wedding present. And it wasn't just any car: it was a Kingswood Estate station wagon. A spectacularly long model with faux wood-grained side panels, it seemed more akin to a Spanish galleon than a personal automobile. He soon understood the reason for the choice. It would be used to transport merchandise, when necessary, and it had to be conspicuous, because the boss planned to put the Perrette logo on the sides. In short, Bouchard was to drive a company car. The only true gift Robert Bazos gave his young employee was permission to use the car for their honeymoon in Pennsylvania. And as a courtesy, he waited till the couple returned before applying the blue and white decals showing Perrette holding her pot of milk.

Alain Bouchard would therefore discover that the car came with a few extra responsibilities. In addition to designing new stores and organizing launches, he was entrusted with renovating older stores. He was named territory supervisor, which involved regular visits to each store and mentoring the managers. The demands on him were clearly too great; there wasn't a moment of downtime.

He realized he wasn't the only one who was becoming burnt out. His work with dealerships had allowed him to see behind the scenes, and he discovered the extent to which the company's operating system was interfering with their functioning. "I saw the numbers," he says. They didn't show Perrette in a rosy light. For one thing, the dealerships had to pay the head office for any products lost due to shoplifting—and it wasn't the wholesale price they wanted for the stolen items, but the retail price. Each shoplifting experience was thus triply costly: the dealers lost the value of the product; they lost the profit that was anticipated from the sale; and they had to pay this unrealized profit to the company's management. It cut into revenues that most dealers already thought were too low. "I lost dealers constantly, and I lost good ones," says Bouchard, who would inevitably find himself with the burden of finding and training replacements.

One day he had the opportunity to speak directly with Robert Bazos, who was passing through to inspect renovation work for the Perrette in his own neighbourhood, the Town of Mount Royal. Bouchard told him that the turnover rate for dealers was much too high and that replacing them was costing the company a lot. "Try to find a formula for them to make more money, and that will make them stay with us longer," he suggested. Bouchard can still hear Bazos' response, as clearly as he did that day: "Mind your own business."

"The next day, I handed in my resignation. And he really took it well," Bouchard recalls with a touch of irony that doesn't mask that the wound is still a little raw. "He said, 'Give me the keys to your car.' I told him, 'I'm not going to steal it, I have to go home, but I'll bring it back to you.' But he insisted."

With no car and no job, Alain Bouchard came home in a taxi that night. He took stock of his five years at Perrette during the ride. The chain had 184 stores, and he had been involved in the opening of about 100. He had learned many things: how to put a store together, how to operate it and how to manage the staff. The experience had also been an extraordinary course in what not to do. Treating people the way Robert Bazos did, he thought, "was no way to run a company. That's why he didn't succeed." As the taxi neared his home, he promised himself he would meet Bazos somewhere down the line and prove that he was right.

CHAPTER 5

A Builder

Maybe fate had given him a sign, telling him he needed to go into business. Or maybe Alain Bouchard had tempted fate voluntarily, more or less, by confronting Robert Bazos; after all, he knew his boss's personality and surely expected that his suggestion would create friction. During those last months with Perrette, Bouchard had quietly gone to visit certain stores that he would have liked to acquire. He had been dreaming of it for years. That's why he'd finally succeeded in putting aside some savings by working long hours and limiting his spending to a bare minimum. He had also found the time (who knows how) to buy a number of cottages in the Laurentians, north of Montreal, which he then renovated and sold for a profit. But he had to admit that he didn't have the necessary capital to go it alone: he lacked both the financial assets and the management experience that would be essential to make his project a success. So where should he turn? At just 24, he had accumulated a unique body of work experience. But was there a market for it?

He decided to put himself up for auction, in a sense, offering his services to a headhunting firm. To his great surprise, he was offered four jobs within a week, and some of them promised to be quite lucrative. Pepsi began courting him actively. The company's representative told him there was no money to be made in retail, that the future was in the mass manufacturing of food products like sugary soft drinks. The argument almost convinced him, but it would have left his dream of being his own boss at a dead end. He would never be a real leader in that kind of company.

Provigo, a Francophone-led grocery store chain that was experiencing massive growth in Quebec, also made him an offer: supervisor for a chain of mid-sized grocery stores under the name Provibec, a kind of hybrid of Perrette stores and supermarkets. The position didn't seem to offer much in the way of challenge, so he declined. Two days later, however, Provigo came back with a new offer. Would he be interested in launching a new store concept within the Provigo family, with the unique feature of being open morning to night, seven days a week? In short, they asked him to help build a banner—Provi-Soir—that would mount an attack against none other than Perrette. "I was the only person in Quebec who had the experience. And they were ready to pay for it. They made me an offer I couldn't refuse."

At Perrette, he had helped start up about 100 stores. At Provi-Soir, he would be present for the opening of the first to the hundredth. The company would give him the responsibility of developing the chain, of building new stores and maintaining them. He was resourceful and bursting with initiative, but he had a long way to go in the area of management. "I didn't even know that you're supposed to sign contracts above your name, not below!" he says. Provigo agreed that he should take evening courses at the business school HEC Montréal, and they would reimburse part of the costs. There he learned the basics of economics and administration, how to read balance sheets, how to manage supplies. He also took away a lesson: it comforted him in his drive to be more than a mere employee. One evening, the professor was speaking about the principles of decision-making. He told the students that the best way to find out how high you can rise in a company is to make decisions that should theoretically come from your immediate boss. "Aiming high is the way to discover whether you've got what it takes. If you fail, at least you'll learn from your mistakes." The notion of "aiming above your position" did not fall on deaf ears.

One day, when his superior was ill, Bouchard negotiated an agreement with an oil company that owned property in the Quebec City region, where excavation work was underway for the building of a Provi-Soir. Soil quality had been improperly evaluated, and the heavy power shovel had become stuck in the swamp-like ground. The project absolutely had to be saved. It was also clear that costs for excavation and stabilization would bust the budget for the construction of the building, which would cut into the store's profitability.

Bouchard therefore came up with an informal arrangement, which he presented to the oil company representative. Another Provi-Soir was set to be built soon after, on company land more than 100 kilometres away. Bouchard proposed transferring half the unforeseen costs for the Quebec City project to the budget for the other building, to distribute the financial impact more evenly. Clearly, he did not have the authority to make such an agreement. One of the company's directors was astonished when he saw unexpected costs for the second project. Bouchard explained what had inspired him to make the agreement, and he managed to convince him of its merits. "I tell my employees that story," he says. "I say 'Make decisions, take initiative and you'll see where it can lead.'"

Many companies discourage this type of behaviour and promote strict rule-following and a hierarchical structure. Bouchard, however, advocates an entrepreneurial attitude at every level. He encourages risk-taking. This requires a high tolerance for error, but he prefers taking an overall position of trust—even when it sometimes backfires—to an overall position of mistrust that will sometimes prove justified.

"No one shows up to work every day aiming to rip off the boss," he says. "In real life, people want to earn their wages, to feel good about themselves, to be able to say they did a good job, to contribute in their own way." To get there, Bouchard says, each individual has to find the zone in which they can make decisions, room to manoeuvre that fits their abilities and gives them a chance to show what they can do. "That's a basic need for all humans. We all want that: to reach the level of importance corresponding to our potential. That's the biggest lesson I learned in my three years doing evening classes at HEC Montréal."

* * *

At Perrette, Bouchard's supervisors would rent a space and then give him the mandate of putting in a store within a few weeks, without asking his opinion on the location chosen. He had definitely faced challenges. Often he even saw them coming beforehand, but no one would listen to his warnings. The years of trial and error had nonetheless paid off. They allowed him to develop the skill that he would later put to use: the ability to identify the best location for a convenience store, which became part of his new role at Provi-Soir. It was a responsibility that he took very seriously. To successfully carry out his task, he developed a mathematical model that he applied systematically to each new project. His basic criteria started with the number of vehicles driving to the site each day. Then he examined the number of residents who lived around the location, in expanding concentric circles to which he assigned a decreasing value according to distance. He also assessed the demographic makeup of the population, the average age, the number of children and the ethnic makup, knowing from experience that some groups are less likely to shop at convenience stores. After having been at the heart of Provi-Soir's rapid growth, this formula, honed over time, would be one of the key elements to the success of Couche-Tard.

Bouchard began to develop sites in partnership with oil companies, starting with Shell, after a strategic agreement was reached between the multinational and Provigo. Shell had a refinery in Montreal, and it had become aware of the trend emerging in the United States of coupling service stations and retail stores. However, it had little experience in this area, and no particular interest in advancing the project itself. The deal with Provi-Soir, a chain of stores with extended opening hours—like service stations—therefore seemed a natural solution, not only to expand the network, but also to increase profitability for existing stations by adding a convenience store. Following the Shell deal, others were made with Esso and Petrofina, until half the Provi-Soir stores ended up selling gasoline. In the process, Bouchard became familiar with the oil business, whose rules were much more complex than those of retail. Obtaining permits and building a gas station that would meet safety and environmental protection standards could take up to a year and a half of work.

"Provigo was a school of hard knocks," says Bouchard, who is well aware of how fortunate he was to be involved in one of the biggest commercial success stories of the era in Quebec, working under seasoned managers like Jean-Claude Merizzi and Pierre H. Lessard. He had a budget and accounts to manage, and objectives to achieve. He would learn to negotiate with suppliers, and build strong relationships with them.

In short, he laid the foundations for what he would need to build his own company one day. He also asked for a Provi-Soir franchise, near his home in Saint-Jérôme. The request was granted.

Bouchard's professional life was moving forward at full speed, like a train unwavering on its track. Soon, he knew, he would have to slow down. A bump was emerging on his wife Diane's belly: he was going to become a father. It would happen in 1977, on the same day—indeed, within the same hour— that the world learned of Elvis Presley's death. Like being born on the 25th of December, the coincidence already marked the child, Jonathan as special. But he was also special in another way: he was not like other children, and would never be.

There is a name for Jonathan's condition: cerebral palsy. In his case, it was accompanied by physical deformity on the left side of the body, hyperactive behaviour and a slight intellectual disability. He was a special child with special needs. His parents quickly got used to heading to the hospital with him for the many surgeries his condition required. It forced them both to slow down—especially his mother, an ambitious woman with boundless energy. Alain Bouchard's son would become an anchor in his life, something that kept him attached to reality. An endearing, playful person with a good heart, Jonathan has provided a source of authenticity for his father. Their relationship has often pulled him out of the bubble in which he can become enclosed when focusing on his many projects.

"I might have never left Provi-Soir," says Bouchard. But he wanted to apply his philosophy to the importance of making decisions that are "above one's position." A temporary absence of his immediate superior due to health problems gave him the opportunity he wanted. While his boss was in the hospital,

Bouchard found independent retailers that Provi-Soir could acquire and quickly transform. Bouchard, in a hurry to capitalize on the growing reputation of the Provi-Soir banner, believed it was necessary to step up the pace in order to win the battle against Perrette. Almost overnight, the brand could strike a major blow and acquire 25 new stores, all in the Montreal area. Even better, these stores were operational, and therefore had a known and quantifiable customer base, which would reduce the risks.

As soon as his superior returned to work, Bouchard gave him his pitch. "I told him, 'We aren't growing quickly enough. So I've made a plan.'" But his superior didn't even hear him out. He had no interest in acquiring stores that didn't have the same amount of space as the standard model built by Provi-Soir. "He said no, so I took my plan and left, and I carried it out by myself. If he had said yes, I would have stayed and implemented it for Provigo."

There was no longer any margin left for Bouchard to become a more important player at Provi-Soir, so he decided to leave. He did so on good terms, however, offering to buy a second Provi-Soir franchise,[13] whose construction was almost finished, in Blainville, north of Montreal. At management's request, he agreed to stay on in his position until they could find a replacement. He expected it would take them a few months. It ended up taking more than a year, and not one but three successors were hired: a development supervisor, a construction supervisor and a maintenance supervisor. He still can't believe the implication. "Like an idiot, I was doing all that work by myself," he says—an amount of work that resulted in personal sacrifice and sometimes resulted in a less than perfect work quality.

---

13. The store still exists in the same location, but it has a different sign: Couche-Tard.

Finally free from his previous position, now responsible only for managing his two franchises, Bouchard was ready to take on new business opportunities. He quickly acquired Marché Jérômien, a small grocery store whose supply source was the IGA supermarket chain, a competitor of Provigo's. Then he realized that with just one independent grocery store he could buy merchandise at a lower price than he could with a Provi-Soir franchise. It was shocking, in fact, that Provigo was selling products to Provi-Soir, members of its own family, at a higher price than IGA was asking from strangers. It could only end badly.

"They kicked me out. That was hard," says Bouchard, who nonetheless understands Provigo's reaction. Franchises must be loyal members of their clan. Obviously, Bouchard had had other projects in mind. "I knew I was going to go out on my own, but they forced me to do it a little sooner than I expected." And it certainly didn't happen in the way he thought he deserved. A bailiff appeared at one of his stores and presented him with an eviction notice—he who had built the Provi-Soir enterprise from its beginning. His wife, red with rage, gave the Provi-Soir delegate a furious warning: "One day, we will buy you out!"

Of course, it was purely emotion that inspired the threat. "Me? I never would have thought that," admits Bouchard.

CHAPTER 6

The Business Plan

Expelled from his two Provi-Soir stores, Bouchard had gone from having three stores to having just one: Marché Jérômien, which he himself had renovated and which was running well. He had hoped to call it Dépanneur Jérômien, but another store had already taken the name. It was an inauspicious start for a man who would one day be a world leader in "depanneurs"! He was able to get back the money that he had invested in the two franchises—just tens of thousands of dollars. That's a small amount with which to build an empire.

He felt very alone in the adventure. It was time to find some associates. His brother Serge was game, and maybe one of his brothers-in-law would be, too. Next Bouchard had to find trustworthy employees to run the store while he took care of developing the enterprise. He immediately thought of Jacques D'Amours, a brilliant young man he had met seven years before when they both worked at Perrette. Bouchard was a replacement manager at the time, and D'Amours—then barely 14 years old—was a jack of all trades. He had no option but to mature early; his father had left the family and his mother was raising 11 children on her own. All of the D'Amours children had to start working at a very young age.

After leaving Perrette, Bouchard had kept in touch with the young man while he took his marketing courses. D'Amours had moved on to work in the oil industry. "He had ambition," says Bouchard. That ambition is the reason he refused the offer to work *for* Bouchard, specifying that he would only work *with* him. "Jacques asked to be my associate instead," says Bouchard. They would be a trio: Alain Bouchard, his brother Serge, and Jacques D'Amours—whose savings would come in handy when purchasing their next acquisition: a food wholesaler located in the town of Mont-Laurier, in the Laurentians.

Jacques D'Amours had just decided to quit his job to devote all of his time to the new adventure, when the owner of the Mont-Laurier wholesaler, Oscar Létourneau, changed his mind and sold the business to someone else. "We had to find a new investment," said Jacques D'Amours. Knowing Bouchard as he did, he didn't expect it to take long. A few weeks later, Bouchard came back with a proposal to buy a depanneur and a super-market that belonged to the same owner, located side by side in a small newly-built commercial centre in a residential neighbourhood of Laval. "The two came as a package deal," says D'Amours.

However, there was a problem. The supermarket was affili-ated with the Metro grocery store chain, one of the biggest in Quebec, and the only other store that the new associates owned, Marché Jérômien, was affiliated with IGA, a compet-ing banner. Then, Bouchard says, IGA (short for "Independent Grocers Alliance") made him "an offer I couldn't refuse." If he transformed the supermarket into an IGA, he would be given a third depanneur for next to nothing in exchange.

They took possession of the stores on February 18, 1980— Bouchard's birthday, and also the day D'Amours returned from his honeymoon. D'Amours was 23 and Alain was 31 at the time. Their relationship, ever fruitful, is still going strong today. However, it had started rather badly a decade earlier when they first met. D'Amours has a vivid memory of the encounter—as one does of some traumatic event. He had been working for a year at "Perrette number 32," near his home in Ville d'Anjou, in the east end of Montreal. After school he would go and fill the refrigerators, and on weekends he would sort empty pop bottles and return them to Coca-Cola, Pepsi and 7Up suppliers.

The tiny room he worked in was also used to store various grocery products. A back door led out to the alley. One day, when bringing out the garbage, he encountered Bouchard, who offered a greeting that did not exude warmth. "If I ever catch you stealing a box of chocolates, I'll kick you out," he promised the young man.

D'Amours would never have suspected that 40 years later he would say of Bouchard, "We're basically an old married couple." And a couple of billionaires, he might add.

Bouchard quickly grew fond of the boy he had taken under his wing. When a Perrette manager was absent, the two would share the role. Bouchard started the day—Perrette stores opened their doors at 9 a.m.—and D'Amours would take over after school and stay until closing time. During the summer, the pair would renovate stores together and set them up to be new Perrettes. Working closely together, their mutual trust and understanding blossomed. Bouchard, says D'Amours, is "an honest and hard-working man who gives his employees freedom to move." For his part, Bouchard praises his younger colleague's loyalty and passion for work. It's as though they were meant for each other.

* * *

Initially, the partners planned to build an enterprise whose mission was twofold. It would have a depanneur division, for which the Bouchard brothers would share responsibility, and a supermarket division, headed by D'Amours. After just over a year, however, they agreed that the two sectors of activity were too different, and that the possibilities for growth were far greater in the depanneur sector. For the price of a single supermarket, they could buy several depanneurs and transform them however they liked, thereby starting to build the DNA of the company. With two types of stores, this wouldn't be possible.

With this new plan in mind, Bouchard set out to knock on the doors of small grocery stores and tobacco shops in the area he knew best: north of Montreal, between Laval and Saint-Jérôme. Many were no more than "living room depanneurs," in the words of D'Amours: small shops in spaces under 90 square metres (970 ft²). These often sold little in the way of food, offering mainly newspapers, games, school supplies and trinkets.

Bouchard would show up unannounced and launch into a discussion of traffic and business numbers with the owners. When the moment seemed right, he would ask whether they might consider selling. He was often met with refusal. "Alain's strength is that he's a developer, a go-getter," says D'Amours. "If you tell him no, he doesn't give up, he tries again a year or two later." This determination would serve the company well on numerous occasions—indeed, it would become one of its distinctive values.

Their company wasn't worth much at the time. It would grow each year by adding one or two new stores—often not the most impressive additions to the enterprise, as D'Amours notes: "Poorly designed stores, a bit depressing, with no walk-in refrigerator." The key was detecting their potential and then actualizing it.

Condition number one: Sign a long-term lease with the owner of the building. What good would it be to launch a successful store if it led directly to an argument with a building owner aiming to exploit the situation by doubling the price of rent? Often, Bouchard would take advantage of negotiations by proposing that he rent an adjacent commercial space, which would allow him to double the size of the depanneur, install a row of refrigerators and create more space between the racks. The company was still counting its pennies, so the work didn't exactly proceed according to construction industry standards. As soon as a deal was reached, Bouchard and D'Amours would get out their tool boxes. "We were specialists in demolition," D'Amours says proudly. The duo tore down walls, ripped out old shelves and destroyed antiquated counters. Sometimes they would have to design a walk-in refrigerator or redo the lighting. Within the space of a weekend, the place would become unrecognizable; airy, clean, bright, more welcoming overall—and, most important, more profitable. "It was easy for us to double the sales," says D'Amours. The important thing was to keep the rhythm going. To do so, they constantly turned to banks for loans and small lines of credit. Interest rates were prohibitive, but so was inflation. "It didn't even require talent to make money," says Bouchard.

CHAPTER 7

Technically Bankrupt

"My banker said something that I'll never forget. He looked at my accounts and told me, 'Technically, you are in bankruptcy.'"

Thirty-five years later, these words still echo in Bouchard's ears. At the beginning of the 1980s, interest rates were around 20 percent, the result of chronic inflation provoked by the decision of oil exporting countries six years earlier to significantly raise the price of their product, which had become absolutely indispensable for the development of modern society. Not all the effects were bad, in Bouchard's view. "I did an economic analysis. The prices were rising every week, so even if interest rates were high, I was making a good profit."

In light of that, he couldn't understand how the manager at the Banque Canadienne Nationale[14]—one of the smallest banks in Canada, operating mainly in Quebec—had reached that conclusion. "My balance was positive, so how could I have been on the brink of bankruptcy?" The banker explained that he only looked at two columns: liabilities, which includes loans, lines of credit, mortgages and other financial commitments, and assets like equipment, inventory and real estate. Bouchard had entered another significant amount in that column: the value he placed on customer traffic. But the banker wasn't interested in that. "That's worth zero," he told Bouchard.

---

14.   Ancestor of the National Bank of Canada.

And yet, the company's business model was founded on the notion that the value of a retail company rests on the support of its customer base and its loyalty. Without customers, a balance sheet is meaningless. That's why Bouchard agreed to pay a premium when he was acquiring an existing store. He wasn't buying just an inventory and some displays; he was buying a location and a customer base that had established habits—a concept referred to as "goodwill."

But the banker refused to see things from Bouchard's point of view. In a case of bankruptcy, he thought, he could only liquidate tangible assets. It was stunningly obvious that the two men weren't speaking the same language. "I only purchase existing stores, and therefore I'll be bankrupt perpetually!" Bouchard argued. Indeed, the possibility of bankruptcy could turn into a full-blown tragedy: At the banker's behest, Bouchard and D'Amours had personally guaranteed the company's borrowings.

This conversation with the banker came at a bad time. Bouchard had just signed purchase commitments to acquire four additional businesses. They would double the size of their company in the blink of an eye; but to do so, they needed to obtain financing. It was this need that had brought them to the bank that day, only to be told they were technically bankrupt. There seemed to be no upside. "He just told me, 'You'll have to find another bank.' And that's how Richard ended up joining us."

It was no surprise that Bouchard turned to Richard Fortin. He had met Fortin a decade earlier, at a party at a mutual friend's home. Neither of them had yet turned 25, but both exuded energy and ambition. They clicked immediately, with such ease that they ended up talking, drinking and laughing together for the rest of the evening. Their friendship was sealed.

Fortin had just begun a career in banking. Bouchard was still working at Perrette, where he was in charge of company development, and was constantly on the road supervising construction and renovation work. Every Friday, he would return to Montreal to write his reports, and the two men would take the opportunity to meet up for lunch in a restaurant downtown. "We both dreamed about running a business, but not necessarily together," says Fortin, who later moved to Quebec City to work for a number of years at the Mercantile Bank.

Ten years after their first meeting, Fortin had become Quebec vice-president of the Société Générale de France (Canada), subsidiary of the large bank headquartered in Paris. That title came with the customary privileges, including an office on the 24th floor of a building at the corner of University and Dorchester in the heart of Montreal.[15]

It was there that he received a call from his friend Alain Bouchard in 1982. "I want to buy stores," Bouchard explained, "but the bank says it's happening too fast and that I'm technically bankrupt." From Fortin's perspective, the problem was fairly simple. The manager at the Banque Canadienne Nationale was basing his response on an oldish view of things that belongs to folklore, when people in charge of commercial loans were often ill-informed and didn't understand the realities of the business world. In all likelihood, they were mainly nervous about the skyrocketing increase in defaults during that recession period.

---

15. Today, the two streets have different names that honour former premiers of Quebec who fought on opposite sides of the battle for Quebec independence. That portion of University Street is now called Robert-Bourassa Boulevard, after the federalist former leader of the Quebec Liberal Party and premier of Quebec from 1970 to 1976 and from 1985 to 1994. Dorchester Boulevard was changed to René-Lévesque Boulevard, after the founder of the Parti Québécois who promoted independence and served as premier from 1976 to 1985.

There was no question of Fortin intervening with the Société Générale to have them grant the loan to his friend: That would be an obvious conflict of interest. Instead, Bouchard asked him to become financial advisor for his company and to act as an intermediary with other banks. He would be paid for the work, of course, Bouchard added. Fortin flatly refused. "I don't need to get paid to help you out. You're a friend," he said. "But if you need an associate specializing in finance someday, I'd be interested in investing." He clearly expected to be treated as Bouchard's equal rather than becoming merely an employee.

It didn't take long to convince the other partners. Designing a depanneur, operating it, making it profitable—they knew how to do all that. But financing acquisitions quickly, so they could compete with existing chains, was an area they knew nothing about. Fortin would give the company two valuable things: the credibility they lacked, and the means to achieve their ambitions. The Bouchard brothers and Jacques D'Amours therefore agreed to have a fourth associate join their ranks, but on one condition. "If you become a partner," Bouchard told Fortin, "You can't stay with the bank. You have to work with us full time." They were all well aware that the company did not yet have the resources to offer him a competitive salary; that would be possible when they owned 10 stores, they agreed. For the time being, Fortin's investment in the company's capital was very welcome. It would make it possible to finance the acquisition of one store. "But I had signed for four of them!" Bouchard recalls. "Now we had to pay."

Up to that point, the company had been developing smoothly, albeit on a modest scale. The three shareholders had their hands full with the day-to-day management of the stores. Bouchard would supervise the stores in the Laurentians, in Sainte-Agathe and in Saint-Jérôme, where he lived. He was also thoroughly occupied looking for new business opportunities, which required regular travel. His brother Serge and Jacques D'Amours would share responsibility for the other businesses and related tasks: inventory, orders, hiring, deposits, paying bills, and taking care of maintenance and repairs.

They were ambitious, but their ambition hadn't much affected their reality yet. Grocery store chain IGA supplied Boni-Soir, the banner under which Bouchard's stores operated. But nothing distinguished them from the other Boni-Soir depanneurs. All that the name really implied was that they were independent convenience stores supplied by food wholesaler Hudon et Deaudelin.[16]

Without significant financial resources at his disposal, Bouchard had to be creative to be able to acquire new stores. The banks were demanding and mistrustful. He was able to circumvent this problem, however, by proposing to sellers that they finance the purchase of their stores themselves. Many sellers saw this as a clever way to facilitate the transaction while also ensuring a significant annual income for themselves, since the interest rate they agreed to for the balance of the sale was close to 20 percent—the same rate the banks would have charged.

* * *

The recession in 1981 and 1982 hit Canada hard—particularly Quebec, which had already suffered a blow when part of the Anglophone community made an exodus to the neighbouring province of Ontario. The election of the sovereignist

---

16. Hudon et Deaudelin was taken over by the Sobeys chain in 1998, when the Nova Scotia-based company acquired the Oshawa Group firm.

government led by René Lévesque in 1976, and the adoption of Bill 101, which made French the only official language in Quebec, had scared off many English speakers; a more promising economic outlook in Toronto took care of the rest. More than 100,000 Anglophones abandoned their position as a minority in Quebec and merged with the Anglo-Saxon majority in the Ontario capital.

Inflation, bankruptcy, the closing of factories, unemployment and poverty were painful realities across Canada, and the banks were becoming increasingly cautious. How could the economy be revived when entrepreneurs couldn't borrow money to carry out their projects? To solve the problem, the Canadian government adopted a program to guarantee loans for small businesses, up to a maximum of $250,000. In effect, the government would act as guarantor in case of default. The project provided concrete support for small businesses as well as a colossal gift for the big Canadian banks.

Fortin discovered that the program offered a solution to the financing dilemma faced by the four shareholders. No problem, he told Bouchard: We'll split the company into separate units and apply for small business loans. The loans would be guaranteed by the government, so the banks would have no cause to refuse them. Following the advice of the Banque Canadienne Nationale, the group chose a different institution to finance its growth: the Bank of Montreal.

Parcelling the company into smaller units would be a timely move for another reason. The Quebec government, wanting to support small food stores, had ruled that only independent retailers would be authorized to sell beer. Supermarkets would obviously be excluded from this lucrative trade. But at what point is an independent retailer undergoing expansion too big to qualify as a small operation? The Quebec government had ruled on that, too: Once it possessed five establishments, a merchant lost the right to sell beer. Perrette stores were operated by independent retailers; Provi-Soir by independent franchises. But the Bouchard brothers, D'Amours and now Fortin owned stores that they managed themselves. To avoid losing the sales bonanza that beer offered, they had to form corporate units of no more than four depanneurs. "We invented the names each time," says Bouchard. "Dépanneur Super Plus, Dépanneur Public, and so on. They all had the same shareholders, but the important thing was that they were individual enterprises on paper."

*　*　*

In 1984, Richard Fortin finally traded his comfortable vice-president's office on the 24th floor of a downtown office tower for a makeshift office in the basement of a depanneur on Villeray Street in the north end of Montreal. "On my first day of work, I had to sit on a case of Coke in a dusty basement." But despite all that, he was happy. It was the happiness that comes with believing you're a part of the very beginning of something big. His confidence was inspired by Alain Bouchard, he says, his charisma and his passion for work.

The arrival of Fortin as a full-time associate made it possible to better define the roles of each member of the team. The game plan required all of them to roll up their sleeves and work intensively. Three would share day-to-day management of the 12 stores the group now owned, leaving Bouchard responsible for expansion projects. "Alain travelled the streets of Montreal and surrounding areas to meet store owners and try to buy their businesses," says Fortin, who was called upon, along with the others, when it was time to renovate newly acquired stores. "We put on our work clothes, and whatever we could do ourselves, we did."

Then, Jacques D'Amours, Alain Bouchard and his brother Serge would put their recipe into action. The ingredients: strategic positioning of products, an aggressive pricing policy, fast service at the cash registers and cost control. "In each case, our operating methods allowed us to increase sales by 15 to 20 percent in the first year. Every time," stresses Fortin, seeming to be still surprised by the simplicity of it all. "It was a gold mine," adds D'Amours. They were becoming experts at extracting that gold, but it was crucial that they keep searching for new veins, without relenting. Their drive could border on absurdity. How else could one describe the decision made by this small company with limited means to approach the biggest chain of convenience stores in Canada—Mac's—with an offer to buy its Quebec network, which was in financial difficulty? The attempt, bold as it was, failed.

* * *

The taste of success that the group had enjoyed only increased their determination and energy. Fortune would also shift their course, pushing their mission in new directions. One weekend, Bouchard saw a new opportunity, and he seized it by buying a company called Recypro. It was worlds away from selling beer, snacks and cigarettes; Recypro, with a tiny factory near Bouchard's home in Saint-Jérôme, recycled automobile parts and used telephones, of all things. In reality, its proximity to Bouchard's home was its only advantage. With no knowledge of production line work, he quickly became overwhelmed. So, Bouchard made a somewhat desperate call to the city's industrial commissioner. Explaining his new and unfamiliar endeavour, he asked whether the commissioner could connect him with an organizational expert who could bring a minimal amount of coherence to its operating structure. His timing, it seemed, was opportune. A man by the name of Réal Plourde, an engineer and a business turnaround specialist, had recently contacted the commissioner to tell him that he was available a few hours a week to help out small business owners in the region, if needed.

Réal Plourde wasn't actually a business turnaround specialist per se. At the time, he was in fact trying to get his own unusual and erratic career on track. Having finished university with an engineering degree, he had landed a nice job at the Quebec Ministry of Transport. The tail end of the 1960s was an active time for the construction of the province's highway network. But on the day marking his first year on the job, when Plourde opened up the letter confirming that he had become a permanent employee of the Ministry, he balked. His future was clearly laid out, on a path as straight and long as an empty highway. He would spend the rest of his life carving lines through the most beautiful farmlands in Quebec, spanning its rushing rivers and slashing into the flanks of mountains, eventually ending up in a blank state of retirement—the only foreseeable culmination of a career devoted to the glory of asphalt. It was too much to contemplate—or too little.

Plourde had a taste for adventure. He craved finding a way to give his life meaning. Less than 24 hours after he was given the permanent position, he quit. He had decided to travel to Africa to work as a volunteer for the Canadian University Service Overseas (CUSO). His colleagues succeeded in dissuading him—but only partially. If he really wanted to help the African continent, why not use his skills as an engineer with Canadian firms that were already involved in projects supported by the World Bank or by the Canadian International Development Agency (CIDA)? He could thereby make a decent living and still follow his dreams. Thus Réal Plourde ended up embarking on a four-year journey in West Africa—mainly in Togo and Congo— supervising road construction. Apparently he had not completely escaped his destiny in roadwork; but the scenery had changed drastically, as he had wanted. Plourde says that experiencing life in Africa helped him rediscover "the values of sharing and cooperation that we're losing today in our modern individualistic societies."

By the time he returned to Quebec, the era of major road-work projects was over, and work on large-scale hydroelectric dams had lapsed. With some effort, he managed to scrape up a few small contracts for work on municipal infrastructure— nothing overly stimulating. Spending four years outside the country had opened his eyes to the world, but it turned out it had also cost him opportunities back home. Réal felt he had hit a wall. Deciding to go back to school to give his career a new direction, he enrolled in a full-time master's in business administration (MBA) program at the business school Montréal HEC.

On a Friday afternoon—Plourde remembers it well—an industrial commissioner introduced him to one Alain Bouchard, whose company was recycling old Bell Canada telephones. "It was a time when Quebec entrepreneurs thought they were good at everything," Réal says with a slight smile.

Bouchard can often appear gruff when negotiating a price or a salary. "I asked him, 'How much do you want us to pay you?'" Bouchard recalls. Plourde's qualifications impressed him: An engineer and an administrator, he was exactly what they were looking for. He also had definite human relations skills, which would be helpful for creating a team that could make the plant profitable. Plourde's response delighted him. "He said, 'Pay me what you can, pay me what you think I'm worth. Once I've shown you what I'm capable of, then you will pay me what I deserve.'"

The two men spoke the same language; they had the same priorities of mutual trust and respect for the work itself. And they both had come a long way to get where they were. Bouchard was from a poor family with six children on Quebec's North Shore, while Plourde was from a family of seven on the other side of the St. Lawrence River, in Bas-Saint-Laurent, one of the poorest regions of Quebec. Having arrived just recently, he and his wife knew no one in the Montreal area. When Bouchard learned that they would be spending Christmas alone and far from their loved ones, he invited them to his home for the 25th of December—"like I was a member of his family," Plourde says with gratitude.

Bouchard quickly discovered that Plourde possessed the skills of a watchmaker: he had a genius for connecting gears and parts in such a way that the machine as a whole would function smoothly and efficiently. He knew how to work with employees, to delegate tasks and responsibilities, to break down steps, to motivate teams to achieve goals that were realistic. He was a master of organization, and had an incredible gift for understanding human nature. Chalk it up perhaps to four years in Africa, which would leave no North American unchanged.

"The company was too small to have so much talent," Bouchard thought. He set about acquiring other small manufacturing companies, and gave Plourde the responsibility for running them. One company manufactured security modules that were installed at entrances to stores to detect theft. Another produced eyeglasses lenses. "We were making money, but it was a major distraction," says Bouchard of these commercial ventures. He found himself outside his comfort zone. He soon decided to put an end to it, particularly when Plourde, having taken over management of the prescription lens company, concluded that competition was too strong in the industry, and that it would be better to sell it as soon as possible. The buyer, a French firm, insisted that he remain in his position for one year. He might have stayed longer, but his employer refused to share equity in the company, prompting him to leave. He then turned to Alain Bouchard, who was happy to make room for him, but Plourde asked him too to be taken on as an associate: He knew what he was worth to the team. He got what he wanted.

In 1984, Serge Bouchard left the company he had founded with his brother, and changed his trajectory. There had been one Bouchard too many in the business, and one too many who wanted to lead. He decided to become a stockbroker. When Plourde joined the organization not long after, the three remaining shareholders agreed to take on the partner even though he lacked the funds to invest in shares of the company. Under the circumstances, the best they could do was offer him a package of stock options.

"Alain told me, "You're an engineer, so you'll take care of building the stores,'" says Plourde. It seemed like a modest task for someone who had overseen major infrastructure projects involving hundreds of workers, but it would work out for him insofar as he would be building something that would be partly his own. Still, Plourde didn't anticipate how much of his time would be taken up dealing with requests from store employees demanding emergency repairs. "My roof is leaking. My counter has tiles missing. Can you fix it?" he says, echoing the endless demands he faced. He started to feel like he had descended a few rungs on his career ladder. "We had to do everything ourselves, since we had no margin, no room to move. I really started to ask myself what I was doing there."

He decided that the company's hierarchical structure was all out of proportion: four full-time partners and managers for no more than a dozen small businesses. It all only amplified his doubts about the endeavour. "I thought it was too top-heavy, even though we didn't have big salaries at the time. But Alain had a vision, a big ambition, and he knew he couldn't do it alone. He wanted to build a team for the future."

They didn't know it then, but they had formed one of the most successful and long-lasting groups of entrepreneurs in Canadian history. Who could have suspected such an outcome for a company of that size—barely able to afford real offices, which they finally obtained by renting space in a commercial building in Laval. Before then, each of the partners had had to find a corner on the second floor, in the back or in the basement of one of the depanneurs. None of the spaces available had been big enough to hold all the partners at once for any length of time, which meant they therefore had to go to Bouchard's home to hold their meetings. This way, business life and personal life were inseparable, which only helped strengthen ties within the team.

* * *

At the end of December, 1984, the partners of the company—which had just opened its first entirely new store, erected on the site of a former gas station—had good reason to celebrate. It had been a long time since Bouchard had felt that unique excitement, a thrill that he loved: the feeling he had when the first customers arrived on the opening day for a convenience store. His confidence was high as he walked to the front of the small reception room they had rented so they could end the year together on a festive note. Facing the several dozen people present, he began to speak. He thanked the employees for their continued efforts. Then he went on to deliver a prediction that left his audience stunned. Their company, he told them, would become the largest convenience store chain in Quebec. "The other partners and I just stared at each other," says D'Amours. "We definitely had a long way to go to catch up with Provi-Soir, which had 200 stores, or Perrette, which had 125. We only had 12!"

Fortin was also in shock. "Bouchard hadn't told us about his announcement beforehand. Réal Plourde and I agreed that it was a very nice goal—but could we actually achieve it?"

CHAPTER 8

The Couche-Tard Banner

Alain Bouchard's partners knew him to be ambitious. They also knew he had a stubborn streak. "As soon as he committed to a project, he absolutely had to achieve it," says Jacques D'Amours. But becoming the biggest in Quebec? This time they thought he was dreaming. What no one expected, not even Bouchard, was that the convenience store industry would soon experience a three-year slowdown, creating plenty of opportunities for new acquisitions.

The problem was that too many players had joined the game at the same time. Watching the success of Perrette and the expansion of Provi-Soir had convinced all the major food chains to develop a network of small convenience stores where they could distribute their products while taking advantage of longer opening hours. Convenience stores were being used as soldiers in a proxy war between the food giants. IGA supplied Boni-Soir. The Metro chain was associated with Sept Jours convenience stores. Grocery stores within the Steinberg family had launched the La Maisonnée concept in 1982, with the will to create "the next generation of depanneurs." La Maisonnée was the first to offer coffee beans and fresh sandwiches, paving the way for the model under which convenience stores provided customers with super-fast food. And then there were the hundreds of small independents, which began to pop up on every street corner, as though Quebec were in the grip of some contagious disease: *micro-entrepre-*

neur-itis. These "bannerless" stores nonetheless found a banner that would unite them as members of one family: They all displayed the name *dépanneur.* It appeared that that was all the affiliation they needed.

In the fall of 1985, Bouchard met with a representative from the Texaco oil company, who told him about a small chain of stores in Quebec City whose owner was thinking of leaving the business. The owner had had the originality to create a distinct personality for his stores. They operated under the name Couche-Tard.

This name evokes happy memories for many Quebecers and French Canadians. At the start of the 1960s, the national public television broadcaster aired a program called *Les couche-tard* that brought amusement to an entire generation. With its jovial pair of hosts, Jacques Normand and Roger Baulu (nicknamed "the king of hosts"), the program was a late-night talk show—the first in Canada—hence its name, which translates as "The Night Owls." The show was a rite of passage for popular singers and actors, as well as for politicians who were anxious to show themselves in a friendly and relaxed light. Some would come to regret the attempt, being blindsided by irreverent questions from Normand, the court jester of the unpredictable duo.

The Couche-Tard sign, featuring a silhouette drawing of a pajamas-wearing sleepwalker, a night-cap pulled over his head, was both a nod to the joyful show and an indication of the stores' extended opening hours. Couche-Tard had four stores that belonged to the owner of the network, used to exploit the privilege of selling beer, and seven other affiliated businesses—franchises, essentially. Ten of the convenience stores were right in Quebec City, and one was several hundred kilometres away in the town of Magog.

Acquiring Couche-Tard would represent the most decisive victory yet for the young company led by Alain Bouchard, which only had 20 stores at the time. With a single deal, the company would expand by 50 percent. But did they have the necessary funds, given the difficult shape the industry was in? How would they succeed in integrating these new businesses, which were outside their standard territory of Montreal's northern suburbs? Their fear was a simple one: taking too big a bite might cause them to choke.

The four partners adopted a strategy that would steer them with all their acquisitions to come. They would start hunting as a pack. The group would be personally involved in assessing the businesses, down to the smallest detail. Once they had mastered every aspect, they would all have to agree before proceeding. Thus they headed together to Quebec City to pay the Couche-Tard depanneurs a visit, to gauge the value of their locations, their current state and their customer traffic. Then they sequestered themselves for a full weekend with the owner's representative to check the books and work out the details of the offer. Being skilled negotiators, they managed to convince the seller to give them a balance of sale—in other words, to loan them part of the acquisition cost.

Two of the four depanneurs belonging to the Quebec entrepreneur were located in buildings that he owned and which he would hand over as part of the deal. Richard Fortin came up with the idea of using them as a bank to finance the operation. The four partners bought the two buildings in a personal capacity and mortgaged them to their maximum value, generating a surplus to use as a down payment on the transaction. They also borrowed money, using equipment for the stores as collateral. In the end, says Fortin, "we came back with cash."

"We were all euphoric on the drive back to Montreal," says Fortin. They had acquired 11 depanneurs and two buildings— with only $20,000 as a down payment. What's more, the four partners had taken on their own brand name—Couche-Tard— which would soon adorn all their other depanneurs.

They came, they saw, they conquered.

* * *

Who had come out on top, in the deal, the seller or the buyer? The answer to that question wasn't clear. The depanneur sector was undergoing a thorough transformation due to changes to the law on beer sales in supermarkets. The Steinberg chain, one of the main players in the food industry in Quebec, had got the ball rolling by employing a clever subterfuge. It had acquired an independent grocer with more than five establishments; the enterprise was old enough that it had a "grandfather clause" to sell beer, according to legislation that existed prior to the introduction of the law protecting small retailers. Steinberg not only bought the small business; it also legally merged with it—a disingenuous move, commercially speaking. The legal fiction on the surface thinly masked the real objective: to claim that the grandfather clause applied to its entire network of supermarkets, and that they therefore had the right to sell beer.

The move triggered a wave of protest from depanneurs and launched a race among the big food chains, all of which wanted to buy up aging grocery stores that clung on to the same grandfather clause. The battle was moved to the courts. Provigo aligned itself with Steinberg and contested the law that gave only small retailers the right to sell beer. Finally, the Quebec government decided to change the legislation: the sale of beer would be allowed in all food retailers, supermarkets and depanneurs alike.

The news meant that depanneurs would lose a substantial portion of their income and therefore of their profits. Traffic slowed and their value dropped. The business model for these small stores started to seem uncertain; the balance of power had changed. Depanneurs still had the advantage of proximity to customers and longer opening hours; but losing the exclusive right to sell beer was a real blow.

However, it was accompanied by a gain: one that didn't make the headlines but that would have a major impact on the development of the sector, and for Couche-Tard in particular. The reform would put an end to the limit on the number of stores a company or individual could own that are licenced to sell beer. Since Steinberg, through a legal sleight of hand, had found a way to have its entire chain exempted from the restriction, the policy no longer made sense.

Abolishing the four-establishment limit gave greater flexibility for the organization of Couche-Tard's corporate structure. It would be possible to build a company that owned hundreds of depanneurs. The news was more than timely: Stores were widely available and nicely affordable.

* * *

Acquiring the Couche-Tard stores in Quebec represented a turning point for the company. Bouchard believed it gave the company "our big C": *credibility*. "It was very important that that deal was a success," Fortin says, "because it gave us confidence in our ability to make more deals."

One thing was certain: The small group of investors were starting to appear on the media's radar. Several newspapers reported on the deal that had led to the birth of a seventh group of depanneurs in Quebec, after Perrette, Provi-Soir, Boni-Soir, Sept Jours, La Maisonnée and Mac's.[17] For the food industry giants that had just won a victory they believed was decisive, the arrival of this new player was merely a source of surprise, and not a cause for worry.

17. Mac's convenience stores, whose biggest presence is in Ontario, belonged to the firm Silcorp, based in the Toronto area.

CHAPTER 9

"A Depanneur Economy"

The company Alimentation Couche-Tard Inc. was officially created on May 4, 1986. Just a few months later, the stock went public.

It became...a laughing stock. Couche-Tard's actions were attacked as an example of what not to do. The company quickly became emblematic of business greed, of companies led by directors whose sole intention is to line their own pockets. All four partners remember that time with a mixture of bitterness and amusement. However, time would prove the critics wrong.

To finance the acquisition of Couche-Tard stores in Quebec, Richard Fortin had had to stretch the elastic of the company's debt dangerously thin. At times, he feared the risk was too great. As the company's finance officer, he had always tried to avoid relying too heavily on the leverage effect, "since it puts us at the mercy of the bankers." But that's exactly what he had done to increase the company's size by 50 percent. The move compromised their capacity to pursue expansion further. They had to find new capital. Luckily the circumstances couldn't have been better: Quebec was gripped with market fever.

A few years earlier, in 1979, the Parti Québécois government had been preparing to hold its 1980 referendum on Quebec independence. To counterbalance the fear of change that prevailed in the province, they had to find a way to boost Quebecers' confidence in their ability to develop their own economy. They needed to incite a passion for entrepreneurship, to encourage venture capital and develop a culture of success.

To achieve this, Quebec Finance Minister, Jacques Parizeau, who had come from the business world, created the Stock Savings Plan, or SSP (in French, *Régime d'épargne-actions*, or *RÉA*). The measure was also a way to reduce the sizeable gap between tax rates for Quebecers and rates in the neighbouring province of Ontario. Quebec's more progressive tax system had led to what Parizeau had dubbed a "revolt of the affluent." The SSP would allow wealthy taxpayers to deduct up to $12,000[18] from their taxable income each year, so long as the funds were used to buy shares in companies whose principal place of business was in Quebec.

Alain Bouchard had always tried to avoid talking politics, but he couldn't hide his admiration for the accomplishments of René Lévesque's government. The first law Lévesque brought in was Bill 101, which made French the official language in Quebec—not only in public administration and the courts, but also for commercial signage and at work. Bouchard believed that the law had had a powerful effect in empowering Francophone Quebecers. To be sure, the Quiet Revolution in the 1960s had started the ball rolling; but Bouchard believed that the Parti Québécois taking power in 1976 and implementing its bold set of reforms had been "an even greater boost, one that gave Quebecers self-confidence and helped them believe they could start their own businesses."

It would take some time before the SSP reached its full potential, inspiring new companies to list on the Stock Exchange and to take advantage of the powerful business opportunity that represented. Along with the tax rebate for investors, the

---

18. All figures in this chapter are in CAD$.

program—in its infancy—also provided financial aid to small enterprises to help them complete the prospectus that would allow them to qualify for the Quebec Securities Commission before being listed on the Montreal Stock Exchange.

In 1984, there were 24 companies that took advantage of the SSP; these companies raised $218 million from investors. The next year, the 55 share issues eligible for the program were able to generate $1.4 billion. When Couche-Tard announced its intention of listing on the stock exchange in the first half of 1986, the 32 public offerings that had already been launched had accumulated more than $1 billion. That amount would double by the end of the year in a meteoric rise.

In 1986, the SSP had become so popular that the government decided to cut some incentives, such as reimbursement of costs for prospectus preparation. Thus, Couche-Tard wasn't entitled to the incentive. The only aid available to them was therefore indirect: a tax "holiday" for taxpayers who chose to invest.

The amount at stake for Couche-Tard's first stock issuance was ridiculously small: less than $2.5 million. Nonetheless, Bouchard will never forget how nervous he was on his way to meet with the brokers to present his project. "I knew nothing about that world. My voice was trembling. Richard was with me and he had to take over so I could calm down a bit. We were out of our comfort zone—way out of our comfort zone. We must have seemed like hapless dreamers at the time."

On June 26 of that year, the newly formed company, Alimentation Couche-Tard Inc.—created one month before by the merger of the four companies[19] owned by the founders

---

19. 118466 Canada ltée, 118491 Canada ltée, Les développements Orano ltée and Dépanneur Super Plus Inc. Alain Bouchard, CEO, owned 56.95 percent of the new entity; Jacques D'Amours, vice-president of operations, owned 28.07 percent; and Richard Fortin, vice-president of finance, owned 14.98 percent.

(the main one being Alain Bouchard's holding company, Développements Orano)—appeared in the newspapers for the first time. There were mere snippets of information on a few lines in the financial pages of the big Quebec daily papers, announcing that Couche-Tard had filed a preliminary prospectus for an initial public offering (IPO). *Le Journal de Montréal* mentioned that the company had "a network of 34 convenience stores in Quebec;" *La Presse* newspaper simply stated that it operated "depanneurs."

A few days later, Jean-Philippe Décarie, one of Quebec's most respected business journalists, published an article in *Le Journal de Montréal*, sarcastically speculating on the next stocks to be issued on the stock exchange. "Let's start with a newcomer in the fast-paced world of high finance: Alimentation Couche-Tard Inc." He went on to describe the company's business plan: to transform their four wholly owned depanneurs into franchises, which would be added to the 30 other franchises located in the Quebec City and Montreal regions. Couche-Tard was a modest enterprise, he wrote, but it was profitable. And above all, with $13 million in sales in 1985, it showed strong growth. On an annualized basis, sales would reach $20 million by May 3, 1986. The profits had followed, climbing to $610,000—an 82 percent increase.

It was the kind of performance dreams were made of; and Alain Bouchard's dreams came in quantified form. A few weeks after Couche-Tard was officially listed on the stock exchange, he spoke with a trade magazine, *Le Dépanneur au Québec*, and revealed that Couche-Tard's goal was to reach 100 stores—which meant tripling in size over the following three years. In five to eight years, he predicted, the company would have 200 stores.

Gaétan Frigon observed the hullabaloo surrounding Couche-Tard's arrival from his vice-president's office at Metro.

"Listen: you don't enter the stock exchange to raise $2.5 million," he said. Although he thought that the SSP was a "stroke of genius" for stimulating Quebec entrepreneurship out of its inert state, he also thought Alain Bouchard was extremely reckless to take that route so early in his company's development.

*   *   *

On August 22, 1986, the Couche-Tard name made its first appearance on the Montreal Stock Exchange, under the symbols DCT and DCT.W. The latter identified the warrant that allowed its holder to buy a half-share in the company at a specified date and price. The 1.1 million shares, issued at $2.25, represented one-quarter of the company's shares; the remaining 3 million shares were divided between the three founders.

Réal Plourde, who had expressed his wish to become the company's fourth partner the previous year, waited impatiently for his moment to come. Having no capital of his own, he had no way to buy a portion of the company. All he owned was a virtual portion in the form of stock options. If the company performed well on the stock exchange, he could exercise his options and convert them into shares; if it didn't, they were worth nothing. In the meantime, he was as free as anyone to buy shares now that they were on the market. He mortgaged his house, which had been paid off, to buy 50,000 shares as soon as they were put up for sale. His wife was less than overjoyed at his decision. Their family home belonged to both of them; the shares, however, were in his name only. He promised to pay off the mortgage, but she worried that the money would come from the family budget.

Then came the storm—the media storm. One after another, some of the most reputable journalists in Quebec began to denounce the "blatant abuses surrounding the SSP." Couche-Tard became a symbol of the offenses.

On October 3, 1986, Simon Durivage opened his daily public affairs show, *Le Point*, which aired immediately after the evening news on CBC, with a comment on the SSP. "We are currently...veering directly away from the original objectives," he declared. "Is it legitimate for individuals to profit from the plan and line their pockets in the process?"

The report he presented looked at six cases of alleged abuses. The second was that of Couche-Tard. The host informed viewers that the "owners of four depanneurs" were issuing for more than $2 million in shares. "To what end?" he asked, before answering his own question. "Essentially, to buy back four depanneurs...that were very heavily mortgaged." Concluding his indictment, he said that in exchange for the $2.2 million invested in the company, shareholders would end up "with these [four] depanneurs, franchises—eventually—and only 21 percent of the shares in Alimentation Couche-Tard."

The thread was picked up the next day in *La Presse* newspaper, in an editorial by Alain Dubuc. His piece was entitled "An economy of depanneurs," leaving little doubt as to how he viewed the matter of convenience stores being eligible for the SSP. "It borders on the ridiculous," he wrote. He urged authorities to ask "By what logic are a significant number of *bineries* [a derogative term used to describe small restaurants serving simple meals] able to profit from this government aid...as though the future of Quebec lay in retail?" The SSP, he concluded, "is a development tool, not a cash cow."

Even the reputable newspaper *Affaires* entered the fray, denouncing "stock savings plan abuses," and singling out Couche-Tard. "Are we actually going to pay $12.5 million for four mortgaged depanneurs and 20 franchises that have existed for less than a year?" the publication asked. The figure of $12.5 million represented not the amount of the issue but the total value of the company's capital.

In the days following this multipronged attack on Couche-Tard, the company's shares dropped, losing 25 percent of their value. Too furious to deal with it personally, Bouchard delegated his lawyer, Michel Pelletier, and his finance officer, Richard Fortin, to meet with the television host Durivage and the editor of the program, to demand a retraction. It wasn't the first such request for Durivage. He had hosted the program *Consommateurs avertis* for a number of years. The show specialized in exposing frauds of all kinds committed by manufacturers and retailers big and small. His methods had earned him no small number of threats of legal action. Durivage had thick skin, and he also had nothing to lose: CBC provided his legal defence, and if a case ended badly, it would pay up on his behalf.

From Couche-Tard's perspective, the damage to its reputation was easy to calculate. The company's shares had dropped by a dollar on the stock market; there were 1.1 million shares on the market. It didn't require a calculator to arrive at the amount that would be sought if a retraction was not given. "I tried to be nice at the beginning," Fortin recalls. But tensions had mounted.

"You said we have four depanneurs, but we have 32," he admonished the host. "You said we were lining our pockets," he continued, and threw on the table the deposit slip for $2.5 million in the company's Bank of Montreal account. "The money's in the bank, and it's going to be used for the company's growth." Durivage refused to admit any error; but the news editor intervened. They would make a retraction.

When the time came, however, it was clear that Durivage didn't have his heart in doing so. It was a few days after the meeting with Couche-Tard that he touched on the subject. Quebec Finance Minister, Jacques Parizeau, creator of the SSP, was a guest on the program to discuss the controversy surrounding the plan. In the preamble to the interview, Durivage referred to his report from the previous week. Clarifying a few points concerning Couche-Tard, he explained that the company had 32 stores rather than four, and that the funds it had raised when it was publicly listed were now in the company's holding. "No one even realized that it was a retraction concerning their report on Couche-Tard," says Alain Bouchard. "But the damage was done, and we had to live with it."

Bouchard could have sued for defamation, but that could have been a double-edged sword and provided more ammunition for critics of Couche-Tard. Moreover, he believed that legal action would divert his energies and prevent him from moving forward. Better to turn the page, swallow his pride and prove that his detractors were wrong to ridicule his project of building a big company out of small stores. The retail trade is mundane; it's all too easy to mock, while standing in awe of more spectacular technological revolutions. "One thing is for sure: depanneurs aren't glamorous," Jacques D'Amours acknowledges. "We're not building airplanes. But we've always made a profit."

*   *   *

Shaking off the attacks, the company jumped into the process of unifying its banners. The Saint-Jérôme depanneur, near Bouchard's home, was the first to be converted to a Couche-Tard. The sign had red letters on a white background, and featured an amiable sleepwalker, smiling broadly, arms outstretched and a nightcap pulled down to his nose.

Listing on the stock market meant coming into the public eye. It also carried new obligations: they needed to ensure rigour. The company now had to be accountable to its shareholders, present its business plan and accelerate its growth. Couche-Tard had taken the fastest route, one that required the least financial resources and the lightest management structure: namely, the formula of franchises. To maximize the performance of each unit, it announced that the majority of its new stores would provide self-service gasoline. Franchises would cost $20,000; Couche-Tard would take five percent of the sales value, in exchange for which the company would offer franchises technical and financial training, as well as marketing support. Couche-Tard would not provide merchandise for its franchise network; it would, however, negotiate contracts for supplies with the wholesaler Hudon et Deaudelin.

One month after it listed on the stock exchange, Couche-Tard bought three new depanneurs. Three months later, it bought three more. It ended the year with a stable of 40 stores. The company's stock was slowly recovering from the bad publicity that had hurt it early on. It reached $3.20 per share in November—a gain of close to 30 percent from the initial price. It was the second-best performance among the hundred-odd new companies listed that year as part of the SSP. The four leaders of Couche-Tard were definitely starting to silence the naysayers.

Emboldened by the progress it had made, and having brought in resources that would allow it to multiply its acquisitions, the company daringly declared its ambitions. It intended to have more than 200 stores under its belt within five years; then it would expand beyond Quebec, to Ontario and the United States.

*   *   *

The next year, in 1987, public support for the SSP came to an end, owing largely to a general market crash. Many of the stocks that had been listed thanks to the program were of questionable value. Their failure led to the failure of other shares. The crisis of confidence resulted in Couche-Tard's stock dropping under $2.00. For Réal Plourde, who had mortgaged his home to buy a block of shares at $2.50, the bitter pill was doubly hard to swallow.

CHAPTER 10

A Marriage with Metro

"Couche-Tard is waking up," *Le Journal de Montréal* announced playfully on January 13, 1987. The previous day, the company's stock had jumped to $4.70, a 20 percent increase, in response to an impressive announcement. The company was acquiring 75 Sept Jours depanneurs that belonged to the Metro-Richelieu chain. In one fell swoop, Couche-Tard would go from 42 to 117 stores, making it the second largest network of depanneurs in Quebec—behind Provi-Soir, which had almost twice as many.

It was undeniably a spectacular coup. Not only had the small company, whose annual sales barely reached $17 million, bought a competitor twice its size; it had bought it from Metro-Richelieu, a colossus 100 times larger, with $1.7 billion in sales.

Even better: The deal wouldn't cost a cent. Metro-Richelieu would effectively hand over all its depanneurs for one million new shares in Couche-Tard, which amounted to 17 percent of the company.

So how did Alain Bouchard and his associates pull it off?

* * *

The Sept Jours chain hadn't been up for sale, but it was something of an albatross for Metro-Richelieu. Like the other big grocery chains, Metro had entered the depanneur game after Provigo launched the Provi-Soir brand. The essential thing was to maintain its market share. "It was basically an obligation. It wasn't about making money," says Gaétan Frigon, who was vice-president of Metro-Richelieu when they made the decision to invest in that sector. "Our hearts weren't in it," he says—no more than that of any other food company. No one really believed in a structured approach to depanneurs. The reason for this, said Frigon in the colourful language that he is known for: "Depanneurs are bullshit!"

Sales were too small, employee turnaround was too high, supervision was problematic given the prolonged hours, and shoplifting and backroom theft was uncontrollable. The list of problems to be dealt with seemed to be ever growing. Metro-Richelieu was losing money.

No stranger to knocking on doors, Bouchard had approached Metro's management in 1986, before Couche-Tard had even gone public. Accompanied by Richard Fortin, he had met with Jacques Maltais, the president of Metro-Richelieu, and his senior vice-president, Raymond Bachand, future finance minister of Quebec. It took a certain amount of chutzpah to tell them that the management of Sept Jours was inefficient, that their model wasn't profitable and, as Fortin recalls, that "They would never succeed with their way of operating the chain of depanneurs."

Hearing this was probably a blow to the pride of Metro-Richelieu's directors; but it couldn't have been a shock. It didn't take long for the two parties to come to an agreement on a purchase price. However, Metro-Richelieu pulled away at the last minute, deciding it too would enter the stock market. But Bouchard persisted, and he made a strong case. Metro-Richelieu had found itself in a new position; it had to be accountable to its shareholders, and it couldn't allow itself to carry the financial burden that its network of depanneurs represented. Better to hand it over to those who had proven they were capable of operating a convenience store chain and making it grow.

Fortin thought he had sealed the deal when a call came in from the senior vice-president of Metro-Richelieu, changing the outlook. The board would agree to let its chain of depanneurs go, but on two conditions. One, it would not be paid in cash, as Couche-Tard had hoped, but in shares in the company. They would therefore become associates, which would allow Metro-Richelieu to maintain its presence in the sector. The second condition flowed from the first: Metro-Richelieu would be given an exclusive contract to supply Couche-Tard/Sept Jours for a period of 15 years. "A five-year contract is already an eternity," says Fortin. "So just imagine, 15 years." But it was the price that had to be paid in order to triple in size.

"Metro-Richelieu's only goal was to obtain the supply agreement with Couche-Tard," Gaétan Frigon points out, and thereby to take away market share from its rival, Steinberg. "It wasn't aiming to make money with the shares." As it turned out, it would be the most profitable investment in Metro-Richelieu's history—by a long shot. The company's 75 depanneurs would go from operating in the red to being worth billions of dollars.

The relationship with Metro has not always been smooth sailing. The process of absorbing the Sept Jours depanneurs and making them profitable would inevitably make some people very unhappy—including the owners of the stores' buildings. Metro's management had made commitments with them; they had signed the leases at prices that Couche-Tard later decided they wanted lowered.

"We had a pretty extreme approach," admits Bouchard, who entrusted the dirty work to his partner Jacques D'Amours. Although rather shy by nature, even taciturn, D'Amours nonetheless proved himself to be a powerful negotiator. He approached the landlords one by one to ask them to change their rents, explaining that Couche-Tard wasn't a billion-dollar company like Metro.

The landlords had taken advantage of a highly competitive period during which all the food chains had wanted to set up depanneurs. They upped the ante accordingly; but times had changed. Some of them were getting anywhere from $40,000[20] to $80,000 per year for their spaces—and certain owners as much as $120,000. In many cases, 20-year leases had been signed, ensuring a comfortable retirement for the owners. "At Couche-Tard, we were paying $20,000 to $40,000 per year," says D'Amours. "That's why we were profitable."

The owners responded as one might expect: They refused to renegotiate their existing contracts. Bouchard recalls, "We told them we would reopen the lease agreements whether they wanted to or not. If they refused, we would close the store and stop paying rent." To put more pressure on them, D'Amours saved the monthly cheques in a drawer until an agreement was reached. The tactic often provoked landlords into showing up at his office, where he would present them with the balance sheet for the depanneur in their location; inevitably, the store was in the red. "If it were you, could you stay in business with a balance sheet like that?" he would demand. Anger would ensue; the owners would invoke their rights and threaten action. D'Amours would reply that the law obliges each party involved in a commercial dispute to mitigate their losses, and then he would propose alternatives: for instance, extending the duration of the lease in exchange for a reduction in rent, or a compensation payment in exchange for breaking the lease. It

20. All dollar values in this chapter are CAD$.

worked almost every time. Couche-Tard never had to appear in court to test their argument that landlords were obligated to make an arrangement. "We weren't sure about the legality of our position," Bouchard admits, "but we took it anyway." Only one store ended up closing. Many owners had called Metro's management—with whom they had signed their original lease—repeatedly, threatening legal action. Even more so considering Metro was profitable and therefore couldn't use the same excuse—the fear of going under—to justify such a drastic measure. "They had a point," D'Amours says.

Pierre H. Lessard, president of Metro, didn't appreciate the approach, and he let Bouchard know it. "You don't have the right to do that," he told him; he was particularly concerned since his company was a major partner in Couche-Tard and had a member on the board. In the eyes of the owners, that meant Metro was still contractually linked to their lease.

Bouchard told Lessard that he was sure he was in the right: "I know what I'm doing, Pierre. Don't interfere," he said. "If the day ever comes when you have to pay, then call me." That day never came.

They may have been unsure of the legality of their tactic, which they continued to use for years, but D'Amours was convinced of its necessity. "If the owners hadn't accepted, we probably wouldn't be around today," he says. "We'd be long gone."

* * *

As the group's engineer, Réal Plourde was in charge of supervising renovations and maintenance, as well as managing human resources, an area he was particularly fond of and for which his partners saw he had a natural talent. The company was tripling in size, which meant the logistical structure had to be reworked, the organizational chart revised, and each person's role reconsidered.

Plourde was astute enough to see that the machinery of the organization fit together nicely, that responsibility levels and expectations—high expectations, to be sure—were well matched. The central structure was minimal, and intentionally so. They were all aware that the heart of their operations was in the stores, in the relationship with the customer. The decision to have no headquarters was a part of that philosophy, and the symbol of it. Too often, in his previous roles at Perrette and Provi-Soir, Bouchard had seen the arrogance and contempt with which the higher-ups at headquarters viewed those who did the work on the ground, be they employees or even the franchisees. He wanted Couche-Tard to avoid that culture completely, and it all started with having no head office. Instead, the base of operations would be a "service centre." As the name suggests, its role would be to serve the stores, by providing training to franchises and their employees, for instance.

Coordinators were appointed, each of whom was charged with overseeing 10 depanneurs, which they would visit regularly to provide guidance in their daily operations. Once a year, the four founders of the company conducted an in-person tour of the stores.[21] It was an opportunity to hear firsthand whatever complaints and concerns the franchisees might have, to discuss the company's workings with them and to listen to their suggestions. Were they satisfied with the attitudes of the staff they dealt with when they called the service centre? Or with the response time for computer problems? What new products or services would they like to be able to offer in their

---

21. The annual visits of the Couche-Tard founders continued until 2006, when the company surpassed 5,000 convenience stores. Clearly making the rounds of that many stores was beyond the realm of possibility.

stores? The owners' approach helped them to stay grounded in reality, to let new ideas emerge, to test out solutions, to anticipate employees' training needs. "We'd all served customers ourselves," says D'Amours. "Problems with the cash register, broken lights, issues with suppliers—we'd experienced it all. We knew what happens inside stores."

Pierre Peters[22] was one of the first employees hired by Couche-Tard management after the Sept Jours acquisition. Put in the role of regional coordinator, he was immediately handed the responsibility of supervising more than 20 franchises in Montreal's West Island area.

Peters was well acquainted with depanneurs. His mother had owned a La Maisonnée franchise, and he had worked there as a teenager. When she left, he was recruited as temporary manager for stores that were struggling, until new investors took over the business. He was an ambitious and talented young man: The position of layout coordinator offered to him was an unsatisfying one. He hoped to become a supervisor, but there were no openings at the time or on the horizon. Times were hard for the depanneur industry; La Maisonnée had to limit its growth. In fact, the director of operations told him that only one company seemed to be on the rise: Couche-Tard. Go talk to them, he was told. Surprisingly, Peters had never even heard of the company.

He was quickly captivated by the energy of the directors of Couche-Tard: men who came from a humble background and who had experienced every side of convenience store work. "It was a small fish that had just swallowed a big fish. They seemed ambitious, they envisioned big things."

---

22. At the time of the writing of this book, Pierre Peters sits as Couche-Tard's vice-president of operations for the Quebec East region, and is responsible for hundreds of depanneurs.

Three months after Peters was hired, Couche-Tard's management had a realization: The Sept Jours network in the Quebec City region had had no supervisor for the last eight months. Left to their own devices, "franchisees tended to do whatever they wanted," says Peters. He was given the mandate of transforming those Sept Jours into Couche-Tard.

* * *

The three years following the acquisition of the Sept Jours chain provided a hard lesson in the difficult craft of blending corporate cultures, especially while righting financial accounts. They had taken an enormous bite, and their challenge was to digest it—under difficult economic conditions, given the collapse of the Stock Savings Plan (SSP).

After a rocky beginning on the stock exchange in the fall of 1986, Couche-Tard shares made a dramatic recovery at the start of the following year. In January 1987, the shares traded at $4.10. Thanks to the value of the warrant, it had shown a 100 percent growth in just six months of existence. But despite being honoured with the award for large commercial enterprise of the year—bestowed by the premier of Quebec, Robert Bourassa, in July 1987—Couche-Tard shares were worth no more than $2.10 in December: a lower price than when they were first listed. By September of 1989, they reached $1.55. That was less than the book value of the company, which was at $2.03 per share.

What had happened to make Couche-Tard take such a beating?

One cause was definitely the gloom felt on markets, which had led to, or resulted from, the disappearance of a number of companies enrolled in the SSP. But there was more. After two years of rapid growth, Couche-Tard seemed to be losing its ability to inspire. Its directors were making confused missteps. In June 1987, they bought Pro-Optic—the largest ophthalmic lenses manufacturer in Quebec—for $5 million, only to sell it two years later. And in 1988, the four founders of Couche-Tard transferred their assets into a holding company called Actidev, through which they would hold their block of shares representing 59 percent of the company.

In one general meeting after another with shareholders, Bouchard talked about the imminent announcement of a major acquisition: sometimes in the United States, sometimes in Ontario. He had already unveiled the name that the chain would take in the Anglophone territory: Wee Hours Convenience Store. The following year, he had to explain that it still hadn't happened, that negotiations had fallen through and that for the time being he would focus on adding new stores in Quebec, at a projected rate of 20 per year. But from the acquisition of the Sept Jours stores, in early 1987, through 1990, Couche-Tard opened barely a dozen new depanneurs per year. And despite an increase in revenue, net earnings began to fall. In 1988, they were at $1.42 million, or 23 cents per share. In 1989, they fell to $1.25 million, or 20 cents per share.

And that was just a prelude to what lay ahead: the perfect storm.

CHAPTER 11

The Perfect Storm

There are moments in life that define us. More often than not, they come during periods of crisis. The same can be true for businesses: critical moments can shape them—provided they don't kill them. Such was the case for Couche-Tard at the start of 1990, when four phenomena occurred simultaneously, creating a storm that nearly destroyed the company.

As a backdrop: There was a global recession, which was particularly severe in North America. Then came a decision by the government of Quebec to allow supermarkets to open their doors in evenings and on weekends, depriving depanneurs of one of their main competitive advantages. That measure alone would lead to a 10 percent drop in sales in the depanneur industry. From the perspective of the grocery chains, of course, it would also restore a certain fairness in the power balance that had shifted for two decades between their stores and depanneurs. In 1974, the little shops held only two percent of the total retail food market in Quebec; 17 years later, with 6,000 points of sale in the province, they represented 20 percent of grocery sales. Even Yves Rondeau, director of operations for Provi-Soir, the largest chain of depanneurs in Quebec, acknowledged the fact: There were too many deps.

Two other measures adopted by governments would impact the depanneur industry. On January 1, 1991, a new tax came into effect in Canada: the goods and services tax (GST), inspired by the European model of value-added taxes. Retailers found themselves directly in the line of fire for the new tax grab. They were forced to invest considerable resources to adapt their cash registers, computer systems and accounting methods. An estimated 85 percent of depanneurs' sales were subject to GST; only basic food items were exempt.

Cigarette sales made up a larger portion of the overall revenue than all the grocery products combined, accounting for about one-quarter of the total sales. And cigarettes were the target of the next blow. In the spring of 1991, taxes on tobacco were raised dramatically. The federal excise tax, to which GST was added, rose by 138 percent. Provincial taxes jumped by 23 percent. With that, as though under a powerful spell, the cigarette market fell by 20 percent, then 25 percent, then 40 percent. It all took a mere six months. The combined effect of the GST and other taxes on tobacco, says Alain Bouchard, "was like getting hit by a train."

It would be one thing if the taxes had been imposed for reasons that were justified. The governments had claimed they were raising taxes in order to promote public health by pressuring smokers to quit the habit—especially young people, who are more affected by higher prices. But the drop in cigarette sales was an illusion; only legal sales had dropped off. Inflated cigarette prices had inadvertently created a new industry for contraband cigarettes. Years later, it was discovered that a number of major Canadian cigarette manufacturers were complicit in the subterfuge that was happening. They were exporting their products to the United States—tax-free—knowing full well that the intermediaries they were selling to were promptly bringing the product back to Canada, usually through the First Nations reserves that straddle the border between the two countries. A network of resellers, as calculated and organized as marijuana dealers, then ensured distribution of the merchandise in bars, restaurants, workplaces and even schoolyards. Another point of sale: under the counter at certain depanneurs. Selling at $25[23] for a carton, half the legal price, these cigarettes fuelled an extremely lucrative business for all involved.

Was there a future for depanneurs? Bouchard seemed to have little faith that there was. In September of 1991, after having completely transformed 162[24] stores into franchises, he announced the opening of the first service station under the name ActiGaz. The new banner, Bouchard said, would have 14 locations in Quebec before the end of the year; it would eventually have 60. Each site would include a self-serve gas station, a car wash and something new: a "mini depanneur," which would not be a Couche-Tard store. The reason for the switch? As Bouchard explained at the opening of the first ActiGaz in Sherbrooke, it was time to be prudent when it came to developing new depanneurs.

This business venture would report directly to Actidev, the holding company belonging to the four Couche-Tard founders and through which they held close to 60 percent of the depanneur chain's capital. The news sent a confusing message to shareholders, who were justified in wondering where the true priorities of the management team lay, at a time when Couche-Tard's profits were continuing to fall. The company's banker shared their concern.

On Christmas Eve of 1991, Bouchard received a letter from the vice-president of the Bank of Montreal. The letter informed him that an expert had been retained to carry out an analysis of Couche-Tard's finances, business model and management team. The bank was concerned about the company's long-term

---

23. Prices in this chapter are in CAD$.
24. 130 Couche-Tard stores and 32 Sept Jours stores.

viability. In the United States, the giants 7-Eleven and Circle K had been placed under bankruptcy protection law. The biggest Canadian chain, Silcorp, was also facing serious difficulties. "Bankers all over were asking whether there was a future in depanneurs," Bouchard says. "I was asking myself the same question."

Late in the day on that December 24th, Bouchard invited his three partners into his office and solemnly placed a bottle of cognac on the table. "Should we sell everything and move on to other things?" he asked them. Richard Fortin, a stocky man with a robust optimism, remembers that moment as "pathetic."

Couche-Tard would post losses; they all knew it. There was no mistaking the regular reports from the stores. Confirmation would come in the next quarterly report. The losses were modest—$150,000 for the quarter ending February 1992—but they were losses nonetheless. Bouchard asked the group to think things over during the holidays. What did they want to do with the rest of their lives?

By the end of the holidays, the four men had come to a conclusion: They should stay the course. The main reason, in Fortin's view as a former banker, was that no bank would dare cut off funding for a company with a cash flow of $3 million. "We should continue operating," he said. But they should also roll up their sleeves, he added, and strive to improve performance.

Taking a more philosophical view, Réal Plourde presented his own argument. "If it was hard for us," he said, "it was even harder for other companies, since we were the best operators around." When Plourde became a partner in the company a few years earlier, he had pledged to stay with the team as long as it was fun to do so. Far from being discouraged by the situation, he saw it as an exciting challenge. "New constraints can also bring new opportunities," in his view. He thought that once the crisis passed, Couche-Tard might be able to snatch up its weakened competitors.

* * *

Sure enough, 1992 opened with some good news. After having spent a few years digesting the acquisition of Sept Jours depanneurs, Couche-Tard announced in January that it had signed a letter of intent to acquire all the 109 convenience stores that were owned by the Ontario firm Silcorp: 72 La Maisonnée stores and 37 Mac's stores. *Couche-Tard becomes the top depanneur in Quebec*, proclaimed newspaper headlines. With 271 stores, the company would then have 20 more stores than Provi-Soir. The incredibly optimistic goal Bouchard had set five years earlier, with a timeline reaching for the year 2000, would already been attained. It was now in their grasp, eight years ahead of schedule.

However, the markets didn't respond as exuberantly as one might have hoped. On the contrary, Couche-Tard lost 10 percent of its value in the days after the announcement, falling to $1.75. The explanation that Silcorp management had given to justify its decision to withdraw from the Quebec market was no doubt a major factor. Vice-president Vladimir Romanchych had declared essentially that, owing to the unfavourable economic climate in the province, the Quebec division was one of the main causes for his group's poor performance. "We simply aren't making money in Quebec anymore," he said.

Alain Bouchard's team knew the precise reason for the division's lack of success. When Steinberg had put La Maisonnée up for sale four years earlier, Couche-Tard's directors had expressed interest; they had even made an offer, knowing full well that the network suffered from serious problems. "They [Steinberg's management] had tried to copy us by buying up existing depanneurs. But they didn't know what they were doing," says Bouchard.

When the auction closed, the person in charge of the sale of La Maisonnée called Bouchard to tell him the results. Sounding extremely pleased, he announced that Couche-Tard hadn't won—it hadn't even come in second (Provi-Soir had done so). The new buyer was Silcorp. "What a mistake that was," says Bouchard. Mac's convenience stores were already losing money in Quebec. Paying far too much for La Maisonnée, whose business model needed to be overhauled, Silcorp stood to lose a fortune. "We took a look at the numbers," says Jacques D'Amours, "and with the price they had paid, we knew it would be impossible for them to survive."

So it was only a question of time before Silcorp contacted Couche-Tard management to offer them the chance to buy the whole thing at a lower price: They needed a way to climb out of their financial hole. In 1991, the call finally came. An agreement was reached, and Couche-Tard took a closer look at the books. It wasn't a financial hole they were in, says Bouchard; it was a chasm.

One of the main reasons for this involved conditions that had been imposed by Steinberg on the sale of La Maisonnée. Steinberg had retained ownership of the buildings that housed the La Maisonnée depanneurs, and had negotiated 20-year leases for the stores. The price of rent was twice as high as the going rate for similar premises. Worse still, Steinberg, experiencing its own financial struggles, refused to renegotiate the leases.

Bouchard was left with the duty of delivering the bad news to Silcorp's boss, Derek Ridout. "You have to close these stores," he told him. "Some of them are losing $200,000 a year. I went through my own ordeal with the Sept Jours stores. I'm not doing it again with La Maisonnée." Simply put, the Couche-Tard team was ready to buy 70 of the 109 Silcorp establishments in Quebec—the ones that stood a decent chance of becoming profitable—but not the others.

Rather than sell its stores piecemeal, Silcorp ended the negotiations. Four months later, the Mississauga company had recourse to the Companies' Creditors Arrangement Act for legal protection, allowing it to break most of the leases. It then proceeded to close almost 40 stores, one by one. Despite having $750 million in sales each year, with its 972 depanneurs distributed across Canada and the United States, and its 197 Baskin-Robbins ice cream stores in Canada, Silcorp was posting losses of $30 million.

The company's decline coincided with that of its main associate in Quebec, the venerable Steinberg supermarket chain, which also sought protection from its creditors. The two companies were like a pair of non-swimmers who had been thrown into a lake and clung on to each other to avoid going under: Steinberg refused to supply Mac's and La Maisonnée stores, despite the fact that it was its appointed wholesaler and landlord.

"The golden age of depanneurs is over," declared Bouchard. The time had come to "open the door for the second generation in the convenience store industry in Quebec."

* * *

Couche-Tard's management kept itself busy during the first half of 1992. The four partners had committed to lowering operational costs: No area was safe from being slashed, no amount saved was too little. They turned over every rock and pored over every contract. The four founders of Couche-Tard also knew they had to personally set an example.

The service centre in Laval had close to 60 employees at the time. "We gathered them all together to explain the situation," Bouchard remembers. He announced that, given the circumstances, each of the partners would lower their compensation by 25 percent. "But first we had to convince ourselves to do it," he admits.

He followed with the announcement that there would be a general and immediate wage freeze for all employees—but this would be conditional. In the event that the company succeeded in getting things on the right path, Bouchard promised them, each would receive a retroactive amount, equal to the inflation rate. Some viewed the promise with doubt; but Bouchard would make good on his word in time.

Bouchard would have liked to take even more aggressive measures. He was inspired by the example of Jack Welch, who had ruled General Electric with an iron fist since 1981. Nicknamed Neutron Jack[25] for his practice of cutting jobs by the thousands—mainly in administrative positions, which he scornfully referred to as "bureaucracy," Welch prescribed a formula as simple as it was ruthless: Each department head had to lay off 10 percent of their employees each year, those they deemed the least productive. Like a high-stakes game of musical chairs, the practice continued year after year. The method appeared to provide a sound example in a time of recession, and Bouchard asked Plourde whether Couche-Tard should adopt it. After all, their company surely had employees who could be considered more chaff than wheat.

---

25. The expression refers to a neutron bomb, which kills animal life (including humans) without destroying buildings and infrastructure.

"Those are management theories that are totally void of sensitivity," his human resources manager responded. So what should be done with the least productive workers? "We'll put them in the right place, where they'll learn to be productive," Plourde told Bouchard. It was the price to pay to obtain loyalty from employees, rather than obedience; long-term commitment, rather than mere submission.

According to Bouchard, this was Plourde's main contribution to defining the corporate culture that would prevail at Couche-Tard from that point forward. It may be true that no amount saved is too small; but some savings aren't really savings at all.

* * *

"I tried to meet with the president of the bank, and he refused," Bouchard remembers with bitterness. Bouchard was particularly furious because not only did the Bank of Montreal decide to commission a study on the company without even consulting them first, but it had also announced that Couche-Tard would have to foot the bill. And to top it all off, the bank flatly refused to provide Couche-Tard with a copy of the result.

Bouchard had put his foot down on that final point, however, and he was glad he did. The report, drafted by Bernard Gouin, concluded with a prophetic line that Bouchard can still recite verbatim more than a quarter century later. "If there is one company in North America that can successfully survive in this industry, it is Couche-Tard."

"That's all well and good," Fortin says regarding that claim, with some amusement, "but afterward, you have to prove it."

But the bank had neither the patience nor the faith necessary to let them make that demonstration. In the spring of 1992, an emissary from the Bank of Montreal visited the Couche-Tard office on Saint-Martin Boulevard in Laval. "Our economic situation wasn't good, but we were confident," says Bouchard. "We had a business plan that we were ready to show him." As soon as they had finished the presentation, the visitor offered a counter-argument. He gave his impression of a typical modern shopper: "I do my shopping at Club Price[26]—I fill up an entire shopping cart there. I don't need to go to the depanneur anymore." His conclusion was brutal and to the point: "Depanneurs are obsolete. They're finished." The directors of Couche-Tard tried to explain the advantage of convenience stores, with their proximity to the customer and short wait times at the cash—Club Price had a reputation for long waits at the check-out—but they got nowhere. "Find another bank," the representative told them. In the meantime, he transferred Couche-Tard's account from the Laval branch to the one responsible for bad loans' cases. The message couldn't have been clearer.

It was time to find more ways to save money, to turn over every stone once more. Cutting costs usually risks bruising feelings. But the action they needed to take then was particularly awkward, since it was one of Couche-Tard's main shareholders that had to pay a price. The Metro group had owned almost 20 percent of the shares in Couche-Tard since it had handed over its Sept Jours depanneurs to the company. As part of the deal, Metro had become the food wholesaler for all the stores. The idea was that Metro would be able to offer better prices, given the combined volume of the two companies. Metro was obviously making a profit on sales, and it also stood

---

26. Club Price is the ancestor of Costco, a warehouse that sells everything from television sets, to car tires to groceries, usually in large formats.

to receive certain other financial benefits that would not go to Couche-Tard. This seemed justified for food products that went through Metro's warehouses, requiring handling and transport, but Metro was also taking a cut from anything that manufacturers delivered directly to depanneurs: chips, soft drinks, milk, bread. The net result was that, even though almost half of what the depanneurs bought did not pass through Metro's warehouses, the company nonetheless received a sales commission on everything. "Each time Pierre H. Lessard from Metro gave me something, he asked what it would bring in *for him*," says Bouchard.

Taking advantage of the renewal of its agreement with Metro, Couche-Tard informed the company that it had created its own department for purchases and accounts receivable. From then on, the company would be negotiating with its main suppliers directly. "Metro wasn't given a choice," says Bouchard. The strategy allowed Couche-Tard to increase profit margins without raising retail prices. With more than 150 stores and annual sales exceeding $100 million, Couche-Tard was able to get some attention from manufacturers—enough at least to show that the gamble would pay off. Metro was furious, says the company's former vice-president, Gaétan Frigon. "But that's how Bouchard made money. He's terrific!"

The Couche-Tard founder had another project in mind, something he'd been thinking of for a long time. His wife had predicted it—threatened it, in fact—on the day when the bailiff came to kick them out of their first two depanneurs. He would buy the Provi-Soir chain, the chain he had helped build from its beginnings. There was only one problem: Couche-Tard completely lacked the financial resources to pull it off.

After months of discussions with suppliers, Bouchard finally managed to convince them to advance the funds to finance the operation. In exchange, he promised some of them that his depanneurs would give them exclusive rights. There would be only one brand for milk products, one supplier for chips and soft drinks and so on. The suppliers decided it was worth the cost of investment. "Alain was responsible for that amazing feat," says Richard Fortin with admiration. "But on the day when we showed up to meet with the president of Provigo, he refused to look at our offer." Fate had played a trick on them. Other potential buyers had also showed up at Provigo headquarters on that day, to look into the possibility of acquiring the entire company. There was no question of selling one of its components for the time being. Bouchard had done all that work for nought.

* * *

In April 1992, Couche-Tard decided to give itself a new identity, a new approach and a new mission. Starting with its 34 depanneurs in the Quebec region, and extending to the rest of its network the following autumn, the company would undergo a facelift. The old Couche-Tard sign, with its smiling sleepwalker, would be put to bed. In its place would be a sign proclaiming "Dépan-E$compte" in big letters, under a drawing of a piggy bank. The name "Couche-Tard" would still appear, but in smaller letters.

It was a massive gamble.

If supermarkets wanted to fight over Couche-Tard's market by opening their doors in the evening and on weekends, so be it: Couche-Tard would take them on by turning its stores into discount stores. No one in North America had ever tried a similar move.

"We had no choice," Bouchard explains. "Our clients were telling us that aside from buying newspapers and lottery tickets, they didn't want to shop at our stores because prices were too high." Couche-Tard's board of directors was divided on the strategy—and for good reason. Bouchard admits that it was "absolutely a roll of the dice." To his mind, however, it's what saved the company and allowed it to weather the biggest storm that had ever struck the depanneur industry.

Making the transformation had required renegotiating agreements with the suppliers and the franchisees. Until that time, Couche-Tard had been receiving royalties from its franchises, ranging from 11 to 13 percent on sales from each store, to cover costs for rent, management, training and advertising. Henceforth, franchises would pay a fixed amount for rent, and royalties would be set at 5 five percent. This added an incentive to boost sales.

That's where the boldest change lay: Couche-Tard was putting manufacturers in competition with each other by offering them exclusivity on store shelves. Space was already limited: Why offer four brands of batteries or potato chips? May the lowest price win. Regular prices were lowered so they would match supermarket prices or beat them. Thus, every month, about a hundred products were offered at a reduced price, often supported by a concerted and aggressive marketing approach, offering two items for a price barely higher than the price of one.

This new incarnation of Couche-Tard was accompanied by an advertising campaign that changed the playing field. For the first time in Canada, a depanneur chain would have television commercials. And the ads were by no means meek. The 30-second spot featured four of Canada's most famous politicians—portrayed by marionettes. There was Prime Minister Brian Mulroney; Liberal opposition leader Jean Chrétien; Quebec Premier Robert Bourassa; and former head of the Parti

Québécois, Jacques Parizeau, founder of the Stock Savings Plan that had allowed Couche-Tard to go public.

The ad also made a tip of the hat to Quebec nationalism, with a line informing viewers "C'est une entreprise de chez nous" ("It's a company from here"). This earned a response from the perpetual adversary of Quebec nationalism, Jean Chrétien, who seemed to both endorse Couche-Tard and mock it slightly. "The Pepsi is cheap," he observed sardonically. Brian Mulroney, in his rich baritone voice, added his own comment, saying, "For once, we all agree"—a cringeworthy reference to his multiple fruitless attempts to bring about a constitutional agreement that would reconcile Quebec with the rest of the country. The latest such attempt, the Charlottetown Accord, was at the time the subject of a national referendum. The advertisement ended on a playful note, making a reference to the recession that seemed to be dragging on endlessly: "Dépan-E$compte Couche-Tard: We help out (*dépanne*) the economy, too."

The provocative advertisements would be awarded four top prizes by the Television Bureau of Canada—gold in every category.

CHAPTER 12

Natural Selection

In October of 1992, a week before the official launch of the new Dépan-E$compte concept, the markets bet on the failure of what seemed like an act of desperation. Couche-Tard shares hit a historic low—$1.00—barely above the shameful level of penny stock. The book value of shareholders' equity, however, was $2.62 per share. It demonstrated a real lack of faith in Couche-Tard's management, despite the extraordinary efforts that had been made to streamline the company. Couche-Tard had lightened the administrative structure, scrutinized every expenditure, tightened control measures for shoplifting and employee and supplier theft and, finally, disposed of its subsidiary of ActiGaz service stations, turning the page on its latest diversification venture into which it had sank $2 million[27]. But what the markets didn't see was that this difficult period had only given Couche-Tard's management team more motivation to win. "It was an incredible time," says Alain Bouchard. "We worked intensely, and it ended up rallying the troops, with great results."

They pushed forward like warriors, driven by the survival instinct and a passion for victory. They simply refused to be beaten.

*　*　*

---

27. All dollar amounts in this chapter are in CAD$.

Despite the drop in sales attributed to contraband ciga-rettes, Couche-Tard had succeeded in maintaining its presence, and even in gaining new market share, with its aggressive strategy of competitive pricing. However the company had to admit that its performance was not meeting expectations. Sales volume had increased by 10 percent, but the profit mar-gin had declined as a result of the attempt. In the end, the net benefit attained was barely half of one percent of sales—half a cent for each dollar received from customers. Still, it was slightly better than the previous year. After a stretch with their salaries frozen, Couche-Tard's employees would receive a ret-roactive raise, as promised. The company's competitors, how-ever, were barely hanging on.

On October 26, 1993, Derek Ridout, president of Silcorp, announced that it would sell its 54 Mac's and La Maisonnée stores in Quebec to Couche-Tard. It had carried out the major cleanup that Alain Bouchard had recommended the previous year, shedding the prohibitive leases it had signed with Steinberg and the stores that were its greatest loss-makers. But the pressures of the Quebec market were still too great. It had to sell—at a bargain price. Couche-Tard had the opportunity to acquire the 54 stores—23 Mac's and 31 La Maisonnée stores—for barely $5 million: less than $100,000 per store, all inclusive. Forty of the stores were franchises and 14 were cor-porate stores, wholly owned by the company, including equip-ment and inventory. Under different circumstances, it might be considered a friendly price—in truth, it was a fire sale. Because of its failed attempt to break through in Quebec, Silcorp had to shave $3 million from its books.

The purchase may have been a bargain, but the Bank of Montreal was reluctant to become further involved in deals with Couche-Tard, unless the company's directors could come up with a significant down payment. The problem was, all of the latter's assets were now in Couche-Tard. Bouchard had to make the decision to ask Metro-Richelieu for help—and the service came at quite a cost. "They made the down payment on our behalf," Richard Fortin remembers with some dismay, "but we had to use the company as collateral." The Bank of Montreal advanced the rest of the amount, but imposed strict conditions "that compromised our freedom of movement," Bouchard says.

It was an all or nothing situation. If something went wrong, if they failed to meet their deadlines, they would lose Couche-Tard, and Metro-Richelieu could seize the company for a low price. Fortunately for them, La Maisonnée quickly became profitable. They were able to pay back the loan from Metro in less than a year, escaping the threat of default with great relief. When the dust had settled, the Couche-Tard network owned 212 depanneurs under three separate banners: Dépan-E$compte Couche-Tard, Sept Jours and La Maisonnée. The company was starting to claw at the heels of Provi-Soir, still the leading depanneur chain in Quebec.

* * *

Cigarette smuggling had been a problem for too long. Public outcry from retailers seemed to fall on deaf ears, however—even despite evidence showing that the tax burden shouldered by smokers had ended up working against the governments that had created it. A Canadian study estimated that between $500 million and $700 million in federal treasury revenue was lost in 1991—the year that the increase in tobacco taxes came into effect. Smuggling had grown to epidemic proportions since then—the practice was so widespread that legal sales of cigarettes in depanneurs had dropped by 60 percent. Couche-Tard estimated that the loss had cost it one million dollars a year in revenue, which equalled twice the company's profits. It was time to draw the line.

The Quebec Food Retailers' Association, an organization that Bouchard sat on, covertly created a group made up of its most active members. They called it MATRAC: Mouvement pour l'Abolition des Taxes Réservées aux Cigarettes (Movement to Abolish Taxes Exclusively for Tobacco). The acronym intentionally evoked the word *matraque*, which means "truncheon" or "baton"; it signalled depanneur owners' desire to strike a serious blow. On January 24, 1994, when the outside temperature was -20°C (-4°F), they set up improvised kiosks in Saint-Eustache, west of Montreal, along the highway leading to Oka. Oka had a First Nations reserve with a flourishing trade in cigarette smuggling, one that was extremely lucrative. Ostensibly justified by the ancestral right to ignore the "white man's tax laws," the illicit industry operated in broad daylight, in brazen contempt for the police and political authorities, which seemed powerless to put an end to it.

Creating a provocative scene to mock the smuggling situation, the depanneur owners brought traffic on the highway to a standstill. Their strategy: Sell drivers cigarettes at the same price as smuggled cigarettes. They attracted hundreds of customers who wanted to take advantage of the discount, but who, by doing so, also indirectly demonstrated their sympathy for the retailers' cause. The media rushed to cover the defiant gesture and broadcast it widely. Alain Bouchard and Réal Plourde were the only owners of depanneur or food retailer chains to participate in the protest. Bouchard had personally called the presidents of Metro, IGA and Provigo to urge them to join in, but none wanted to risk being arrested and charged with a criminal offence. But it was a risk that Couche-Tard's management was willing to take; they believed the future of their company depended on it.

Instead of landing him in front of a judge, the protest brought Bouchard to the office of Claude Ryan, the Quebec minister of public safety. Bouchard was accompanied by Michel Gadbois, president of the The Quebec Food Retailers' Association. Ryan carried a lot of weight within the government. His influence reached well beyond his responsibilities as "Minister of the Police." Convincing Ryan of the justice of the retailers' cause—showing him that the issue was truly a matter of law and order—was therefore crucial.

The visit started with a confrontation. Ryan challenged Bouchard's account of the extent of the problem: that smuggling had affected their sales by more than 60 percent. Bouchard responded by telling him that the problem was so widespread that in the entrance to almost any building in downtown Montreal, you could find a concierge who would sell you black market cigarettes.

"You're exaggerating," the minister shot back in his typically abrupt manner.

"Even in this building," Bouchard insisted. "Someone in your own office is selling smuggled cigarettes." Impossible—not at the ministry responsible for law and order, Ryan objected. "Just come with me," Bouchard told him. "We'll go downstairs and buy some."

His aide interrupted the conversation. "Mr. Ryan, you can't do that," he said. The minister stared at him; the truth was written all over his face. "Mr. Bouchard is right," he continued, stammering slightly.

The Mafia had stretched its tentacles so far they reached right under the feet of Quebec's protector of law and order. The aide had been forced to speak up out of fear that the unthinkable would happen: that the stern minister himself would be seen purchasing smuggled cigarettes, even if only for the purpose of demonstration. Ryan had to know the truth.

In February of 1994, the federal government's budget granted depanneurs what they had been clamouring for. In a concerted action with the Quebec government, it announced a significant reduction in cigarette taxes, which would allow its retail price to be cut by half or more. A pack of 25 cigarettes had cost $6.25; it would henceforth cost as little as $2.75. A month later, a full front-page photo of a smiling Alain Bouchard appeared in *Le Journal de Montréal*, along with a triumphant headline: *The customers are back*. The article reported that Couche-Tard stores had seen an increase of 600 customers per week on average; in some cases, as much as 800. In-store cigarette sales tripled and sometimes quadrupled. And once customers were inside a depanneur, they were naturally likely to take the opportunity to buy other products: a newspaper, some candy, milk. It was a huge victory: The worst was over and the best was to come.

The four partners making up Couche-Tard's management chose that moment to send a message to the market: a sign that they had complete faith in themselves and their company. In May, they announced that they would put an end to the confusion created by the existence of the two public companies, Actidev and Couche-Tard. Actidev was Couche-Tard's controlling shareholder, and the Couche-Tard shares were its only asset. Why were there two companies on the stock exchange for a single business? Which was a better option to buy? Where would the profits end up? "There will no longer be a dilemma for investors," Richard Fortin declared when he presented Actidev's purchase offer for all of Couche-Tard's outstanding shares at a price of $3.00, just higher than its $2.90 market value that day. The price was triple what it had been a year and a half earlier. Actidev—a management company controlled by the four Couche-Tard founders, but also traded publicly— would tie its destiny to that of the depanneur chain. The company would later adopt a name based on what it had been called since birth: ACT, for Alimentation Couche-Tard.

Invigorated by his success in the fight over cigarette taxes, Bouchard announced that he would be turning to other battles with governments and their agencies. The first opponent would be Quebec's liquor board, the Société des Alcools du Québec (SAQ), with the goal of expanding the range of wines offered in depanneurs. The foul taste of these wines had made them a frequent target for bitter ridicule. Jealously protective of its monopoly on wines with the Appellation d'Origine Contrôlée designation, a French certification, the SAQ resisted pressure from grocery stores and depanneurs that wanted to offer their customers better quality wines. The conflict of interest was obvious. Bouchard also announced that he planned to confront Loto-Québec, another monopoly and a government cash cow, so that retailers could achieve a better profit margin on lottery tickets.

* * *

On Tuesday, March 21, 1994, an executive from Perrette called Bouchard on the phone. He didn't mince words. "Do you still want to buy our company?" he asked Bouchard. "We're on the brink of bankruptcy. We have to sell."

Bouchard most certainly did want to buy the chain where he first cut his teeth in the industry. Each year, he had invited Robert Bazos to meet him at a restaurant so he could make his interest clear. But the Perrette owner had always answered that he wanted to give the company to his son, who was still in school.

Bazos had waited too long; the perfect storm had spilled the proverbial milk. Even though it had closed its least profitable stores, Perrette was sinking. Its food wholesaler, IGA, had just announced it would cut them off unless they paid in cash, knowing full well that this was impossible, and hoping it could therefore buy the chain for a song. Clearly they had misjudged Robert Bazos.

Unaware of the urgency of the situation, Bouchard told Bazos that they could discuss it the following week. "No, it has to be today. Now, in fact," was the reply.

At Perrette headquarters, not far from Couche-Tard's own office in Laval, Bouchard was handed a document describing each of the group's stores. A meeting was set with Bazos and his attorney for June 22, the following day. Bouchard didn't even have time to prepare an offer; but it wasn't necessary. For $15 million, he could buy all 86 stores and their inventory, 56 buildings that housed the majority of them, and the dairy in Laval. Take it or leave it.

Perrette's biggest creditor, IGA, which wanted to get its hands on the struggling company, would be fully repaid, as a priority. This was necessary to get IGA out of its status as a creditor, to remove the possibility that it would try to block the deal. IGA would end up being taught a lesson for its aggressiveness. After receiving protection from the Companies' Creditors Arrangement Act, Perrette would then offer its other suppliers compensation ranging from 50 percent to 75 percent of the amounts owed to them, once the preferred creditor—the CIBC bank—was fully repaid the $3 million it had loaned Perrette. The outstanding debts were gigantic: in the range of $20 million.

The following day, June 23, 1994, Perrette declared bankruptcy after 30 years of existence, and dismissed the 180 employees at its dairy in Laval. The company announced that management of its 84 stores would be transferred to Couche-Tard, under a purchase that was conditional upon an examination of the books.

On June 24, the day of Quebec's national holiday, Couche-Tard took control of Perrette's stores, becoming the biggest depanneur chain in the province, with 300 establishments—60 more than Provi-Soir.

Alain Bouchard had achieved his dream. At the start, however, it seemed more like a nightmare.

Couche-Tard didn't know what to do with a dairy. This uncertainty was compounded by the overproduction of milk in Quebec at the time. The company also lacked the $15 million necessary for the purchase; and it was short on time. No one wanted to deliver merchandise to the bankrupt stores, which the company was trying to run without yet owning them.

Fortunately, Metro was willing to help. More than happy to pull the rug out from under IGA and backed by major financial resources, the food company agreed to supply Perrette stores and to be patient when it came to having the bills paid. That was a great help, since all cash from daily sales had to be handed over to the trustee in charge of managing the bankruptcy. Oil company delivery persons would sometimes call Bouchard at home at 3 a.m., demanding immediate payment for supplying one of its 32 Perrette-affiliated service stations. Stocking a gas station with fuel is expensive, however, especially when you have no access to sales revenue. Couche-Tard was stuck sinking into debt while it searched for a solution.

The price to acquire Perrette was incredible, says Fortin. Nevertheless, the banks weren't lining up to finance the operation; on the contrary. "I would leave a bank office thinking that it had all been sorted out," Fortin says, "then the file would be sent to Toronto, and everything would change." The Canadian banks had been burned by a number of bankruptcies in the convenience store sector and had lost faith in the industry, convinced that the future lay in large food retailers. Faced with refusal from the Bank of Montreal to loan them more money, Couche-Tard turned to a new financial institution: the National Bank, the smallest of the major Canadian banks and the only one whose principal place of business was in Montreal. The bank agreed to take over the existing loans made by the Bank of Montreal and to cover the acquisition costs for Perrette. "Luckily, some solid Quebec financial institutions believed in us," says Fortin. Thinking that it was a bluff, the Bank of Montreal refused to change their position. It resulted in their loss of the Couche-Tard account for good.

The race against the clock had begun. On June 28, a meeting was held for managers of Perrette depanneurs in a Laval hotel. The goal was to reassure them: Couche-Tard would stand by them, and depend on the stores to help the company get through the period of uncertainty they faced together. All but two of the depanneurs would be saved. Their supervisors and district managers would keep their jobs. Downsizing would take place at the head office, where half of the 60 positions—senior executive positions—would be eliminated.

A deal was quickly reached with Sealtest dairy, which agreed to pay $5.6 million to buy the factory previously owned by Perrette; the deal was a way for Sealtest to get rid of a competitor. The Laval plant never reopened, and Sealtest moved some of the dairy's machinery to its Montreal factory.

Couche-Tard could finally submit its formal offer, on July 4: It would pay $9.5 million, which would include the repayment of $5.5 million on unpaid mortgages. The 56 commercial buildings Couche-Tard had acquired would cost it an average of $100,000 each, and each of the 86 stores would come in at $50,000. Those that were rented had leases, in some cases still valid for 10 more years, with fantastic rates: under $1,000 per month. It was a bargain that IGA would have loved to take advantage of. IGA's president, Pierre Croteau, contacted Bouchard directly, almost threateningly. "Get out of there. It's ours. We'll compensate you," he told him. But the head of Couche-Tard had no intention of being intimidated. "Perrette is starting to get back on track," he told Croteau. "Cigarette smuggling has ended, the banner is recovering. The company was going to survive. But you did everything you could to make it tank. I'll never let it go."

IGA turned to the courts to try to block the deal. It claimed it had been prevented from making Perrette's creditors an offer that would be more favourable at the meeting held on July 21, during which the majority had accepted the settlement proposal.

The theatrical scene at the meeting in question had had a touch of vaudeville. Perrette's 500-odd creditors had assembled in the main room of the Bill Wong restaurant on Décarie Boulevard in Montreal. The city was in the throes of a heat wave, and the restaurant's air conditioning was broken. People were practically shouting to get the vote over with so they could get out of that oven. Others complained that IGA had already been shown favour: Every last cent owing to it had been repaid, even though it wasn't a preferred creditor, while others were offered only 30 percent of what they were owed. The more experienced among them knew that rejecting the proposal spelled bankruptcy, pure and simple, which would mean they stood a strong chance of receiving nothing.

As the meeting dragged on, several creditors started calling for extra efforts. A tacit understanding exists in the business world: Everything is negotiable if you apply a little pressure. "We needed to add $500,000," Bouchard says. The meeting was adjourned for a few minutes, which provided an opportunity for Bouchard to negotiate with Bazos in the hallway. Bouchard proposed to split the additional sum between them, fifty-fifty. But Bazos too knew the golden rule of negotiating; he refused.

While all this was happening, a bride in a white dress was pacing the corridor, on the verge of tears. The cause for her distress: The endless meeting was holding hostage the room that had been booked to be her wedding hall.

The deadlock was finally broken when Sealtest, reached by telephone, was persuaded to contribute to the extra amount. Bazos would put down $100,000, Sealtest $150,000 and Couche-Tard $250,000. The creditors approved the proposal by 90 percent. The marriage celebration was finally able to proceed, and Couche-Tard and Perrette were able to move forward with their union.

The lawsuit later launched by IGA only pushed the honeymoon back. The deal simply had to wait for a green light from the courts.

Bouchard thus had two reasons to be happy, instead of one. He had struck back at IGA; and he had gotten back at Bazos—the man who had once forced him to take a taxi home after firing him. The victory over Bazos was all the more gratifying for how long it had taken him. Bouchard says that the day left him charged with emotion—a mixture, no doubt, of pride and the satisfaction of revenge.

Others would have been satisfied to become leaders in their market. With 300 depanneurs and more than 1,600 employees, and annual sales of $325 million, Couche-Tard was starting to carry some serious weight. Nonetheless, Bouchard launched a new front just a few weeks after the deal was made. In an interview with *Entreprendre* magazine, he declared his next target: acquiring Couche-Tard's main competitor, Provi-Soir. "For us, it's a matter of time," he said. It was a bold enough declaration, but he followed it with an outright provocation. "I don't understand what Provigo is still doing in our business: the depanneur market."

But why stop there, for that matter? "The franchise formula has had its day," Bouchard told the magazine. An interesting comment indeed, given that the vast majority of the 300 Couche-Tard stores were franchises!

*　*　*

While depanneurs were the only ones selling grocery products in the evening and on weekends, customers were prepared to pay a premium to shop in them. But once supermarkets had been granted the right to stay open late, seven days a week, the price gap could no longer be justified. Even pharmacists had thrown their hats in the ring. The Jean Coutu pharmacy chain had changed its formula. The stores, previously centred on a rather austere drug counter, were transformed into a veritable bazaar, offering an array of products: stationery, gifts, electronics, games, books and newspapers, lottery tickets, film development, beauty and hygiene products, and dry, canned and frozen foods. Customers could find pretty much anything they wanted—"Anything, even a friend," the advertising slogan proclaimed, adding an odd twist. And somewhere within their stores' expanse, you could even find a feature that some surely found useful in a drug store: a prescription counter.

The end result was a depanneur under another name, one that didn't offer beer, but which nonetheless sold cigarettes—an absurdity, given that the principal function of the business is linked to health.

The metamorphosis of Couche-Tard into Dépan-E$compte, with prices that could compete with those of supermarkets, had had the effect of reducing the profit margin. Under the previous formula, the profit margin had ranged from 26 to 28 percent, according to Jacques D'Amours. After the change, it was between 20 to 22 percent. "Profitability had disappeared for the merchants. Our franchisees were not happy. They started calling us, wanting to sell."

But there weren't many buyers for these stores during that period, when merchants of all kinds were using the commercial franchise formula. Fast food, cleaners, automotive accessories, clothing—franchises were the flavour of the month, and supply exceeded demand. As a result, Couche-Tard began buying back the contracts for its franchises and operating more and more depanneurs itself. Eventually, it bought them all.

This required a major reorganization of the company, a reform that was led by Réal Plourde. "What we needed to do was build an entire operational system to ensure that we could manage the corporate stores by ourselves," he says.

The learning curve was steep, recalls Pierre Peters, an executive who was involved in the transformation. "At the beginning, we were losing money," he says. "We were unstructured. We didn't have controls in place." It boiled down to one problem: How could they make sure that every element in that commercial network worked to its maximum potential—without having a boss on site, as they had had in the franchises? The answer to this question, he says, was what allowed Couche-Tard to become what it is today.

Generally, depanneur managers haven't received a university degree or certification from leading business schools. More often than not, their life's path simply ended up leading them there, with barely a high school diploma under their belt. "They lacked training. That's why we opened 'Couche-Tard training centers,'" says Plourde with pride.

Classrooms were set up in the company's office. Full-time teachers were hired. Courses were offered in accounting, customer service, inventory management and marketing. Couche-Tard had decided to make a massive investment in the skills of its workforce, devoting 3.5 percent of its payroll budget to the cause. "When you train your employees," says Plourde, "they become better operators. But it's also a motivator for them, knowing that the company is ready to invest in their development."

For those who show an interest in climbing the ladder, the program offers a career plan and supplementary courses in finance, human resources management and leadership. The most motivated students receive scholarships to study in university and even to obtain an MBA. Couche-Tard became associated with Montmorency College in Laval for the creation of a program in retail management. More women than men took advantage of the training, the reason being that depanneur positions primarily attract two types of employees: One is students, for whom the job is their first work experience, a part-time employment that provides them with spending money; the other is women over 40 who are returning to the job market after having left it to raise children. They often lack training, but not ambition.

Pierre Peters says that it would be a mistake to assume that since a franchise owner has a direct financial interest in the business, he or she can do a better job managing the depanneur than a salaried manager. Many franchises suffered from a lack of training and adequate tools; they were unable to juggle work schedules, theft and cost overruns. "It seems like a franchise owner should be able to control things better than a manager could, because it's the owner's money that's at stake. But that's not the case. The control system we implemented allowed us to do much better."

Couche-Tard installed computerized cash registers and scanners, put in cameras to control theft, and introduced the release of financial statements at a higher frequency: every four weeks instead of every three months. Each manager had to present a business plan and an operating budget, with a grasp of all the variables. "Our approach was pretty cutting edge," says Plourde, who admits that some weren't sure about the transparency the approach required. "It was argued that managers who only made modest salaries would start realizing that their store was making a good profit, and they would say that we weren't paying them enough." The training played an important role in heading off any problems in that respect. A fundamental lesson had to be instilled in Couche-Tard employees: They were part of a network in which the most profitable contribute to those that are still developing.

* * *

Another part of the transformation involved installing a new computer system that could produce a perpetual inventory, a tool that was essential for keeping operations tightly controlled. This change led to a revelation for Bouchard during one of his annual "presidential visits."

A number of managers were unsatisfied with how the system worked in its early stages, and told Bouchard that they often received calls from the "head office" to resolve different problems. At the end of his tour of the stores, Bouchard rented a reception hall so he could address all the employees from the service centre in Laval, who had become so numerous that none of Couche-Tard's buildings could hold them.

"I'm not here to tell you some good news," he told the assembly. "We all need to understand that in this organization, today and always, you and I are at the service of the stores. Not the other way around." And that, he said, should be reflected in their vocabulary. "There is no *head office* in this company, and there never will be," he insisted. "So, I don't want to hear the words *head office* or *headquarters* anymore. We are a service centre and a training centre—that's it."

Couche-Tard would always insist on this principle in the years to come, in all of its divisions, anywhere in the world. It would be a distinctive mark of the company, a basic element of its personality and culture.

CHAPTER 13

A Hostile Bid to Reach Other Provinces

The Couche-Tard recipe was working like a charm. At the end of 1995, the company announced record profits of $3.2 million[28]—almost 10 times higher than the previous year. The value of its stock had quadrupled in four years, passing the $4.00 mark. The future was so bright that Fidelity, a gigantic American investment fund with USD $300 billion in assets, decided to acquire 10 percent of the shares in Couche-Tard. It was a clear display of confidence.

At the time, two large convenience store chains of equal size shared the market in the neighbouring province of Ontario. Their success was limited. Becker's, a member of the Bazos family, that owned 560 stores, had been accumulating losses for four years. Three years earlier, its competitor, Silcorp, had been forced to seek protection under the Companies' Creditors Arrangement Act, in an attempt to regain financial health. This operation had cost the company dearly, resulting in the loss of half of its stores. Silcorp still held on to 528 stores, under the Mac's and Mike's Mart banners, to which they added 50 Hop In stores in Michigan. The reduction in federal tobacco taxes the previous year had helped increase profitability, but the company's problematic incursion into Western Canada had been a counterweight to the balance sheet.

---

28. In this chapter, all numbers are in CAD$, unless otherwise stated.

In the summer of 1996, taking advantage of a drop in Silcorp's shares, Couche-Tard presented an unsolicited purchase offer of $16.50 per share—the equivalent of $74 million. It was a premium of 26 percent over the previous month's average stock price. Silcorp's share price immediately jumped to $17.00: A sign that the market anticipated a higher bid. That expectation was accurate.

Buying Silcorp was not Couche-Tard's first choice. "Our game plan was to purchase Provi-Soir first," admits Richard Fortin. Along with Alain Bouchard, Fortin had met with Pierre Michaud, chair of Provigo's board, and Pierre Migneault, president and CEO of the food giant, in a private club in downtown Montreal. They hoped to find a more receptive ear than they had encountered during Couche-Tard's last attempt.

However, the two Provigo directors wouldn't loosen their grip on their chain of depanneurs. Richard Fortin would be the last to say they were making the wrong decision; after all, it was well known that Provi-Soir was the most profitable chain in Quebec. Offering an alternative, Michaud and Migneault proposed a merger between the two groups, with the parts divided according to the asset value of each. It was a fool's bargain. "We had fewer stores than they had," Fortin explains, "and ours were less profitable. We would have had 30 percent of the company, even though we were the ones who knew how to operate it." The offer was rejected on the spot. "So then we saw that we had no choice. We were a public company, we needed growth. We had to see about Silcorp," Fortin says.

"We had to see about Silcorp" is a mild way to describe what would in fact be a frontal assault, one that required plenty of ammunition: close to $75 million. Fortin and the brokerage firm, Gordon Capital, began long and difficult negotiations with a number of banks to raise the necessary funds. The main support came from the National Bank and the Caisse de Dépôt et Placement du Québec. That institution, created at the time of the Quiet Revolution in the 1960s, had over $100 billion of capital at its disposal. The Caisse managed pension funds for the province's public sector employees and the Quebec Pension Board, to which all Quebec workers contribute—among other things.

Despite the backing from the National Bank and the Caisse, they were still short. The doors of Toronto's big banks remained closed. Couche-Tard had to call on an outside player to cap off the financing: the Tokyo-Mitsubishi Bank.

Financing preparations were almost settled when Becker's management approached Couche-Tard. The company hoped it could find a lifejacket that would keep it afloat before it sank for good. From the perspective of Couche-Tard's management, however, it was too late. Their efforts to acquire Silcorp had advanced too far; the financing agreements had already been made. On top of that, Silcorp was profitable, therefore a more desirable target.

On the evening of Saturday, August 24, the four Couche-Tard founders found themselves at Bouchard's home, sharing a nice meal to celebrate the start of the pan-Canadian adventure that was opening up before them. Now they had to plan their implementation schedule. In the middle of dinner, Fortin's telephone rang. It was his contact at the Caisse de Dépôt.

There was good news and bad news. The institution's credit committee had agreed to finance the operation, but on the condition that it would raise Couche-Tard's interest rates. Fortin swiftly took a hard stance, even though it risked scuttling the deal. There would be no question of renegotiating the agreement in principle that had been reached. If the Caisse didn't stand by it, their word meant nothing. When the call ended, the mood at the gathering had lost its sparkle. If the financiers didn't back down, they would have to abandon the project.

Bouchard and Fortin would be flying to Toronto the following day. They had hoped they would be presenting their surprise offer to Silcorp's president—who still knew nothing of their plan—on Monday. It was good that he was unaware, given the new circumstances. Would the meeting even come to pass?

Fortin spent Sunday morning pacing at home, waiting for the telephone to ring. Had his refusal to allow the Caisse to change the deal at the last minute pushed the powerful financial institution into backing down, or made them dig in their heels? The answer came before noon: The initial agreement would be respected. They had the green light to start the acquisition process. It had been a close call, but their plan was still on track.

Bouchard and Fortin headed for the airport. They waited until they were in the air to call Silcorp's president, Derek Ridout, to schedule a meeting early the next morning to present their offer. They couldn't reach him, but they succeeded in getting the board's chair on the line. The chair gave them the private number for the president's cottage. An appointment was made for the following morning.

* * *

Couche-Tard was making an ambitious gamble: It was aiming to buy a company twice its size, in a market—Ontario— the directors didn't know well, in a region where they barely spoke the language. "I was so uncomfortable in English," Bouchard says, "that I wrote my questions down before I had a conversation with a supplier." Thus he wasn't entirely at ease as his first contact with Derek Ridout drew near. Luckily, he and Fortin were accompanied by their broker at Gordon Capital, who could help move the discussion along.

They knew the issue thoroughly, had scrutinized every detail. They had even reserved a car to take them from their downtown hotel to the company's headquarters in Scarborough, a suburb of Toronto. When the car arrived, they were flabbergasted. The white limousine was so long it could have seated the company's entire board of directors. What first impression would they give, showing up in that monstrosity? The vehicle looked like something that would transport Mafia dons on their way to a family marriage. Their only hope was that they would be lucky enough that only a Silcorp parking attendant would notice them.

Fate had other plans. The Couche-Tard directors arrived at Silcorp at the exact same time as Ridout, who realized who they were immediately. They could only imagine how arrogant and tacky they must have appeared to Ridout as he watched them pull up in a carriage that only the nouveau-riche would choose. Their own discomfort at the situation no doubt exceeded any that Ridout himself might have felt.

The meeting was courteous, and not much more. Bouchard and Fortin presented their purchase offer: $16.50 per share. The two visitors were thanked politely. Their offer would be submitted to the board of directors, who would consider it. Have a nice day.

The same day, Couche-Tard management announced in a statement that it had presented an unsolicited offer to Silcorp, an offer its president said was a surprise. His comment highlighted the language barrier: Couche-Tard hadn't hidden its desire to penetrate the Ontario market. A year earlier, during the general meeting of Couche-Tard shareholders, Bouchard had specifically mentioned Becker's and Silcorp as the two most likely targets that would help him reach his objective of expanding beyond the Quebec market. Analysts hadn't been sure how to describe this strategy, unusually forthright for the business world. Was it candour, or was it arrogance? One thing was certain: It was direct.

The proposal was unveiled a few days before the Couche-Tard annual general meeting. The mood was ebullient. Once the deal was made, the company would become the leading depanneur chain in Canada, with almost 1,000 stores and around $1 billion in sales. Bouchard announced to his shareholders that he would be moving to Toronto with his family, along with Réal Plourde, the partner in charge of operations, in order to supervise the integration of the new group over a two-year period. Managing the transition remotely wouldn't be possible, he said. Mac's stores that had belonged to Silcorp would take on the yellow and blue colours of Couche-Tard. The battle had ended; the conquerors prepared to raise their flag.

*　*　*

But it wasn't that easy. On September 19, 1996, Silcorp announced that its board of directors had unanimously rejected Couche-Tard's offer, since, in their eyes, it didn't reflect the real value of the company.

This was war. Silcorp refused to grant Couche-Tard access to its books, but it opened them to any other group interested in making a better offer. It refused to submit the proposal to its shareholders to allow them to decide. It withheld its list of shareholders. It threatened to go into debt to pay a hefty dividend to its shareholders, in order to empty its value and become less desirable.

And all that was only a start. On September 30, Silcorp announced its merger with Becker's, effective mid-November. The offer to purchase its main Ontarian rival from the Bazos family had been $33 million; Bazos would also be given 20 percent of Silcorp's capital and thus become its main shareholder.

It was neither a marriage of love nor a marriage of convenience—it was a shotgun wedding. Having been rejected by Couche-Tard two months earlier, Becker's decided that Silcorp's offensive was a good pretext for uniting with the strong partner. Being hunted by Couche-Tard, Silcorp saw its merger with Becker's as an opportunity to expand its waistline to the point that it would lose its appeal.

At least, the directors of the two Ontario companies believed this would be the effect. Though they denied it publicly, Couche-Tard management seriously considered the possibility of swallowing up the happy couple—a move that would have a price tag of more than $100 million. "We looked closely at the question and we were preparing to make a higher bid for the two companies," confirms Fortin, who was Couche-Tard's treasurer. "They thought they had scared us off, but that wasn't the case."

In fact, once the offer from Couche-Tard had expired, Silcorp let them know discreetly that it would consider an offer for $19 a share. Bouchard believed that the Silcorp leaders were incompetent. He had also declared publicly that they had "neither the expertise nor the vision" to make Becker's profitable, adding that their depanneurs were 15 years behind those in Quebec. Let them deal with their problems, then. "I said 'They can try to clean up the mess, and then we'll see.'"

There was another, more important reason to abandon the Ontario project, according to Fortin: "In the meantime, the telephone had rung. It was the people from Provigo. They told us, 'If you're still interested in Provi-Soir, we're ready to talk.'"

The game that they were playing had its limits: Couche-Tard couldn't gobble up companies endlessly, like in a corporate Pac-Man. Acquiring the 1,000 Silcorp/Becker's stores in Canada and the 300 Provigo-owned stores in Ontario, Alberta and mainly Quebec, was simply too much. Moreover, the prospect of buying the Provi-Soir chain, and thereby consolidating Couche-Tard's operating base, was much more attractive than moving to Toronto to do the necessary dirty work there.

"Provigo's directors had lost their confidence," says Bouchard. Couche-Tard's low-price policy had forced them to reduce their margins, and they were unable to make their operations profitable. Their belief was that if Couche-Tard acquired Silcorp, it would put such a strain on the organization from Laval that it would be a long time before they had the resources to purchase Provi-Soir.

However, no other company seemed capable of buying them either. They felt it was necessary to act quickly, before the situation worsened. Provigo's president, Pierre Migneault, didn't attempt to bluff. "I don't like the depanneurs, neither does the board of directors. The industry is going under," he told Bouchard, who was delighted at the events unfolding. "I had wanted to buy it for ages," Bouchard says.

For Bouchard, it was more than a business decision. He felt like he had built Provi-Soir with his own hands. He knew every location by heart. He had even helped pick the mascot: an owl giving an exaggerated wink, an insomniac that was a rival to Couche-Tard's sleepwalker. He no longer harboured a need for vengeance, no matter how badly their relationship had ended. He knew he would have done exactly as Provi-Soir had, were he faced with a rebellious franchisee like himself. Ultimately, he felt simply happy and excited that he had finally acquired the company that, as he puts it, he "had always loved."

Eighty-five million dollars: That's the amount Couche-Tard was ready to put on the table to buy its main rival in Quebec. The purchase would include 245 Provi-Soir stores, along with 21 Winks convenience stores in Ontario and 28 more in Alberta, which operated under two banners: Winks and Red Rooster. Their combined sales were around $300 million— almost a trivial amount for Provigo, which accumulated annual sales of $5.7 billion. The high price per store was explained by the fact that this was, above all, a real estate transaction. Provi-Soir possessed prime locations on busy streets and roads. Even better, 40 percent of its stores we equipped with service stations.

Provigo wanted to sell, but they weren't exactly holding a fire sale. "They didn't give us a gift," as Bouchard puts it. Other players were approached, including Silcorp, which had its hands too full to start a new project, and the big oil companies: Shell, Ultramar and Petro-Canada, all of which had depanneurs coupled with a number of their service stations.

In the end, it was Couche-Tard that submitted the best offer, wholly financed by a bank loan from the three institutions that had agreed to support its offensive against Silcorp. The agreement stipulated that Provigo would remain the supplier for food products for its former stores, while Metro would continue to supply the other Couche-Tard stores.

Provi-Soir franchisees were nervous, and with good reason. For 15 years, a number of them had brought legal proceedings against Provi-Soir. They felt the company had been using unfair practices—criminal, perhaps—against them, with the aim of extracting maximum profits. And then along came Couche-Tard, a competing company that was more dynamic and aggressive, stepping in as boss. The franchisees feared the worst. Plourde saw their concern starkly expressed when he met with those in the Montreal region, after the Provi-Soir purchase had been finalized. Plourde presented the company's philosophy and explained that all existing contracts would be respected to the letter. Then he told them that Couche-Tard would be prepared to buy the franchises from anyone who wanted out. "So, do any of you want to leave?" he asked them. He remembers their response: "Half of the room raised their hands," he says.

So many of them were ready to abandon ship that an order of priority had to be established. Those who had already informed their former owner, Provigo, of their intention would be first in line.

*   *   *

Meanwhile, Bouchard's personal life was also taking in water: His marriage was foundering. His wife, Diane Rioux, who had furiously admonished the bailiff 20 years earlier, vowing that one day they would buy Provi-Soir, left the family at the moment her prediction came true. Taking no luggage with her, she left behind the two children born during the marriage: Jonathan, who had required so much attention over the years, and Karinne, born two years later, in 1979—the year when Bouchard had opened his first depanneur.

Karinne's memories of childhood are inseparable from the early years of Couche-Tard. She remembers the smell of her father's cluttered office above the depanneur in Saint-Jérôme, where she often would accompany him to sit on an old crate of milk containers as he worked. While he combed through his accounts again and again—this was the period when the banker had told him he was technically bankrupt—Karinne would amuse herself by emulating her father and juggling numbers. "When I was in kindergarten," she says, "I didn't like to play. My father had given me a little notebook with calculations to do. That's what I did while my friends were playing!" The apple truly didn't fall far from the tree. In fact, maybe in some ways it didn't fall far enough: "My father taught me to haggle on everything," she says. "I never want to pay full price, for anything. It drives my husband crazy."

Karinne was an adolescent when her parents separated and her father assumed sole custody of the children. Despite all his work obligations, Bouchard was never an absent father, Karinne says. "He was always home for dinner."

Indeed, a late-day visitor to the Couche-Tard service centre in Laval—the very heart of a multibillion-dollar multinational company of extended-hours stores—would be astonished to find the premises looking like a ghost town at 6 p.m.: The vast parking lot empty; everyone having gone home for the day.

The example came from the very top. Bouchard had personally reproached employees "caught in the act" of working too many hours. One night when he passed by his office to pick up a file, Bouchard found an attorney, recently hired by Couche-Tard's legal department, busy preparing a contract. He lectured him at length. "You have a family, a wife and kids. What are you still doing here at this hour? Go home!" he ordered. The young employee explained that it was normal for lawyers to work long hours, and that he'd been taught to stay late in the private firms he'd worked in before coming to Couche-Tard. "To me, it isn't normal," Bouchard responded. "You have to have a balanced life to be able to reach your potential. I'm paying you to have clear ideas. Go home to your family, and don't let me see you in the office this late at night again."

* * *

Merging Couche-Tard and Provi-Soir was not without its challenges. But that came as no surprise. The two companies, similar in size, had been rivals for years, in a period during which the depanneur industry had gone through the worst crisis in its history. The battle had left scars; a reconciliation was needed. It would start with a symbolic gesture: The Provi-Soir owl would become the emblem for the entire group, and the Couche-Tard sleepwalker would finally be put to bed. The calm but alert Provi-Soir owl—a predator waiting for the best opportunity to snatch its prey—would be a better representation of what Couche-Tard had become than the sleepy wanderer, as likeable as he was.

The management team then started doing what had worked best in its recent acquisitions. It involved going out into the field, meeting employees, setting objectives. Crucially, it also meant providing the means, offering training—and learning. "We don't approach it like a clean slate and say 'Here are our policies and here's how it works,'" explains Jacques D'Amours. "We look for what's working well and import it into our stores." Couche-Tard's most effective practices would be integrated into the new acquisitions, and vice versa.

This attitude is an integral part of Couche-Tard's philosophy; it was built into its DNA by the company's four founders. It's the secret of their success. "Operations have always been our strong point," says Richard Fortin. For the group, each store should be considered a laboratory where the best ideas can germinate. It is therefore necessary to harvest them and disseminate them, rather than trampling on new growths.

Their purchase of Provi-Soir stores in Ontario and Alberta would test that openness. The cultures were different, and so were the operational models. Working too hard on creating continuity, a uniform structure, was doomed to end in failure. Indeed, *different* can be just as good, and can sometimes even lead to better results. Accepting diversity—considering it a strength rather than a weakness—would one day be one of Couche-Tard's greatest assets. To start with, though, the thing for the leaders to focus on was learning.

There was a lot to consider. What could they possibly do with a small group of 28 Red Rooster and Winks convenience stores stranded in the middle of the vast plains of Western Canada? Bouchard and his partners put the question in negative terms; the answer seemed predetermined.

They travelled to Alberta, where they had gathered the directors and employees of the tiny operation. "It's too far away. We don't have time," they thought. It had to end. In broken English, Bouchard told the employees that Couche-Tard's ambition was to build an enormous network that could stand up to its biggest rivals. There was only one way to get there: growth—constant growth. In Alberta, however, Mac's and 7-Eleven dominated the market. What good would it do them to keep these 28 stores? The Couche-Tard leaders revealed their intention: to sell the business.

But the Albertans protested. Considering their reaction, Bouchard decided to give them an opportunity. "Okay," he said. "So help convince me that it's not the right move." He gave them two hours, and left the room so they could deliberate.

When he returned, the employees presented him with a business plan—an aggressive one—and told him they were on board with Couche-Tard's goal of constant growth. Even better, their plan was rooted in initiatives they had wanted to take in the past—initiatives that Provigo had opposed, preferring to lay down the law from thousands of kilometres away.

Alain Bouchard was won over by their enthusiasm, their desire to push the store concept forward. Why not give them a chance to run with it? He returned from the trip ready to discuss the possibility of opening 70 new depanneurs in Western Canada.

He was also thoroughly convinced of one thing: He had to improve his English if—as he had insisted to his Albertan employees—he truly wanted to make Couche-Tard grow. His recent experience at Silcorp had been indisputable proof: If he had only been fluent in English, he could have called the company's CEO, Derek Ridout. "He would have talked to me," Bouchard says, and they could have found a common ground. "I was ill-equipped because of that handicap, my lack of English." He hired a private teacher and began an intensive education in the language of business. Being able to communicate with his employees outside Quebec—"*See you next time in Toronto!*"—would make all the difference.

CHAPTER 14

The Start of a Business Model

In 1999, Alain Bouchard gave himself a memorable present for his 50th birthday: Silcorp, a company twice the size of Couche-Tard.

Since the unsuccessful attempt to buy the parent company of Mac's convenience stores two years earlier, both Couche-Tard and Silcorp had spent time streamlining their operations. Couche-Tard had integrated the Provi-Soir chain; Silcorp had done the same with Becker's. Each had consolidated its position as the leader in its own market.

Bouchard had asked a trusted ally in Ontario, Peter Flach, to keep in touch with Silcorp's vice-president, Joe Lewis, during this period. Flach had been charged with overseeing Couche-Tard's aggressive expansion in the rest of Canada. In the fall of 1998, he gave Bouchard the news he'd been waiting for: Silcorp was ready to accept an acquisition offer.

Bouchard placed a phone call to Silcorp's president, Derek Ridout in December. Bouchard had made progress in English, but he was still far from capable of holding a conversation fluently. In preparation, he wrote out what he wanted to say beforehand.

To Bouchard's great surprise, Ridout showed his cards during the call. He admitted straight out that he had never liked the convenience store industry. Bouchard wasn't sure he understood. "You don't like what you're doing, and you continue to do it day after day?" he asked, incredulously.

"It was unbelievable," Bouchard says. "He was president of the company, and he hated it. He hated convenience stores. He never went in the stores, he never attended operators' meetings." His attitude and actions were completely opposite to those of the Couche-Tard founders. For them, visiting stores— their own or those of competitors—was one of the most interesting part of their job.

Bouchard proposed that he and Ridout meet in Toronto so they could talk in person. They could discuss whether it might be possible to start negotiations for an acquisition—one that would be amicable, this time around. He knew that Silcorp's management team wouldn't throw sand in the gears as long as Couche-Tard applied enough oil to keep its parts moving happily. In other words: It was a question of price.

* * *

It was clear that the National Bank would continue to back the financing of the operation. But since Couche-Tard's failed attempt to purchase Silcorp two years prior, the bank had bought a brokerage firm, named after its founders, Lévesque, Beaubien, Geoffrion Inc. The bank hoped that the firm would act as consultant for the transaction. And, unfortunately for that plan, Bouchard had a long memory.

Bouchard sourly remembered how Lévesque, Beaubien, Geoffrion Inc. had treated Couche-Tard a few years earlier. The haughty attitude with which the firm's directors had looked down on the small retailer had left a bad taste in his mouth. Réal Raymond, then vice-president in charge of corporate banking for the National Bank and later its president, in

2002,[29] said "Our chances of getting the contract weren't very good." Still, he convinced Richard Fortin to allow him to meet with Bouchard to try to persuade him to change his mind.

Raymond had first met Richard Fortin by chance, during a round of golf a decade earlier. It was not long after Fortin had left the vice-president's position at the Canadian branch of the Société Générale de France—to manage depanneurs from a basement office.

The decision seemed puzzling to say the least. "I said to him, 'You have to explain why you're doing this.'" Fortin told him about Bouchard and his project of building the largest chain of convenience stores in Quebec. "He's an extraordinary guy," Fortin told him. "He offered to make me a partner, and I jumped at the chance. Because I believe in him."

The years proved him right. Then the time came to move on to the next step: the move that would make Couche-Tard the top convenience store network in Canada and one of the 10 biggest in North America.

Raymond wanted to get involved in that massive project. Financing such an operation could be extremely lucrative; but he had no illusions that it would be easy. He would have to break down Bouchard's resistance. "Before meeting with us, he had said, 'There's no way I'm hiring those guys,'" Raymond remembers.

Nonetheless, against all odds, Raymond won the contract. From there, things moved very quickly, and everything was settled in less than two months.

The process gave Raymond the chance to get to know Bouchard's entrepreneurial qualities: his intense desire to make his company grow, his talent in surrounding himself

---

29. Réal Raymond was president of the National Bank from 2002 to 2007. At the time of writing, he is chair of the board for Metro.

with strong colleagues and his skill as a negotiator. Raymond remembers, "Alain told me, 'You're a banker. You charge for financing and consultation. I earn money half a cent at a time, selling bubble gum. Stop billing me!' He came from a world where every half cent's worth of efficiency is everything."

The purchase offer was filed on March 1, 1999. It was for the hefty sum of $220 million[30] for the 974[31] Silcorp stores, located mainly in Ontario, but also in the Western provinces. The offer, which came to $23.00 per share, represented a 45 percent premium to the average closing price in the 60 days previous. Unsurprisingly, the deal was unanimously supported by Silcorp's management, which saw it as a win-win situation.

"We paid a high price, but it was worth it," says Bouchard. In a single move, Couche-Tard had tripled its stores, now owning 1,600 in total, and doubled its sales, reaching the $1.6 billion mark. It had also jumped from 22nd to 9th position among the largest convenience store networks in North America. Its staff went from 4,500 to 11,500; and owing to the fact that the two companies operated in different territories, the "marriage of convenience"[32] required little in the way of job cuts.

"The acquisition is for growth, not for streamlining," Bouchard told a press conference, accompanied by the president of Silcorp, Derek Ridout. Ridout reassured investors by pledging to stay in his position for a few more years. That didn't happen. On June 1, 1999, less than a month after the transaction was concluded, Ridout, Joe Lewis, the director of operations, and Mike Rousseau, the director of finance, all left the company.

---

30. In this chapter, all figures are in CAD$, unless otherwise stated.
31. The stores operated under various banners: Mac's, Becker's, Mike's Mart and Daisy Mart.
32. English-language newspapers reporting on the event tended not to miss the chance to employ this pun.

* * *

Two years earlier, while they were hoping to acquire Silcorp, Couche-Tard's founding team had decided that they would split in two to operate the new entity. There seemed to be no way around moving to Toronto for at least a few years. "Réal Plourde and I said we would go together. He would be the operator, I would be the builder," says Bouchard.

But when the time came, they felt differently, for a number of reasons. One of these was a personal one: Bouchard was in a relationship. He had met Sandra Chartrand three years earlier, while Chartrand was working for Centraide of Greater Montreal. She had initiated the meeting with the hope of recruiting Bouchard as a volunteer for the charity's financing campaign. He had accepted and continued to participate in the event each year after that.

After his divorce, Bouchard started dating Chartrand, who was 12 years his junior and the mother of a young girl, Camille. Bouchard, who had always wanted to have another child, had found his ideal partner. He appreciated Chartrand's good heart, her openness to others, her generosity and her sincere affection for his son, Jonathan. She was 38 years old; there was little time to lose to make additions to her family. No time was wasted; the following year, the couple welcomed a daughter, whom they named Rose.

Réal Plourde had no more interest than Bouchard in the possibility of moving to Ontario. In fact, he dreamed of creating a more decentralized mode of operation for the company, one that would incorporate local expertise. During the negotiations (which were friendly), Plourde and Bouchard went to Toronto to meet with Silcorp's directors. "Réal's English was even more patchy than my own," Bouchard recalls with amusement. "He had an accent you could cut with a knife." Despite this limitation—or maybe partially because of it— Plourde quickly concluded that Silcorp's upper management was part of the problem rather than the solution.

Bouchard says that Ridout, Lewis and Rousseau "could hardly fit through the doors" due to the size of their egos. They took a condescending attitude toward the Quebecers who believed they could do better than the current owners had done. Indeed, Silcorp's management seemed to them like monarchs governing a kingdom that they never bothered to visit. They were surrounded by members of their court who informed them of the situation in the villages in their territory.

Plourde had been struck by his encounter with one of the main people in charge of Silcorp operations. Plourde had asked the man to describe what his job was. He had responded that, unfortunately, half of his time was spent preparing charts for the board of directors. "That's the problem when a company becomes too bureaucratic and hierarchical," says Plourde. "It turns into a factory for producing reports and analyses. The concrete aspects are forgotten—like the customer who comes into the store, and who needs good service so that he'll return."

"We concluded that the whole top organization wasn't functioning as it should," says Bouchard. He assembled all of Silcorp's operators who worked on the ground: the managers from different geographical sectors, from northern Ontario or downtown Calgary. These were the people who thought the same way Bouchard and his team did. They were motivated by the daily challenges of making the company run well. They were willing to fight for it. "The decision we took then still applies throughout our organization today," says Bouchard. "We took a decentralized approach."

The Toronto office had been decapitated, losing its status as headquarters. After all, why have one in Ontario, when Couche-Tard didn't have one in Laval? Bouchard repeated it endlessly to his new team: "Head office doesn't exist." Toronto would become a service centre; Calgary was given one as well.

The company was organized into three divisions: Quebec, Ontario and Western Canada. A meeting with the Calgary directors, Kim Trowbridge and David Rodgers, played a determining role in this decision, says Plourde. "I asked them what we could do to improve the company," he said. Their response was strangely familiar to the men from Quebec. *People in Ontario come up with all the marketing,* they told him. *They don't know our clients. They send us promotions that aren't relevant here. We should be figuring out our own strategy.*

It was an approach that was all too common for pan-Canadian companies: They would translate their ads into French for Quebec, without bothering to understand the cultural codes of that unique market. Couche-Tard's founders thus instinctively shared Trowbridge and Rodgers' frustration.

They decided to adopt the inverse strategy. In Richard Fortin's view, it was the most important decision in the company's history: to delegate power to the regions. "It's the model that would end up allowing us to buy convenience stores around the world."

* * *

Richard Fortin will never forget the press conference on March 1, 1999, at which Bouchard announced the acquisition of Silcorp. It started when the first question that a journalist asked took him aback, says Fortin. The question was: *What's next?* To Fortin, it was as though that day's deal wasn't important enough in and of itself, and all eyes were already turned to watch for the next deal. "It bothered me, because we had worked so hard to bring the operation together."

But it was Bouchard's response to the reporter that really made Fortin's eyes widen. He delivered the answer with directness: "We're going to enter the United States."

If Fortin was worried—*was Bouchard bipolar, in the throes of a manic episode?*—the markets seemed to share his feeling. Couche-Tard's shares lost 7.5 percent of their value that very day, dropping to $18.50.

In fact, however, the United States market was the logical next step. Having become number one in Canada with the Silcorp deal, Couche-Tard had to look south to continue its growth. It was the very fact of its dominating the Canadian market that opened up the possibility of venturing over the border. The company had finally acquired the necessary credibility, in Réal Raymond's view. "Without that deal, I don't think Couche-Tard could have entered the American market. It lacked the size, the expertise and the market recognition needed to find financing."

In the meantime, however, Couche-Tard had to show it was able to operate its 1,000 new stores outside Quebec. Its program to update facilities was ambitious. The company planned to triple the number of convenience stores equipped with service stations; change the interior design, with the goal of offering an expanded selection of fast-food; increase the presence of ATMs; and install scanners connected to the service centre, where purchases would be grouped to take advantage of the economies of scale made possible by the company's size.

Couche-Tard would thus become the first fully connected network of convenience stores in North America. It allowed the company to control inventory more effectively, and to adapt purchases to real customer needs. It was a way to practice micromarketing: They could adjust the selection, store by store, according to the tastes and habits of each market.

Plourde began to visit the new stores one by one, with Bouchard in tow. They spoke with managers, listened to their suggestions and assessed their needs and their potential. "You have to take the pulse in the store," he says. The only problem was that there were now about a thousand pulses to be taken.

When Plourde became the fourth musketeer in the Couche-Tard founding team almost 15 years earlier, he didn't envision spending his whole life with the company. Despite pressure from Bouchard, who worried that it was a reflection of his loyalty to the company, Plourde had said he would stay only as long as it was fun for him. Since then, Couche-Tard had weathered many storms and undergone many transformations. There had been no time to become bored, but he was beginning to feel that he had been around the block.

Then the Silcorp acquisition had happened, and just in time. It piqued his interest once again, and also strengthened the bond between the leaders of Couche-Tard. "What held us together was the thrill of the project of getting outside Quebec," he says. It was the perfect challenge to match their combined talents.

* * *

Typically, says Bouchard, the stronger a company becomes, the more it tends to impose its procedures on all of its components. Couche-Tard's strength lies in taking almost the opposite tack. "Our DNA is the local business model," Bouchard says. "It's the most important element. It's what allowed us to build everything we've built."

He's such a firm believer in the importance of this principle that, during his many travels, Bouchard has been known to respond with a certain amount of heat when local management spends more than a few hours in its offices to present their results, plans or forecasts. "Where should we spend the week?" he would ask rhetorically, before answering the question: "In the stores, since that's where the company's culture and best practices are transmitted. We have to be taking notes."

Bouchard may have an accent that places him as unmistakeably from Quebec, but he speaks an entrepreneurial language that is universal: the language of people who deal directly with customers on a daily basis. "That's why we have such a great organization," he says. "We're constantly learning. My ego doesn't prevent me from buying another company with 20 stores that do things better than us and transferring their ideas to all of our own stores."

This philosophy was put to the test when Silcorp was purchased and Bouchard had his first meeting with the directors at the company's administrative office in Scarborough. After having explained how Couche-Tard operates, he asked them whether they had any questions. An executive spoke up: "We have a powerful IBM AS400 computer that provides us with extremely detailed reports on our operations," he said, "but in Quebec you have a number of smaller computers that aren't well integrated. How are you planning to coordinate everything?"

"It was more of an editorial than a question," Bouchard says. But he didn't take offence. He simply burst out laughing and told the man flatly that he wasn't an IT specialist. "But what I can tell you is that we have always kept the best elements from any new company we buy, and we will continue to do so." His answer diffused the tension; the tone helped earn the support of the directors. This wasn't a game of hockey—the Montreal

Canadiens vs. the Toronto Maple Leafs, to complete the analogy—where a victory on one side is achieved by scoring against the other side.

The IT experts in both Toronto and Montreal ended up deciding that both sides' computer systems were outdated; all the computers would be replaced. There were no losers: It was a win-win.

* * *

Give more power to the regions. Acknowledge that it's the store employees who know most about what the customers want. All well and good: But it's also important to have direction. Each store can't simply do whatever it wants and act essentially as an independent retailer. The Couche-Tard founders knew their stores down to the last shelf. They weren't about to start signing blank cheques.

So the question was how to reconcile these two seemingly contradictory imperatives: on the one hand, to regionalize decision-making powers and delegate a maximum of responsibility to the stores; on the other, to allow the company to exercise tight control of operations in order to increase efficiency and profitability.

As a starting point, Plourde implemented a standardized reporting system throughout the company, one that was already being used by Couche-Tard in Quebec. It would provide the directors with an overview of their network and of each store's individual performance. But he was met with a certain amount of resistance. Some made the valid point that all the stores weren't on an equal playing field. Quebec stores had a huge advantage, being able to sell beer and wine. Plourde was swayed by the arguments he heard. He set about developing a more refined system for benchmarking, one that would allow them to measure store performance within each division. The goal was to create a healthy emulation culture. "That's how we became effective," he says.

Of course, more had to be done. Accounting requires a certain amount of regularity to be effective; the same goes for establishing team spirit. For that reason, Couche-Tard instituted a mandatory meeting during which each division would report its results every four weeks. Holding the meetings in person was impossible: The territory to cover was too vast, the distances too great and upper management's time too valuable. Telephone was overly impersonal; it wouldn't help unite the senior management team effectively.

They decided on video conferences. These virtual meetings—innovative then—would become an integral part of Couche-Tard's business cycle. They would involve comparing gross margins earned on each product line: gas, food, cigarettes, etc. Earnings, however, were not the only measure for business performance. Was store traffic growing? Did the manager turnover rate exceed the limit, fixed at 20 percent annually? "If a division is at 30 percent," says Plourde, "there's a problem with human resources management. You're either picking the wrong people, failing to integrate them or not training them properly." It's a signal that it's time to look closely, to find the root cause and make the necessary corrections. Failing to do so will inevitably start to affect morale at all levels. This will have an impact on customer service and, in turn, store performance. The same logic can be applied to many other indicators: the number of workplace accidents, absenteeism rates, use of overtime, employee attendance for training offered by the company. All variables were measured, compared and discussed in Couche-Tard's meetings.

Thus Couche-Tard became an immense laboratory. Each store and each division was encouraged to take initiative. When they did, the results would be studied by other parts of the company, in order to foster a dynamic of constant improvement. Through trial and error, Couche-Tard found that each market manager should supervise no more than 10 to 12 convenience stores. Overseeing more would make it difficult to meet existing needs, to give the right support to managers and to ensure that employees are properly trained. Too many stores per market manager would result in a false economy—the numbers proved it.

By measuring the effects of adopted strategies, the benchmarking system allowed the network to correct itself. Administrators in Laval would no longer be making the decisions and handing them down to their branches. The best ideas, no matter where they originated, would inspire the other components of the company. In reality, the approach meant treating everyone in the company with dignity and respect. That's something Plourde remains extremely proud of. "If we showed up in Toronto and said, 'Here's how it's going to work,' we wouldn't have had the same success as we did by explaining our vision to people who worked in a specific environment. So they ended up adopting the system and became the carriers of it."

Indeed, the vice-president of operations for each region was asked to develop his own business plan—a description of what they would do if they were owner of their own company. Advertising, marketing, human resources, accounting—they had authority over all of it. Bouchard would reserve just one prerogative, one that touched on an aspect he excelled at: developing stores. Whether it was to make an existing store bigger or to build a new one, no major investment could be made without it passing through his office first, where it would be scrutinized and considered in light of demographic information.[33]

* * *

Couche-Tard quickly developed a model that would guide its future stores. "Strategy 2000" is no doubt the best example of the four founders' willingness to use the best ideas developed by other members of the Couche-Tard group as inspiration. The project was originally developed by the Mac's division, just before Silcorp was taken over by Couche-Tard. It was then known as "Store 2000."

The model store was somewhat larger than most existing ones, sometimes as big as 280 square metres (3,000 square feet). It included a self-serve food court, with a coffee and bakery counter, as well as a fast-food section that was often concessioned to a well-known chain like Pizza Hut or Subway. Its most original feature was its decor: it could take the look of an old-time general store, mirror a European bistro or even an exotic jungle. Each establishment would determine its own interior design, based on its customer demographics. The idea was to make it an attractive destination, rather than a last resort that was convenient and nothing more.

* * *

At the end of 1999, Bouchard was the focus of a series of glowing articles in a number of newspapers and magazines in Canada and abroad. *The Wall Street Journal* published a long

---

33. At the time of writing, while Alain Bouchard is no longer in the role of CEO of Couche-Tard, this practice continues.

interview with the businessman, portrayed as a prodigious success, who had skyrocketed to the top of the business world.

"We have decided to enter the American market," Bouchard, as forthright as ever, told the interviewer. He gave himself a two-year timeline to find and purchase a company that was big enough to achieve this: a company that counted 200 to 300 stores and management strong enough to serve as a springboard from which he could develop a national chain in the United States. Close to 100,000 convenience stores existed in the United States, and the biggest player only held six percent of that huge market. "There is room for a consolidator," declared Alain Bouchard, "and it is my intention to take a leadership role to achieve this."

Clearly, the man was afraid of nothing—except water, perhaps, a fear that lingered from a childhood trauma that he couldn't overcome. One day while swimming, his uncle had playfully pushed his head under the water, and held it there for too long; the boy was overwhelmed with panic, believing he would drown. Many years later, as a leader who had tested his mettle in the business world, he was a fighter and a survivor; but he wasn't the type to dive into a new venture without first testing the depth of the water and the power of the current.

In another interview, conducted on the eve of the millennium, he quantified his ambitions. Within 10 years, he predicted, Couche-Tard would have 2,000 to 3,000 stores in the United States; within 15 years, 1,500 to 2,000 in Europe. His appetite seemed limitless. Where would it end? *At what age would he choose to retire?* asked a journalist from the Canadian Press. The response was delivered with an air of absolute certainty: *Never.*

He wasn't being entirely serious, of course. But the quip had an effect on Réal Plourde. As the thinker behind Couche-Tard's organizational structure and head of human resources, he was concerned with preparing a new generation to take over for the four founders of the company—Bouchard included, regardless of what he said to the contrary. The process would take time; Plourde needed to know how much. During their annual retreat, devoted to anticipating the challenges and projects—both personal and professional—that lay on the horizon, Plourde put his cards on the table.

"We have to decide when we're going to retire," he said. Bouchard was dumbfounded. "Are you out of your mind?" he answered. "I'm still young. I don't know when I'll want to stop." Richard Fortin, however, thought the discussion was worth having. Plourde led the way, and announced that he planned to retire at 60. Fortin said that was an excellent idea, and he would do the same. Jacques D'Amours asked for some time to think about it; but his first instinct was that retiring at 60 would be good for him as well. Bouchard felt like he was on the spot: He had to commit. He told them he would retire at 65…but he wouldn't leave the company. It was what he truly loved to do. His role would evolve, but it wouldn't end.

According to the schedule of departures they had made, Fortin was going to be the first to leave, followed three years later by Plourde. That meant two heavyweights would need to be replaced.

CHAPTER 15

Small Strides
in the United States

On May 16, 2001, Couche-Tard announced its entry into the American market with the acquisition of 225 stores. They operated in Illinois, Indiana and Kentucky, under the name Bigfoot.

The company that owned the group, the Johnson Oil Company, was founded in 1957 by Dick Johnson. It started as a simple distributor of petroleum products. In the 1980s, Johnson Oil began equipping its service stations with convenience stores until they all had one. Johnson Oil had never had a deficit year. It was profitable—as predictable as a metronome—but the Johnson family wanted to get out, since the new generation had other interests than to run and to develop convenience stores.

However, the company was very involved in its community, and it wanted some conditions on the sale. The buyer had to commit to maintaining the 65 jobs at the company's headquarters in Columbus, Indiana, and to keep the name Bigfoot for as long as possible. And above all, the Johnsons wanted to sell the company to a player who would be determined to ensure the company's growth. That part fit Couche-Tard to a T.

Bouchard had been travelling east to west and north to south across the United States for two years, trying to find the perfect jewel for the Couche-Tard crown. There had been serious discussions with four or five companies, but each of them had stalled. He was looking for a profitable company and was ready to pay for it. But he also wanted to find a strong administrative team that could transform the enterprise into a bridgehead for his invasion of the United States: a country in which the convenience store market amounted to USD $250 billion a year. He made no secret of his objective: Within five years, Couche-Tard would own more stores in the United States than in Canada—even though the number of Canadian stores was growing at an annual rate of 20 percent.

At the start of 2001, Bouchard received a phone call from Alan Radlo from the American investment fund Fidelity, one of Couche-Tard's main shareholders. "You're ready for the American market," he said. "And we'll support you." If the Couche-Tard recipe worked well north of the 49th parallel, why not south of it?

Since it had acquired Silcorp, things were running quite smoothly for Couche-Tard in Canada. The "Strategy 2000" stores were a great success. The company began building a massive distribution centre in Laval that would take over from Provigo and Metro when the agreements with the two food giants expired in 2002. Couche-Tard had grown big enough to become its own distributor. The gesture of independence would lift its annual earnings by some USD $7 million.

Bouchard, however, is not known for being easily satisfied; despite his success, some things rankled. He had built his company without the help of government subsidies. His convenience stores—like all convenience stores—had become gigantic harvesting machines, raking in tax dollars. This was particularly true for gas, alcohol and tobacco, not to mention lottery tickets. And yet, governments were adopting increasingly severe laws and regulations to limit sales of these products. As a result, if, for example, a clerk decided to ignore the law and sell tobacco products to a minor who was an acquaintance from the neighbourhood, it could lead to heavy fines that would be charged to the owner of the company.

In a fiery speech before the Board of Trade of Metropolitan Montreal, Bouchard criticized the two levels of government for requiring retailers to play the role of police after having first turned them into tax collectors. "As convenience stores, we are sick and tired of being the scapegoats for a society that doesn't take responsibility except through hypocritical acts of legislation."

Soon, however, he would find a way to turn the paternalistic attitude of governments to his advantage.

* * *

In the summer of 2000, Couche-Tard incited a minor revolution in the world of slushies—the sugary mixture of crushed ice and sweet flavours adored by children. Up to that time, convenience stores in its network sold products from the American company Slush Puppie. As in many other areas, Bouchard felt he needed to impose his own brand with the hope of making another profit margin grow.

Couche-Tard invested millions of dollars in acquiring hundreds of slushy distributors, developing flavours and creating an irreverent advertising campaign intended to make a big splash. Couche-Tard's "Sloche" was named in reference to a substance well known by Quebecers in their oft-frigid northern climate: the dirty muck found along streets when the snow melts in spring. *Sloche* is part snow, part water and thoroughly filthy.

And with a name like that, why not take things a step further? Raspberry Sloche, scarlet-red in colour, was christened "Sang-Froid" ("Cold Blood"). Grape was "Full Zinzin"

("Completely Insane," with a play on the sound of the French word for grape, *raisin*). Blueberry was named "Schtroumpf Écrasé" ("Crushed Smurf").[34] Another flavour, unsettlingly black in colour, was called Goudron Sauvage ("Wild Tar").

Clearly, the target was a young audience, in that rebellious zone between the ages of nine and 17. The advertising campaign that accompanied the launch of the product put more weight on that strategy. The ads brazenly mocked common public health messages. Banners on busses proclaimed that a Sloche "contains eight non-essential elements," and announced that it constitutes "a good source of crushed ice." Their sarcastic approach went so far as to parody the advertisements imposed by Health Canada on cigarette packages, featuring graphic photos showing the ravages of cancer caused by tobacco use.

Couche-Tard's referential advertisement showed a discoloured face, with the caption "Sloche can cause colouration of the mouth." Then there was the ad showing the interior of a human skull, with the phrase "Sloche temporarily freezes the brain." The ad campaign for "Rosebeef" Sloche won five awards from the advertising association Publicité-Club de Montréal, including its highest distinction, the Grand Coq d'Or.

The formula's success was explosive. Sloche sales went through the roof, reaching 400 percent of Slush Puppie sales in just one summer. Gross margin on the product reached 60 percent.

Everything Couche-Tard touched seemed to turn to gold. Its shares were trading at 20 times earnings, a sign that investors were confident in continued growth. They would not be disap-

---

34. Failing to obtain rights to use the name, the flavour was renamed "Winchire-wacheur," a neologism based on the French pronunciation of "windshield washer."

pointed. Despite the widespread stock market collapse in 2001, Couche-Tard shares posted one of the best performances of the 300 largest Canadian companies that year. Its stock doubled in value between April and November, sales were up 56 percent, and profits leaped by 84 percent.

So why risk everything with a venture in the United States, knowing that a number of other Canadian retailers had lost their shirts doing the same? Was acquiring the Bigfoot chain a smart move? Couche-Tard's board of directors was clearly worried. Richard Fortin shared its feeling. "I told my partners we needed to find a way to finance the purchase without putting the Canadian operations up for collateral." Thus, they figured out how to pay for the American firm without chaining that purchase to the good ship Couche-Tard; should the new vessel spring a leak, it was crucial that it not end up sinking their entire fleet.

Taking inspiration from the coup they had pulled off in the company's infancy—the purchase of their first 11 Couche-Tard stores in Quebec City—the four leaders managed to finance the transaction by leveraging the real estate assets owned by their target for purchase. They found an American buyer for all the buildings owned by Johnson Oil, and Couche-Tard would become their renters. The money they raised from this sale of assets was sufficient for an American bank to agree to extend them a loan that would cover the balance of the purchase cost without requiring additional collateral.

It was all coming together. They would not dive recklessly into the waters of the United States market, but, entering with some measure of caution, they were prepared to get wet all the same.

* * *

Happy times, before misfortune struck the Bouchard family: Alain Bouchard, age eight, sitting on his father's truck in Chicoutimi.

A rock band formed by Alain Bouchard and his friends, performing in Micoua, northeast of Quebec City. Bouchard, at left, played the drums.

In 1985, Alain Bouchard and his partners acquired 11 Couche-Tard depanneurs in the Quebec City region. The Couche-Tard name would become their trademark.

Official photo of one of the most successful and long-running entrepreneurial teams ever created. Left to right: Richard Fortin, Alain Bouchard, Jacques D'Amours and Réal Plourde in 1987.

In the summer of 1986, Couche-Tard was listed on the stock market, only to end up a symbol of the greed of business people in Quebec. From left to right, the three founders of the company: Jacques D'Amours, Alain Bouchard and Richard Fortin.

Despite Couche-Tard being the subject of ridicule the previous year, in 1987 Bouchard received the Dunamis award for the large commercial enterprise of the year from the Laval Chamber of Commerce from Quebec Premier Robert Bourassa.

Top, a Perrette store in Montreal's Verdun neighbourhood.
Bottom, the same store converted into a Couche-Tard after the incredible
acquisition of the Perrette chain in 1994.

Alain Bouchard with Derek Ridout in 1999, during the acquisition of Silcorp, which doubled the size of Couche-Tard: "It was unbelievable. He hated convenience stores," said Bouchard.

In 2001, Couche-Tard made its first breakthrough in the United States with the acquisition of Bigfoot. At left, Brian Hannasch, who ran the operations of the company in the United States Midwest. At right, Alain Bouchard with Dick Johnson, the founder of Bigfoot.

Caricature of Alain Bouchard in the trade magazine *Your Convenience Manager Magazine* in 2003. In that year, Couche-Tard acquired 2,000 Circle K stores in the Southern United States, becoming the fourth largest convenience store chain in North America.

A bold and provocative ad for the "Rosebeef" Sloche, aimed at adolescent consumers.

A Mac's convenience store in Ontario, featuring the Couche-Tard owl, in 2004.

One of the stores based on the "Concept 2000" design, in 2005. This store has a racecar theme, an activity popular in the Indianapolis area.

Space exploration was the inspiration for this Couche-Tard store in Quebec City, shown in 2001.

Alain Bouchard has been a passionate fisherman since he was a teenager on Quebec's North Shore. He pursues the hobby in different locations all over the world.

The four founders of Couche-Tard on one of their annual fishing trips in the Laurentian Mountains. They have good reason to celebrate: In 2000, less than 15 years after it was created, Couche-Tard became the biggest chain of convenience stores in Canada. From left to right: Réal Plourde, Alain Bouchard, Richard Fortin and Jacques D'Amours.

Alain Bouchard with his four children, Rose, Karinne, Camille and Jonathan, together in 2015 for the announcement of the creation of the Jonathan Bouchard Intellectual Disability Research Chair.

Sandra Chartrand and Alain Bouchard at the announcement of a one-million-dollar donation from the Sandra and Alain Bouchard Foundation for the expansion of the Musée National des Beaux-Arts de Québec, in 2013. (Photo by Isabelle Le Maléfan)

For the biggest acquisition in Couche-Tard's history, Alain Bouchard poses in front of a Statoil Fuel and Retail (SFR) service station in Norway, in 2012. At right is Raymond Paré, vice-president and chief financial officer for Couche-Tard, and Brian Hannasch, who would succeed Bouchard as president of the company.

Alain Bouchard, accompanied by SFR employees, during a store visit in 2013.

More than just a chain of convenience stores, SFR is involved in transforming and distributing petroleum and gasoline products. Shown is Alain Bouchard in 2013, accompanied by Brian Hannasch (at right) and Raymond Paré (front left) during a visit to the company's facilities in Europe.

Alain Bouchard tries to visit his company's stores regularly around the world, to talk with employees. Here he visits a Circle K store in the United States, in 2005.

Circle K has an international network of franchises, including this store in Malaysia.

In 2015, the company decided that to achieve global reach, it would have to unify its different banners. All of its stores adopted the Circle K brand—except those in Quebec. At left, Brian Hannasch, president and CEO of Couche-Tard, accompanied by three of the company's founders: Richard Fortin, Réal Plourde and Alain Bouchard.

The conversion of SFR stores in Europe under the new global brand began in 2016.

The Couche-Tard banner and its friendly owl are still present in almost 600 stores in Quebec, including this one in Saint-Canut, in the Laurentian Mountains.

Acquiring Johnson Oil and its Bigfoot stores would add USD $350 million to Couche-Tard's annual sales. The USD $66 million price tag was therefore fairly modest—particularly since the company was already making a profit.

As soon as the deal was announced, Bouchard declared that Couche-Tard's objective was to increase the number of establishments in its new American Midwest division from 225 to 600. It would take place through small acquisitions, and by building new convenience stores inspired by the "Strategy 2000" concept. To succeed, they had to rely on the management team already in place in Columbus, whose jobs Couche-Tard had promised to protect.

The head of the team was Brian Hannasch, an American with a background in the oil industry. Hannasch was very unconvinced of wanting to work for the group of Quebecers, who seemed a little strange to him.

After 12 years working for British Petroleum (BP), headquartered in London, Hannasch had returned to the United States to take care of his father, who was ill. Seeking a less demanding job, he found himself head of the Bigfoot stores, just nine months before the Johnson family chose to get rid of it. By his own admission, Hannasch knew nothing of Couche-Tard at the time. "I didn't even know how to pronounce the name!" he says.

His meeting with the company's founders in a hotel in Indianapolis, before the deal was announced, didn't leave him reassured. "Richard Fortin's English was pretty good, but Jacques, Alain and Réal...it was marginal. So, I thought *I don't know about this*. I figured I would just stick around for six months for the transition and go do something else." In any event, he thought, the leaders of Couche-Tard must have wanted to keep him in his position—simply by default, maybe, or because they had to, having no one else. After all, it was their first incursion into the United States.

But he was mistaken about their reasoning. Réal Plourde, along with Hannasch and Bouchard, had spent two days visiting the group's stores and the Quebecers had agreed: Hannasch had to be their man. He had all the right entrepreneurial qualities, and the same natural ease with interpersonal relationships that had made the success of Couche-Tard possible. Jacques D'Amours explains: "In all our acquisitions, if the owner has no plans for succession, we say 'thank you very much,' and we close the books—we don't even look at them. We need people we can trust." In their eyes, Hannasch was one of Bigfoot's most valuable assets.

* * *

At the beginning of July 2001, two weeks after the purchase was concluded, Hannasch headed northward: The founders of Couche-Tard had invited him to join them for their annual fishing trip. The prospect of spending several days with the men, trying to converse despite their overwhelming thick accent, had not left him trembling with excitement. But how could he refuse? They were his new bosses.

During a stopover between flights, Hannasch went to the airport bar, where he ended up in a conversation with people at a neighbouring table. As it happened, they were David Rodgers and Kim Trowbridge, two directors from Silcorp, the Ontario firm bought out by Couche-Tard a year and a half earlier. What they told him was remarkable.

"They both said the deal was the best thing that ever happened to them in their career, and they encouraged me to give it a try." Hannasch asked them why they thought so. The answer: because Couche-Tard management did what they had said they would do, they told him. They invested in the stores, took care of their people, worked to grow the business. And, they told him, since the company had acquired Silcorp, Couche-Tard's management hadn't broken its word—not once. "They're four very humble guys with a vision of growing and doing the right thing," said the two men, who added that in the business world, that's "very refreshing."

Hannasch boarded his second flight determined to find out for himself whether what they had said was true.

He had expected an American-style fishing trip: a few boat outings, for formality's sake, interspersed with long sessions of beer drinking and card games lasting well into the night. But he was in for a surprise. For one, the four men took fishing very seriously. Beer was conspicuously absent. There were, however, plenty of excellent wines, Hannasch recalls. After a meal washed down with a number of bottles, Réal Plourde went to the other room. He returned not with a deck of cards, but with a stack of songbooks. "I thought it was a joke," says Hannasch. "We were going to sing. And I DO NOT sing! They almost lost me with that one," he says with a laugh.

Nowhere in his mind was the possibility that 12 years later he would replace Alain Bouchard as head of Couche-Tard.

Nor did he imagine that during that time, the company would grow to 10 times the size it was then.

The eventful trip was an initiation for Hannasch to get into the inner circle of the builders of Couche-Tard. All members of this circle share one character trait: sincerity. The genuineness Hannasch saw would be born out in the relationship he developed and sustained with Plourde, who was always ready to listen to his problems and help find good solutions, and who could be relied on to treat people with respect. Over the years, Plourde became more than a mentor to Hannasch; he became something like a second father to the man who lost his own father a few months after Couche-Tard purchased Bigfoot.

* * *

It was Pierre Peters, one of the longest-serving executives at Couche-Tard, who had the responsibility of going to Columbus and explaining to the management of the group's fourth division how Couche-Tard operated—the administrative procedures they followed. The 225 stores had to be grouped into smaller units of 10 to 12 stores, with a market manager placed in charge of each unit. The market manager would act almost as an owner of the micro-chain of stores; he or she would be expected to visit two stores a day to ensure they were running well and to resolve problems as soon as they appeared. This would give the store manager time to focus on customer service. "The efficiency of an operation doesn't come from offices," says Peters. "Any problem is going to be found in the store, and so that's where the solution will be."

But good diagnostics tools were still necessary. For that reason, the network and all of its cash registers had to be computerized as quickly as possible. Cognos reports[35] provided the coordinators with all sales data by product category, helping them target interventions in areas where profitability wasn't meeting expectations. This culture of transparency and accountability, so rare in the retail industry, required not only a reorganization of the hierarchical structure, but also a major ongoing investment in staff training.

---

35. Cognos is a Canadian based company specializing in management and analysis of financial data.

Thus, one of Couche-Tard's first actions was opening a training centre for its employees in Columbus. There were many internal controls to be put in place, and new computer tools to master. "A convenience store is a retail business," Peters told the staff, "and the money is made in the details."

When you impose change, you end up meeting resistance; that's just human nature. But aside from a few people "who had developed the habit of sleeping in their offices," says Peters, he was astonished by the openness and enthusiasm of the executives. Clearly aware of Couche-Tard's success in Canada, they were intrigued. "They were extremely interested in learning what we did differently to maximize each store's performance. I didn't sense any rejection whatsoever."

As it had with its previous acquisitions, Couche-Tard lightened the company's upper structure, an area where some expenditures seemed excessive. After returning from one of his first visits to Bigfoot's headquarters, Fortin mentioned to Bouchard that the small network with just over 200 stores possessed two private airplanes to transport senior executives, while the four founders of Couche-Tard still flew economy. He knew the man too well to expect the answer he'd hoped for. He was pleasantly surprised, however, when Bouchard at least agreed that the four partners could henceforth fly in business class.

The arrival of Couche-Tard was a breath of fresh air for Bigfoot, and a much-needed one. The numbers spoke volumes. The annual turnover rate for store managers had reached an astronomical 100 percent; on average, a manager didn't last more than 12 months. The proportion made sense when you considered the turnover rate for other employees at the stores: 250 percent per year. "That's insane," says Bouchard. Employees quit after less than six months, and it was necessary to constantly train new staff members.

* * *

In the years following the acquisition of the Johnson Oil Company, Bouchard developed a friendship with the founder, Dick Johnson, and his son, Rick, who had taken over leadership of the company from his father—a leadership that ended with the Couche-Tard buyout. The two wealthy businessmen were very active in their community. It was for that reason that they asked the new owner to keep the jobs in Columbus, as well as the Bigfoot name: People in the region had gotten used to it, they said, and it had become a part of their daily lives.

A few years later, in 2009, Bouchard attended the funeral of Dick Johnson, wanting to offer his condolences to the family he had gotten to know. He was genuinely surprised to hear Dick's son, Rick, express his gratitude that not only had the jobs at the Columbus headquarters been maintained as promised; they had been increased. His father had died knowing that the company he had built, a company that helped hundreds of others in the area make a living, had not withered away, but indeed had flourished.

It was such a comfort to the elder Johnson at the end of his life that his son had wanted to acknowledge Alain Bouchard with a concrete gesture. But what do you give a multimillionaire who already has everything? He proposed that since Bouchard didn't personally need money, there were no doubt organizations in his community of Laval that couldn't say the same. Those of us who succeed, he said, have a duty to help the people around us.

As a result, $50,000 was awarded to the Sandra Chartrand fund for the Laval Symphonic Orchestra, a donation that was matched by the Sandra and Alain Bouchard Foundation.

Bouchard has donated a chunk of his fortune to this foundation, which is mainly devoted to two causes that he and his wife both care about deeply: culture, and intellectual disabilities.

CHAPTER 16

The American Wave

The leaders of Couche-Tard gave Brian Hannasch the task of expanding the Bigfoot banner to 500 stores in the American Midwest—in just five years. Hannasch's response was more than fair: "This company is 25 years old with 200 stores, it's quite a challenge. " He never thought the goal would be reached in a few short months.

Dairy Mart, a chain with almost 500 stores spread across seven Midwestern states, had been under bankruptcy protection since September 2001. No one was rushing to buy it, and for good reason. Its accumulated debts—the mammoth sum of USD $220 million—exceeded its book value. In the previous year alone it had lost USD $60 million. Its stores were outdated and were taking a beating from fierce competition with chains that sold high volumes of gasoline, like Costco and Walmart.

As they were wont to do, the Couche-Tard founders visited the stores themselves to get a sense of their value. Richard Fortin remembers, "Often the coffee machine would have a sign saying 'Out of order.' That's unacceptable." In the course of their multiple American expeditions over the years, they would find again and again the same state of neglect in which the stores had been left, while the company's corporate headquarters were gleaming. "The way they were operating made no sense," says Fortin. "Alain and I always said we could increase sales by 15 to 20 percent simply by making minor changes, without investing a lot of money." The solutions seemed utterly self-evident, and they applied them again and again: a clear, well laid-out interior, proper lighting, nice colour and general cleanliness, no lineups, well-trained and welcoming employees and the elimination of useless jobs in the administrative offices.

In the beginning, Hannasch may have harboured doubts about the sophistication of the four founders of Couche-Tard—an easy assumption since their fluency in English was weak at best. But he soon realized that in the areas of trade and finance, acquisitions and synergy, they were as savvy as they come. The Dairy Mart purchase would be his first lesson in negotiation using the Couche-Tard method, under the supervision of chief negotiator Alain Bouchard.

Bouchard presented an initial offer of USD $80 million. It was in the lower end of the range of the stores' value, due to the frailty of the network, which was verging on bankruptcy. The trustee in charge of the matter informed the Couche-Tard directors that another buyer had offered $90 million; if they matched the offer, he said, they would secure the purchase, since Couche-Tard better fulfilled the other criteria they had established for a potential buyer.

Bouchard flat-out refused to increase the offer, a position that left Hannasch incredulous. "Alain, this is a golden opportunity. You can't pass it up," he told him. It was his job to double the size of the American division, and this transaction would accomplish that singlehandedly. Would they give it up for a mere $10 million?

You have to be careful, Bouchard answered: There are often hidden costs in a chain that's struggling financially. Better to pass up an opportunity than rush into one too quickly. And besides, how did they know the trustee wasn't bluffing?

In the end, Couche-Tard carried away the prize with a hybrid proposition. Rather than buy Dairy Mart altogether, the company took only the best 287 locations. For the other 150 stores in the chain, Couche-Tard offered to take over management for two years, during which time they would see whether it was possible to make them profitable—by renegotiating lease agreements, for instance. If they succeeded, Couche-Tard would buy the stores; if not, they would be sold or closed. The deal would cost USD $80 million (CAD $120 million)— a bargain, insofar as it would allow them to increase the company's annual sales by USD $500 million (CAD $700 million). Couche-Tard's management felt sure it could get the chain back on track.

By applying the Couche-Tard recipe, Hannasch's team soon succeeded in integrating Dairy Mart stores under the Mac's banner, which they exported from Canada, and made them profitable. In the process, the company also bought up several small networks—including Handy Andy Food Stores and Bruce Miller Oil—and started to build new stores inspired by the Strategy 2000 concept. "That gave me—and the four founders—the confidence that we had a formula that could work in the United States. That was the start of the journey," he says.

* * *

In January of 2003, ConocoPhillips, the largest petroleum refiner in the United States, announced the sale of its vast network of convenience stores under the name Circle K. The chain had 2,000 stores in 16 Southern states, and had 14,500 employees; sales approached USD $4 billion per year. It was a colossus.

It was also a colossal headache for ConocoPhillips. The multinational's assets—valued at USD $50 billion—were concentrated on exploration, exploitation and the refining of petroleum products—all highly technical operations. It was a world for engineers, not retailers. ConocoPhillips didn't need to run convenience stores, with all the ensuing complications, to sell their oil. They decided to get out.

"History will eventually show which one of us was smarter," says Hannasch. Encouraged by his success breathing life back into Bigfoot and Dairy Mart, he believed he was up to the task of doing the same with Circle K. Moreover, ConocoPhillips wanted to sell the chain in separate pieces to make it easier for potential buyers to digest. "So we took a shot at it," says Hannasch.

On Friday, May 9, 2003, Couche-Tard management and other interested groups received a document with confidential information. It described the lots being put up for auction, divided by territory: Florida, the Carolinas, and the centrepieces, Arizona and California. There was high population growth in all these states, and sales in the stores were higher than the industry average: over a million dollars per year. Copies of the document were made at the Couche-Tard office in Laval so the four founders could study it over the weekend.

It was arranged for Couche-Tard's directors to go to Circle K's headquarters in Tempe, Arizona, the following Monday, for the formal presentation of ConocoPhillips' offer to sell. They decided to arrive the day before so they could visit as many stores as possible. When they did, they discovered that barely one in three stores was computerized, and that their profitability was strangled by indirect costs that were too high—up to USD $80,000 annually per store—the result of a heavy and ineffective bureaucratic structure. For the average investor, this would diminish their value. For an operator like Couche-Tard, however, it was a measure of their hidden potential.

When the presentation was over, all the interested groups were granted access to a room containing all the company's data: contracts, leases, financial results, accounts, employee records, technical assessments. Each potential buyer had two days to dig into the massive amount of information. Réal Plourde remembers a funny scene at the marathon. "The seller was pretty impressed to see the founders of Couche-Tard with our noses in the books, while the other groups had sent lawyers and accountants."

This type of exercise was nothing new for the Couche-Tard team—although they were used to a more modest scale. They had become experts in their unique choreography: Jacques D'Amours handled leases and distribution, Richard Fortin examined the financial records and debts, Réal Plourde analyzed human resources and the operational structure, and Alain Bouchard looked at real estate and the global business plan. Each team member was important, each had his own strengths. It was a given that no decision of that scale could be taken unless they all agreed.

At the end of the two-day marathon, the four founders took stock of their findings. Logically, Couche-Tard would be primarily interested in Arizona, the crown jewel of Circle K with 500 stores. It would give them an entirely new division, comparable in size to the four divisions the company already had.

That would be the reasonable thing to do. But was being reasonable the right approach? "It was a once in a lifetime opportunity: 1,663 stores in the most dynamic region in the United States," says Richard Fortin. "So we went for the home run," adds Réal Plourde.

Plourde asked Fortin straight out: "Can we afford it?" Fortin said they could; but there was a touch of uncertainty in his voice. "I was convinced we could do it," Fortin clarifies in retrospect. "I just didn't know exactly how."

Five months later, on Monday, October 6, Bouchard told the press that Couche-Tard was making the biggest acquisition in its history, at the cost of CAD $1 billion. Once again, the company would double in size with a single purchase. Its revenue would leap from $3.6 billion to $8.8 billion. Couche-Tard would become the fourth largest convenience store network in North America, with 4,600 stores—only 1,200 fewer than the leader in the industry, 7-Eleven.

Negotiations between Couche-Tard and ConocoPhillips had been concluded late at night the previous Friday, in New York; extraordinarily complex, the talks had taken several weeks. At the opening of the first session, Michel Pelletier recalls, "We had zero credibility." Circle K's team included over 20 lawyers and experts of all kinds, while Couche-Tard, represented by Bouchard and Fortin along with Pelletier, were essentially on their own.[36] "But things turned around quickly when they saw that we really knew the data."

Still, Bouchard says that the American company had serious doubts about Couche-Tard's ability to finance an operation of that scale. "We told them that our bank was the National Bank. They asked us, 'What's the National Bank?' We said it is a regional bank in Canada, but to them, Canada is by itself a region. So you can imagine their impression about a regional bank within a region!"

One day, negotiations became so strained that the Couche-Tard team left the table. They walked on Broadway for hours.

---

36. In fact, Michel Pelletier was assisted by a young attorney, Philippe Johnson, son and grandson of two former Quebec premiers, both named Daniel Johnson. Philippe Johnson's work was mostly behind the scenes, and he was rarely present at the negotiation table.

A good place for a Coup de theatre. "When we came back, we ended up negotiating until midnight. The discussion centred on environmental questions, and the issue of the employees' pension plan. Couche-Tard insisted that Circle K provide full funding for the employees pension plan, and that the company would give compensation for its obligations concerning soil contamination from old reservoirs.

"We got up early and we went to bed very late," says Bouchard, who believed that Circle K's lawyers were dragging things out merely to impress their client. The president of ConocoPhillips had wanted to close the deal quickly, before the end of the year; to get there, however, he had to give Couche-Tard enough time to find financing in the American market. "It was clearly their main worry," says Hannasch: "Would we be able to find the cash we needed in time? It put a lot of pressure on Richard Fortin's shoulders."

But Bouchard saw an opportunity. He spoke to the ConocoPhillips representative to complain about the tactics of the company's lawyers, who, he believed, were trying to inflate the bill. "So he got personally involved," says Bouchard, "and started giving orders." The dark spell was broken, and the wheels started to turn.

One of the stumbling blocks in the negotiations has since entered Couche-Tard lore. As part of the due diligence process following acceptance of the offer, ConocoPhillips offered the prospective buyer the right to visit 30 stores of its choosing. In the oil company's view, it was a big enough representative sample to give the buyer a good sense of the state of the network.

For Bouchard, however, the stores were the heart of the company—its raison d'être. Trying to judge the way it operated, to gauge its human resources—in other words, its very value—based on a sample of just 30 stores out of 1,663, was out of the question. It's not as simple as judging the freshness of a massive cluster of grapes by tasting a single one. Bouchard pushed for more, wanting to visit 300 or 400 stores, but ConocoPhillips' attorneys clung to their original offer. "Fine," said Bouchard. "Couche-Tard won't buy it."

Bouchard finally won out, on that point and on the issue of bearing responsibility for facilities in terms of complying with environmental regulations. The latter question had been lingering unresolved, and Bouchard had expected a tough battle. "We were ready to go to war. I thought it would last hours, but we resolved it in 30 seconds."

* * *

With the announcement of the deal, Couche-Tard's stock jumped by 23 percent, reaching CAD $21.00 per share—a new high for the company. The markets were impressed with the hunger the management team showed, and its ability to find bargains. The cost of acquisition for Circle K was just 5.4 times its operating costs—20 percent less than the purchase of Silcorp a few years earlier. All in all: a great deal.

To finance it, however, the reliable Couche-Tard elastic had to be stretched thin once again. It began with a 15 percent increase in the number of shares outstanding, by way of a procedure that raised the ire of some investors.

Over the course of the summer, confident that they would close the deal, Couche-Tard's management had quietly approached certain institutional investors to look for a private investment of CAD $223 million, conditional upon the success of the operation. The market's exuberant reaction to the announcement of the purchase of Circle K garnered them instant profits—to the extent that some thought it smacked of insider trading. But shares had risen for all shareholders; thus the protests were soon lost in a din of general rejoicing.

However, for the biggest chunk of the financing for the acquisition, Couche-Tard had to borrow a gigantic sum: CAD $1.1 billion. This amount exactly equalled the total value of its corporate assets prior to the Circle K purchase. It would drive up Couche-Tard's debt ratio, from 38 percent to 64 percent of its book value—a nervous-making situation for the banks.

Negotiations with the bank syndicate responsible for financing the acquisition—made up of the National Bank, CIBC and Scotiabank—were long and difficult. One day, it reached the point where Richard Fortin abruptly broke off discussions. "The deal is finished," he told them in frustration, overwhelmed by the growing pile of obstacles. "We can barely agree on anything."

Later, he started to regret losing his temper. How would he tell his partners the news? He faced a great deal of guilt for having let them down after promising them he could find the money for the operation. As he drove to work the next morning, Fortin called the directors of the three banks to try to save the project from an untimely end. "They must have been surprised, because it was very, very early," he says. But the timing gave him a certain advantage: It placed Couche-Tard at the top of their list of priorities for the day. The attitude of their representatives at the bargaining table underwent a drastic change that same afternoon. The financing was finally able to go through.

The bank syndicate was responsible for issuing USD $500 million of bonds, with USD $350 million reserved for the American market. That gave Couche-Tard the opportunity to start spreading the word about its company in the United States. A whirlwind nine-day tour was organized, bringing Bouchard and Fortin to the four corners of the country. The goal: to find people who had large fortunes at their disposal and were interested in good investment opportunities.

To carry out their proselytizing mission, Couche-Tard rented a private jet from Laurent Beaudoin, the CEO of aircraft manufacturer Bombardier. This allowed the team to travel around the United States with ease, spreading the good word about their company—a company which, while Canadian-owned, had in some senses become more or less American. After all, once the deal would be completed, three quarters of its revenue would be coming from the States.

In the middle of the tour, not long before one of his presentations, Fortin's phone rang. He had to answer; it was from the handler for his file at the National Bank, Couche-Tard's principal financial partner. "Where are you?" the caller asked when the conversation began. Fortin told him he was in the Rainbow Ballroom: a large hall at the top of the Rockefeller Center in New York City, where he was preparing to present Couche-Tard's business plan to the cream of the crop of American finance. "Do you realize that you've made it to the top of the world?" the banker asked him with admiration.

Suddenly it all dawned on him: how astonishingly far they had come on their journey. "We were two guys from Quebec, and we had made it as high as you can go," he says. That realization increased his nervousness, just as looking down from a great height can induce vertigo. The shock is in seeing how far you are from where you started. "It clearly didn't make me more intelligent, however," he says. He immediately shared his thoughts with Bouchard, who ended up gripped with the same feeling of being overwhelmed. Neither would deny that their knees were shaking as they approached the microphone to begin their presentation.

In the end, the sermons given by the visiting missionaries were persuasive, judging by the demand for Couche-Tard bonds: It ended up being three times the size of the offer.

* * *

Couche-Tard was allowed to visit many Circle K stores as part of its due diligence, and it didn't waste the opportunity. Nine Couche-Tard teams patrolled the entire south of the United States, from the Atlantic to the Pacific. In all, 460 convenience stores received visits from the Couche-Tard ambassadors. After all, it wasn't just a chance for them to inspect the locations; it was also a public relations operation. Plourde even referred to it as a "charm campaign."

Such is the effect it seemed to have on convenience store staff, at any rate. Plourde often heard the same comments: *I've worked for the company for 10 years, and this is the first time someone from upper management has visited my store.* The visit also helped confirm the directors' feeling that in the regions far from the headquarters in Arizona—from Florida to California—the employees felt ignored, left behind. The idea of decentralizing the organization and inversing the roles by creating service centres that actually listen to the stores was warmly received. All that remained after the deal was concluded in December was to carry through with the plan.

Alain Bouchard was then passed the baton. With Brian Hannasch as a partner, he had hundreds and hundreds of stores to visit, thousands of employees to meet. He hoped to connect with them, to listen to their complaints and suggestions and then integrate these in the plans for reforming the company. It was also an opportunity to transmit Couche-Tard's culture, which centres on the values of entrepreneurship—and, they hoped, to gain support for that culture from the troops.

Bouchard's first appearance in Florida did not go unnoticed. When the big boss of a company heads out to "inspect" his new possessions, the arrival tends to entail a certain amount of pomp.

The clerk, the manager, their supervisor, the regional coordinator; the entire chain of command is mobilized, all of them slightly nervous about falling under the scrutinizing gaze of the indisputable overlord of their workplace. The overwhelming priority is to avoid displeasing him. And it generally comes tinged with resentment: What did they do to deserve ending up as actors in a suspenseful and unpleasant movie?

Employees are alerted a few days ahead of time. A major cleanup of the premises takes place, and everything is organized so it's as orderly as possible. The day arrives. Everyone holds their breath, hoping their freshly washed and ironed clothes serve to hide their anxiety.

But not with Couche-Tard. When Bouchard arrived at the first store on his Florida tour, he split from his entourage of senior executives and went directly behind the counter to chat with the clerk at the checkout. "I don't do these tours to inspect buildings. I do them to talk to people, to learn about their reality," he says.

As he left the store, he asked the district supervisor if she could drive him in her car and act as a guide as they continued their store tour. Shocked and a little embarrassed, she told him she couldn't because her car was in terrible shape, dirty and messy. But he insisted: "I'd like to chat with you, learn about who you are," he said. Thus they visited the next three stores together, giving them plenty of time to get acquainted.

Bouchard notes that it probably was no coincidence that for the rest of his Florida trip, all the supervisors' cars he saw seemed to sparkle inside and out. Word seemed to have gotten out about the boss's transportation preferences.

* * *

It was Brian Hannasch who was given the task of integrating Circle K into the Couche-Tard group. The company was split into four divisions: Florida, Arizona, the Carolinas and California. These would be added to the four older divisions: Quebec, Ontario, Western Canada and the American Midwest. Circle K headquarters in Arizona was made lighter, with its staff reduced by a third. "Alain bristles when he hears the term 'headquarters,'" says Hannasch. All four of the Couche-Tard partners would repeat the same maxim: "We don't sell anything in our offices." Limiting the size of these offices went hand in hand with that principle.

Therefore, in line with the Couche-Tard philosophy, the relaunch of Circle K had to involve the local employees: those who knew their market best. Discussions were held with the most promising employees from each region, to assess their potential. Couche-Tard needed four strong candidates to oversee the company's new divisions. These four would have carte blanche to train their team, and to show—through concrete results—that they deserved to be trusted. Their reliability was essential for the size of the task that lay before them, and also for the jaw-dropping amount of funds that would be at their disposal to reinvigorate the operations: a billion dollars over four years.

In the beginning, Hannasch says, he had a hard time grasping the decentralization concept that the Couche-Tard directors espoused. It seemed to go against many of the common management principles used by large companies. "We didn't really understand what it would mean," he says.

For instance, when it was time to prepare the first annual budgets for the new divisions, Bouchard asked the directors how they planned to go about the task. They told him they would set profitability objectives, and then set targets for each store in order to reach the desired performance.

"Don't you think that reasoning is backward?" Bouchard asked them. The stores, he said, operate in an environment that they don't completely control. Their region could be affected by an economic slowdown or, inversely, by inflationary factors or by intense competition. "They deliver the profits that they're capable of delivering," he explained; and that's why the people who are in the best position to define their profitability objectives are managers and their supervisors. That's where the projections for each division should start.

Such an operation obviously requires more work than a decree handed down from the top. In fact, the consultation process would have to be launched in January to be ready for April. "It was a complete education for people in operations and the stores, to empower them and teach them open-book management," says Bouchard.

"We stepped on some toes at headquarters," adds Plourde. "But we also made a lot of people in the network very happy. For the people working in the stores, it was a blessing. Finally they had bosses who were taking them into consideration, actual retailers who looked after stores and customers."

That's what Paul Rodriguez[37] felt as well when he was regional director of operations for Circle K in Tucson, Arizona.

---

37. At the time of writing, Paul Rodriguez is the vice-president of Couche-Tard's Arizona division.

Not long after the company was acquired by Couche-Tard, he and other colleagues gathered at the central office in Tempe to meet Bouchard and Plourde, who were representing the new owners. "We were a little nervous about having a Canadian company buy us, because we weren't as familiar with them," he remembers.

The situation hardly improved when the new leaders began to speak. "In the beginning, their accents were much harder to understand," he says of the Quebecers. But their audience was impressed with the decentralized management philosophy they encouraged. They also seemed authentic: They dealt with others sincerely, and they seemed frank and open. They didn't act like billionaires, he says with approval.

Their meeting ran late, so the group continued at a restaurant. Paul Rodriguez found himself sitting across from Bouchard, who, to the surprise of Rodriguez, immediately ordered a beer. Rodriguez promptly followed suit, drawing a disapproving look from his immediate supervisor. "My boss looked at me like I was crazy," says Rodriguez. Five decades had passed since the era portrayed in *Mad Men*; norms for drinking during working hours had changed vastly in the United States. Rodriguez admits that the appropriate thing might have been to abstain—at least in the presence of the leader of the company, and at the very least before knowing him very well. "But I said to myself, 'I can't let him drink alone!'" he adds, laughing.

CHAPTER 17

An Appetite for Donuts

It seemed like Bouchard and his team could do no wrong. Data compiled by the firm Deloitte Touche shows that Couche-Tard had more growth in five years (1998 to 2003) than any other large company on the planet. Its annual average increase in sales—an incredible 55 percent—was double that of Starbucks, and just edged out the darling of online commerce, Amazon.

But there were clouds on the horizon. Awareness campaigns against tobacco use were starting to have an impact, and cigarette sales represented a significant portion of convenience stores retenues. "We increasingly worked on developing our fresh-food services to compensate for the lost cigarette sales," says Réal Plourde.

Couche-Tard stores tried to find a winning solution through trial and error. The company attempted operating franchises of well-known brands like A&W and Subway. Its experience with Pizza Hut was a disaster. Their ovens were capable of cooking a pizza in seven minutes; but during off-peak hours, it would be too much to ask the sole employee present in the store to operate both the oven and the cash register. Even if the clerks could manage to run the ovens, says Plourde, "Seven minutes is a long time in a convenience store. The reason you go there in the first place is to save time."

One of the solutions Couche-Tard came up with was to offer fresh prepared food such as sandwiches and submarines. Even without a recognized brand with which to draw customers, this solution had the advantage of allowing them to achieve better profit margins. They used dynamic promotional campaigns to boost sales. Aiming to attract a working clientele looking for a quick, cheap meal, Couche-Tard advertised a trio deal—a submarine, Pepsi and chips—with the audacious slogan: Be a man: choose the easy way.

* * *

In the summer of 2003, Couche-Tard management caught wind of a bargain. Dunkin' Donuts, owned by the British consortium Allied Domecq, was on the rocks in Quebec. The fast-food chain had been the first to set up shop in the province in the 1960s; but it had aged poorly. Its pink and orange colours had never been updated, nor had its menu, mainly composed of sugary donuts and low-quality coffee.

A much more dynamic Canadian giant, Tim Hortons, threatened to wipe out Dunkin' Donuts. Founded in Ontario in 1964, Tim Hortons had 2,300 establishments in Canada. Only 200 of these were in Quebec, where it had just announced a major offensive. For its part, the Dunkin' Donuts chain had just over 100 outlets left; half of its franchisees had jumped ship over the past few years. Faced with the Tim Hortons steamroller and their own chain's apparent inability to respond, the other franchisees wanted only to follow suit.

And as the lyric goes, when it rains it pours. The American chain Krispy Kreme had just landed in Canada and was making a big splash. During its first week of operation, the first Canadian Krispy Kreme store, in Mississauga, Ontario, sold one million donuts—a record number.

But, as another saying goes, every crisis is an opportunity. Couche-Tard suspected that Dunkin' Donuts' stretch of difficulties could turn into an excellent business solution for Bouchard and company: It could mean that they had a chance to buy the master franchise for the territory of Quebec, for a very attractive price. The existing franchisees would now operate under the direction of Couche-Tard; Couche-Tard would also obtain the right to open and manage its own Dunkin' Donuts restaurants or food counters.

Bouchard was proud to have pulled of the deal. Just before it was finalized, he had commissioned a survey on brand awareness. "It came out very strong," he says. "Everyone knew what Dunkin' Donuts was." Unfortunately, however, the survey didn't ask the right question: What was their perception of the product?

On August 28, when the deal with Dunkin' Donuts was announced, Couche-Tard stated its intention to double the presence of the brand in Quebec. "We made a firm commitment to have 100 new restaurants in five years," said Stéphane Gonthier, Couche-Tard's vice-president of operations for Eastern Canada. Some of these stores would be set up within the company's convenience stores; others would be in independent facilities, more spacious and contemporary feeling than its older stores.

The repositioning operation would be conferred to Pierre Peters, one of the pillars of Couche-Tard. Peters had been appointed director general of the franchise. "It wasn't doing well when we bought it," he says, "and it didn't do much better while we were operating it."

For one, the franchisees hadn't exactly welcomed the arrival of Couche-Tard. Some tended to be unwilling to proceed with the transformations that the company asked for. Changing the colours, the decor, the menu—it all cost a lot of money.

Couche-Tard developed a new restaurant concept—with a European flair, they said. At 300 square meters (3,230 square feet), it was much more spacious, and featured a large dining room, a healthful menu, premium coffee, a terrace and a drive-through window. The first such restaurant opened its doors in August 2004—exactly one year after the agreement with Dunkin' Donuts' parent company was signed. No doubt impressed with Couche-Tard's momentum, the multinational signed another agreement with Couche-Tard, entrusting them with the development of its franchise in Ohio. Negotiations were underway to expand to other American markets as well. But then:

"The banner's lack of credibility was just too deep," says Peters, and the resources gap was too wide. "We had a marketing budget of CAD $2 million, while Tim Hortons' was over $12 million. We couldn't regain market share." They needed bigger advertising budgets to revive the brand. But they also needed Tim Hortons to back down a little; the tough Canadian company wouldn't yield an inch.

"They tracked our every step," says Bouchard. "Each time we opened a store, Tim Hortons opened one next door—even if the location wasn't good for them. We invested in it for years, we tried hard, but we couldn't succeed."

In the summer of 2008, at the end of the five-year agreement with Dunkin' Donuts, Couche-Tard handed the master franchise back to its parent company and closed the restaurants it owned. Some were sold, and others were rented to McDonald's—and Tim Hortons. As for the best sites—those with drive-through windows: "They took them all!" says Bouchard, with a mixture of pride and envy. "They pay us rent, and they're doing well. We're happy for them. It shows we were right about those sites."

The end of this unhappy chapter for Couche-Tard coincided with the announcement of a deal with Irving Oil, the firm that operated Canada's largest oil refinery, in New Brunswick. Through a 20-year agreement, the company gave Couche-Tard administrative control of its 252 convenience stores. Half of these were located in the four Atlantic provinces in Canada; the other half were in New England. Before that deal was made, Couche-Tard had had almost no presence in those territories. After the failed attempt to turn around Dunkin' Donuts, Peters was given the task of revamping the new network, which sorely needed it.

Just hearing the year 2008 mentioned causes nervous tension in the business community. It was the year the American housing bubble crashed due to the scandal surrounding subprime mortgages. The economy plummeted. The United States, along with the rest of the world, entered a recession. There was no way for Couche-Tard to avoid it entirely.

CHAPTER 18

7-Eleven in Trouble

After purchasing Circle K in 2003, Couche-Tard's sizeable appetite seemed to be satiated. It was time for the bear, amply fattened up, to hibernate in its cave and metabolize some of the abundant mass it had taken on. To reduce the weight of its debt, Couche-Tard would shed some of its less profitable stores, and hundreds of real estate properties. In March 2004 alone, it sold more than CAD $500 million worth. The paring-down of the former Circle K headquarters—which Alain Bouchard compared to the Taj Mahal—helped halve the overhead and administrative costs for each store.

Couche-Tard also decided to unify its American banners under the Circle K name. It wanted to create a major national chain that would consolidate the convenience store market in the United States and position Circle K as the main rival of 7-Eleven, the world leader in convenience stores.

Created in Dallas, Texas, 7-Eleven had come close to bankruptcy a few years earlier, before being bought at a low price by its own subsidiary in Japan. There were 5,800 7-Eleven branches in the United States; with 3,000 stores, Couche-Tard had only about half that number in the American market. However, there was a major difference between the two networks. Couche-Tard owned more than 80 percent of its convenience stores, while 7-Eleven owned only 40 percent of the stores operating under its banner, with the rest belonging to franchisees. In other words, 7-Eleven didn't actually own many more American convenience stores than Couche-Tard. Couche-Tard possessed a significant number of franchises elsewhere in the world, through its Circle K subsidiary—3,000 in Japan, 600 in Taiwan—but they contributed little to its profits, and the company rarely mentioned their presence.

Now, with the unification of its banners in the United States, Couche-Tard/Circle K would become a contender for the largest network of convenience stores. Hostilities with 7-Eleven were not far below the surface.

While busy opening a service centre in each division, training employees and renovating American stores—and spending hundreds of millions of dollars a year doing so—Couche-Tard was nonetheless making profits. From 2004 to 2005, net earnings almost tripled, rising from CAD $75 to $199 million. The sales curve was impressive: from CAD $5.8 billion in 2004, it climbed past the $10 billion mark the following year.

Couche-Tard's financial officer, Richard Fortin, made the calculation: "With something like 2,000 fewer stores than 7-Eleven, we had higher profits." It was indeed so. Having become a giant in the United States, Couche-Tard was outpacing its rival in terms of performance. With sales of USD $12.8 billion, 7-Eleven only eked out a profit of USD $123 million, or one percent of sales. Couche-Tard's profits were not only higher (USD $161 million), but its profit margin—1.9 percent—was double that of its rival. Feeling confident, Fortin told anyone who would listen that "Couche-Tard is ready for a major acquisition," for a billion US dollars, "or more." There was little doubt that Couche-Tard wanted to buy out one of its rivals—a big one, maybe even 7-Eleven—and then surpass it.

"I would have been interested in buying 7-Eleven," Bouchard acknowledges. He even flew to Tokyo to meet with the CEO of the group, in the hopes that he would agree to sell the American portion of his empire, which had more than 20,000 stores around the world. "But the Japanese aren't sellers," he discovered. He would have to take them on in a different way, and using patience.

* * *

In the fall of 2005, around the time when Bouchard was given the Retailer of the Year award from the National Association of Convenience Stores, Couche-Tard threw itself into a long series of acquisitions in the United States. That was no coincidence. The company had built a team of 35 whose sole objective was to scour the country in search of bargains. Each project had to be approved by Bouchard, who had to resign himself to living out of a suitcase as he endeavoured to scrutinize all the stores personally before purchasing them.

If the rumours about that period are true, it gave him ample opportunity to update his wardrobe. Bouchard is said to have systematically forgotten clothes in each hotel room he stayed in, frequently along with his passport or cellphone, which he constantly told people had been stolen. He knows that their disappearance was really a result of his legendary distractedness. "He's always in his own head," says his wife, Sandra Chartrand, who believes he inherited the trait from his mother. Chartrand tells the story of how one day, hoping to give her children a fun surprise on Easter, Rachel Bouchard had bought live chicks to give the kids. Wanting to hide them until the right moment, she chose an ill-advised spot...the freezer.

Couche-Tard bought 16 Conway Oil stores in New Mexico in September 2005; seven Fuel Mart stores in Ohio and 26 BP stations in Memphis in October; 40 Shell branches in Indianapolis in February 2006; 90 Spectrum branches in

Georgia and Alabama in April; 24 Stop N Saves in Louisiana in June; 24 Sparky's Oil in Florida in August; and 236 Shell service stations and convenience stores in Colorado, Louisiana and Florida in October 2006.

As is often the case in the business world, each of these deals comes with its own story—some happy, some tragic. Businesses that have sometimes been painstakingly built over several generations may have to be handed over because of financial problems or a death without a plan for succession, or else to realize the dream of a comfortable retirement. Whatever the reason, the key is to find the right buyer at the right time. Through its active presence on the ground, Couche-Tard positioned itself as a smart choice for anyone wanting to dispose of its stores. The owl was hunting, and its appetite was endless.

At the end of this frantic shopping expedition, Couche-Tard had more than 5,000 convenience stores in North America. It was renovating 450 every year, and building new ones as well, based on the Store 2000 concept. In the Southern states, Circle K stores started to appear with "Western"-themed decor, or in the colours of a local basketball team. The chain even had a store entirely devoted to the actor John Wayne.

For Bouchard, the whirlwind of activity seemed to contain a whole lifetime's worth of experiences and memories. One of these started with a trip to Memphis, Tennessee. While visiting one of his stores, he hit it off with a friendly, talkative manager, an African-American woman, who eagerly shared her enthusiasm for the business and possible projects for the store. As the conversation continued without losing pace and started to interfere with the schedule for the day, Bouchard's entourage started to grow impatient. With his group insisting that they had to move on, Bouchard invited the manager to join them so they could continue their animated conversation.

Not long after their encounter, she was promoted to a supervisor's position. When Bouchard returned to the area two years later, she was his guide for the store visits. In one of the stores, the woman proudly introduced Bouchard to the manager, another African-American woman, in her fifties, for whom the job was the culmination of a lifetime of hard work. During his conversation with the woman, who displayed a beaming smile the whole time, he complimented her on her hair and even kissed her on the cheek.

It was a friendly gesture that is common in Quebec, no doubt a vestige of French traditions, but it can be shocking for some in the Southern states, particularly when it comes to an encounter between two people from very different cultures. Bouchard only realized that he may have crossed a boundary later, when the supervisor told him she couldn't believe what he had done in there. "But I often give women a kiss just out of kindness! There was nothing inappropriate," he protested. No, she said, it wasn't the kiss that was unusual. It was what he had said to the woman. "You commented on her hair," the supervisor told him. Before he could shrug off the remark, she explained that the woman had only been to a hairdresser twice in her life: thirty years earlier, on her wedding day, and on the day of Bouchard's visit. That showed the importance she placed on her boss's visit to her store. Making a good impression had meant that much to her.

* * *

Circle K had gone through five different owners in just over a decade, three of which were oil companies. The impact showed in company morale. But after the initial shock from the acquisition by Couche-Tard, things were starting to improve.

Circle K's employees were given the chance to focus on their mission: operating a retail business, and expanding.

7-Eleven was forced to react. In 2007, the company unveiled an ambitious plan to relaunch activities in the United States, investing USD $2.4 billion into renovations for its 6,000 stores. It would also add 1,000 more stores.

Another major development would shake up the convenience store industry. The British company Tesco invested USD $500 million to launch the chain Fresh & Easy, a hybrid formula somewhere between a convenience store and a supermarket, offering an array of prepared foods and fresh products in its 1000-square-metre (10,765-square-foot) stores—three times more spacious than Couche-Tard's biggest convenience stores.

With that, acquisitions became more difficult, and more expensive. Couche-Tard's pace was slowed. Investors started to suffer pains of withdrawal from the regular doses of headlines they were used to receiving proclaiming Couche-Tard's expansion. But still, quarter after quarter, the company continued to post profits.

Couche-Tard management had been making big promises about their next conquest; but they couldn't deliver the goods. Prudence, Bouchard urged. Patience, Richard Fortin added. "Our logo is an owl," says Fortin. "We perched on our branch, looked at the numbers, and when we spotted prey that seemed weak enough, we swooped down on it."

But bad news was piling up around them. With the global rise in gas prices, competition between American retailers was intensifying, tightening profit margins. In January 2008, Couche-Tard stock reached CAD $16.50, or 11.6 times earnings: its lowest ratio in 10 years. Investors started to think the game of Pac-Man was no longer operating.

Their confidence took another hit in June 2008, when Canada's Competition Bureau brought charges against 11 companies and 13 individuals suspected of conspiring to fix gas prices in a number of Quebec markets, including Sherbrooke, Magog, Victoriaville and Thetford Mines. Couche-Tard, the largest gas retailer in the region, and two of its employees, were among the accused.

Bouchard protested. Gas prices are displayed for everyone to see, he said. Therefore, "you'd have to be naive to think that retailers need to stoop to collusion." Nonetheless, some of the accused pleaded guilty, including the oil company Ultramar, which had to pay a fine of $1.85 million. As part of "Octane Investigation," the Competition Bureau had intercepted hundreds of telephone conversations that took place in 2005 and 2006, which they believed revealed the existence of a cartel aimed at reducing competition and keeping prices artificially high in its territories.[38] In the weeks that followed the accusations, Couche-Tard shares dropped to $10.85, its lowest price in six years—but there were more serious explanations for the fall.

The case seems wholly insignificant alongside what was happening in the United States, where household debt was reaching alarming proportions. The real estate bubble was ready to burst, taking with it first banks, then businesses, then services. The United States and the rest of the world entered the worst recession it had faced since the Great Depression of 1929.

Couche-Tard, which had 80 percent of its sales in the United States at the time, braced for the worst. Management

---

38. At the time of writing, the Competition Bureau has withdrawn its charges against Couche-Tard. The cases against the two employees in question are still before the courts.

set about cutting costs systematically and extensively in every sector. Its benchmarking mechanism was tightened to assess a wider range of variables. To trim costs, the company switched to smaller cars that would reduce gas consumption. ATM machines installed in most convenience stores were supplied with cash from the cash registers rather than by a specialized company, in order to avoid paying commission. The number of telephone lines was reduced and maintenance costs for administrative offices were slashed.

Management also resolved to impose a hiring and wage freeze in the service centres. As they had done at the height of the crisis in the 1990s, the four Couche-Tard founders announced a reduction in their own salaries, in the range of 10 percent. In return for the demands they made on their employees, they committed to granting a retroactive raise the following year, if Couche-Tard's economic situation improved.

The share price for the company, as was the case for many other companies, took a beating during this period, although Couche-Tard took on very little debt. In fact, its value neared a record low in proportion to profits. This prompted management to launch a massive share buy-back program. In two years, Couche-Tard acquired 20 million of its own shares at an average value of $14 per share, then delisted them, thus increasing shareholder equity. This time, to weather the storm, the Couche-Tard founders were placing their bets...on Couche-Tard.

Despite a 19 percent decline in sales, primarily due to the drop in gas prices, Couche-Tard succeeded in rounding out the last quarter of 2008 with USD $38 million in profits: almost double the previous year's results. This was largely due to the USD $30 million reduction in operating costs thanks to its self-disciplinary measures. It was time for the company to follow through on their word and give employees the retroactive wage increase it had promised them. "The Americans were amazed," says Bouchard. "When they received their cheques, they told us they didn't believe it would happen. After all, it was millions of dollars."

Believing that the worst was behind them—but remaining cautious—Couche-Tard management started making some acquisitions that didn't carry a lot of risk. In April 2009, it acquired 450 franchisees from Exxon Mobil in 28 states, and 43 other stores in Arizona. In November, Couche-Tard created a joint venture with Shell to operate 100 stores in the Chicago region.

* * *

You would think Alain Bouchard had learned his lesson during the failed attempt to buy Silcorp a few years earlier. And yet, on March 9, 2010, he attempted a hostile takeover of the chain Casey's for close to USD $2 billion. Founded in 1959 in the small state of Iowa, Casey's was a model business. Well managed, well maintained, profitable and debt-free, it had 1,508 corporate stores in the American Midwest, with 13,000 employees. Added to those of Couche-Tard, its annual sales of $4.6 billion would give the group a combined weight of more than USD $20 billion. "We would have passed 7-Eleven in the United States," says Bouchard.

However, Casey's management rejected the offer for USD $36 a share, barely a 14 percent premium to the last market price. It did everything it could to resist—going so far as to adopt the poison pill technique, sinking $500 million into debt to purchase one-quarter of its own shares at a price higher than what Couche-Tard was offering. It also took Couche-Tard to court, accusing it of having manipulated the markets to its advantage.

In the middle of this months-long battle, Réal Plourde left his position as vice-president of operations, as planned. He was replaced by American Brian Hannasch, who years earlier had been persuaded to give Couche-Tard a chance during a fishing trip. Plourde, credited with having invented the decentralized formula that is Couche-Tard's trademark and its greatest strength, would nonetheless remain close to the company, becoming chairman of the board of directors. He was the second member of the group of four to step away from the company's daily operations, following Richard Fortin who had done the same three years earlier. Fortin too had remained on the board, in the role of chairman, allowing Bouchard to concentrate on his task managing ongoing business matters.

And he certainly had his hands full. The battle to buy Casey's was extremely demanding. Twice Bouchard sweetened the offer, hoping it would meet with the shareholders' approval. Couche-Tard's financial backing was solid. In Canada, it had Scotiabank and the Caisse de Dépôt et Placement du Québec; abroad, HSBC in London and Rabobank in the Netherlands, strong allies who would continue to be useful later on.

But in September 2010, 7-Eleven, Couche-Tard's rival, presented a surprise offer for USD $40 per share. Casey's management said the offer was attractive—attractive enough to enter into negotiations. These negotiations lasted up until the last offer from Couche-Tard expired, at the end of September. At that point, Casey's rebuffed 7-Eleven's advances, even when the offers became more generous. As Bouchard put it, if it were a matter of dating, no one could say Casey's was "easy."

CHAPTER 19

A Battle in Quebec

Alain Bouchard hates conflict. That's why, he says, he has rarely started legal battles with his opponents. "It's negative. And being negative has always prevented me from moving forward." Unfortunately, negativity was about to come to him.

When the employees of Couche-Tard in Beloeil, on Montreal's South Shore, showed up to work on the morning of Friday, November 6, 2009, the store where they had been employed no longer existed. The Couche-Tard and Dunkin' Donuts signs had been removed during the night. The gas pumps were gone, the windows boarded up. There was an air of finality to the scene. However, according to Quebec's labour standards, eight weeks notice must be given to both employees and the Ministry of Labour when closing an establishment.

So what happened? The 25 employees of the store, their jobs unceremoniously scrapped, didn't take long to conclude that the action had more than a coincidental link with their attempt to form a labour union. The first union membership card had been signed two days earlier, on Wednesday. Before even half the employees had joined the movement, the store shut its doors without a word of explanation.

A month earlier, a young employee had been fired from his part-time position as a clerk at the depanneur. The student was suspected of having solicited employees during working hours to try to form a union—an action prohibited by law. The

Confederation of National Trade Unions (CSN), considered the most militant union organization in Quebec, had taken the young man under its protection. The body paid part of his former wages while he waited for his complaint for wrongful dismissal to be heard. While being paid by the CSN, however, the student had returned to Beloeil to urge his former colleagues to sign union membership cards: He felt sure he could get the support of 13 of them—a majority. Two days later, the depanneur closed.

The vice-president of the CSN, Roger Valois, quickly drew his own conclusions. "Couche-Tard is a worse employer than McDonald's and Walmart," he charged; at least those companies had waited for the union to file an application for accreditation before closing the doors of some of their establishments. Couche-Tard's management refused to comment specifically on the Beloeil case. However, the company said that it regularly made assessments of its stores and closed the least profitable. Eight depanneurs had been shuttered already that year, while 20 new stores had opened their doors. It was simply a matter of good management. In sum: the Beloeil store wasn't covering its costs; the burgeoning union activity was unrelated.

The CSN protested before the Quebec Labour Relations Board, with no success. In October 2010, less than a year after the sudden closing, Couche-Tard opened another store on the same site and hired new employees. It was a humiliation for the CSN. The story would not end there.

* * *

Bouchard has a theory to explain why Quebec has the highest proportion of unionized workers in North America.

For a long time, he says, the bosses in Quebec were Anglophones, while the employees spoke only French. The language divide only amplified the class divide. Quebecois workers were forced to organize and form unions to make their needs heard, understood and respected. "In retrospect, I think we needed unions. They were necessary to move Quebec forward, to act as a counterbalance," says Bouchard.

Then came the Quiet Revolution in the 1960s and with Quebec's public sector phenomenal growth, the unions expanded quickly as well, in government services, schools and hospitals. Developing in lockstep with this sprawling employer that is the government, unions took on an enormous, sometimes paralyzing power—that they made abundant use, and abuse, of, particularly during the 1970s. In Bouchard's opinion: "It was messy."

He admits, however, that his opinion on unions is "biased." He believes his viewpoint has its origins in animated discussions he had with his first wife's father, a machinist who worked for the CBC. Like a unionized Tower of Babel, the organization housed almost 25 different unions at the time. Each profession had its own union. A job, an employee, a union: It almost seemed to be a motto within the walls of the national broadcaster. Work, break and meal schedules varied from one union unit to the next; synchronizing them perfectly was impossible, making it almost entirely unworkable to produce a major television program without incurring extra expenses amounting to 30 percent of regular salaries, or more. These costs came from penalties and overtime worked by many of the craftspeople.

For Bouchard, the situation was appalling, particularly as he witnessed his father-in-law relishing the nice regular pay cheque he received as he hung around at home—"just in case" his services were needed. The man argued a strict division of labour has a positive result: It "lets other people work" and thereby leads to job creation. Bouchard thought this idea was beyond absurd. He hated his father-in-law's negative attitude, the role he embraced as dead weight and his resistance to change. Bouchard quite naturally began to associate these faults with unions.

At the end of the 1980s, Bouchard nonetheless worked side by side with a union for a common goal. Under pressure from Provigo, the Quebec government wanted to allow large food chains to extend their opening hours on weekday evenings and even on Sundays. This move would obviously have a huge impact on traffic in depanneurs. Couche-Tard opposed the change. The Quebec Federation of Labour (FTQ), which represented a number of grocery store employees unions, also objected to the measure, saying it would be a major disruption for many families, forcing mothers and fathers to work hours they should be spending with their children.

These arguments were picked up by the Quebec Association of Retail Grocers (ADAQ), representing both large supermarkets and local grocery stores and depanneurs. Michel Gadbois, a teacher at HEC Montréal business school, acted as a consultant for the association in the battle—he would later become its president. "I was pretty vicious," he says without regret. "We put up signs showing a child looking out a window and crying because his mother had to go to work on Sundays. We didn't shy away from being manipulative." The association even made sure to align itself with the Catholic Church on the issue. Working on the Lord's day? *Sacrilege.*

The dispute was finally settled with a compromise. The big grocery stores could keep a very limited number of employees outside of normal work hours. The result: few cash registers open and long lines. Choosing to shop at a depanneur became much more attractive; as Fortin observes, depanneurs "sell time, more than anything."

The battle gave Bouchard the opportunity to rub shoulders with members of the labour movement. He even had a conversation with one of the FTQ's directors, who told him, "You're getting pretty big. Maybe your employees should unionize." He quickly changed his mind, however, when Bouchard showed him some figures. Most depanneur employees worked part-time, often because they were students looking for a small income or their first job experience. They were generally paid minimum wage or a little more. It was no surprise, then, that the annual turnover rate was in the range of 50 percent. Each establishment had only a handful of full-time employees— five or fewer—excluding the manager, who couldn't join a union, being considered a manager. The head of the FTQ got Bouchard's message pretty quickly: *Okay, it's not for us. There isn't enough revenue in it.*

*   *   *

The leaders of the CSN must have nearly choked when, in the summer of 2010, Alain Bouchard's photo graced *Les Affaires* magazine, in a special edition on the best employers in Quebec. Based on a study by Quebec's order of human resources specialists, the ranking put Couche-Tard in second position in the large companies category, "because it established a culture of listening to its employees," the article specified.

The workers interviewed gave Couche-Tard a score of 4.58 out of 5 for the statement *My immediate superior treats me with respect.* The score for the company's honesty and integrity was 4.4. In spite of the notoriously low wages in that type of store, 81 percent of Couche-Tard's employees said they weren't actively looking for a different job. The evaluation also gave Couche-Tard good results for its mechanisms to solicit suggestions from employees and their response to those suggestions, for the improvements to the employee support program, for the training courses provided and for the many incentives for employees to build careers within the company.

In short, Bouchard says, there were plenty of reasons justifying the absence of a union. Six months later, however, the CSN would attempt to prove him wrong.

On January 11, 2011, the CSN announced that it had filed an application for union certification in the name of 12 employees from the Couche-Tard depanneur on Jean-Talon Street, in Montreal's Villeray neighbourhood. It was a first for the billion-dollar company, and a first in the world of North American convenience stores. "This is a major breakthrough in Quebec retail," proclaimed the CSN, vowing that this was only a start and that the battle would continue. "The CSN is launching a massive organizing campaign to support employees in hundreds of Couche-Tard depanneurs who experience terrible working conditions and receive pitiful wages," said Roger Valois.

Couche-Tard clerks, he lamented, had no pension plan, no paid sick days, no medical leave coverage. Their pay was too low, their personal safety inadequately protected from robbers. Therefore, he announced, the CSN had created "teams" in an attempt to mobilize the 7,000 employees from the 550 Couche-Tard depanneurs throughout Quebec. It was an open declaration of war. Representatives of the central union entered the depanneurs, pretending to be clients. When they went to the cash to pay for a snack or buy a pack of cigarettes, they gave employees a card inviting them to call their delegates after work. *A CSN union will get you the respect you deserve,* the message read.

Couche-Tard called the Public Service Labour Relations Board, hoping it would condemn the recruitment campaign as illegal—but to no avail. Meanwhile, the CSN was making headway. In the following months, it filed another application for certification, this time in the name of employees at the Couche-Tard store in Saint-Hubert, on Montreal's South Shore. A few days later, on February 9, the labour relations board recognized the union at the store on Jean-Talon Street: the first in the history of the company.

How would Couche-Tard react? Management refused to comment publicly. Internally, however, Bouchard was livid—a reaction that risked costing him, since the law sets limits on the behaviour of employers who face a union movement.

He therefore decided to address his employees through an internal video message—which didn't take long to end up in the hands of the media. Five minutes of the seven-minute recording were devoted to the union question. "A high number of our branches would be unable to sustain the major increase in costs that a union would cause," the president of Couche-Tard declared. If the union movement ends up moving forward, "any scenario could be possible."

Was it a threat—prohibited by the labour code—or merely a presentation of the facts by an employer concerned with preserving a company whose profit margin is no more than one or two percent? Labour law experts were divided on the issue; everyone, however, understood the message the video contained.

Nevertheless, on March 11, another application for union certification was submitted, this one in the name of 11 Couche-Tard employees at the intersection of Saint-Denis Street and

Beaubien Street in Montreal: the third in less than month. Three weeks later, the store closed. Another three weeks later, the company announced the sale of its store in Saint-Liboire, immediately after the labour relations board recognized the union there.

Officially, Couche-Tard maintained its position that the closures had no link with the presence of unions; they were merely implementing responsible administrative measures. After all, had it not closed 10 establishments in Quebec and 89 in its entire network the previous year?

But Couche-Tard found itself accused of intimidation and obstructing a union movement. The CSN called for the Public Service Labour Relations Board to force Couche-Tard to reopen the depanneur at Saint-Denis and Beaubien, and to grant $1 million in compensation to the employees it had laid off. The issue made waves in the Quebec media.

The impact was intensified by the decision in September to close the store on Jean-Talon—the first store in which, six months earlier, the employees had formed a union. Having not yet reached a work agreement with Couche-Tard, the workers showed up that morning with union stickers on their shirts, hoping to put pressure on their employer. At 5:30 p.m., security guards gave them two minutes to collect their personal belongings. The building was boarded up and sold. The site is now occupied by a high-rise apartment building.

The issue was becoming personal. The CSN organized demonstrations in front of Bouchard's office, accusing him of acting like an anti-union thug. It asked that he be forced to reveal the figures on the profitability of all depanneurs in the Montreal region, so that the labour relations commission could better judge the merits of Couche-Tard's defence. This request, however, was rejected.

The commission also gave the unionists another disappointment. Drawing on a decision from the Supreme Court of Canada, commissioner Jacques Vignola commented: "An employer has the right to close its own enterprise, no matter the reason." No one could force Couche-Tard to keep a store open that was en route to being unionized or was already so; and no one could force the company to prove the economic necessity of its decision.

Couche-Tard thus came out of the struggle on top—except when it came to its image. Its reputation, particularly that of its president and founder, was battered. It was all the more unfortunate that the crisis took place at home in Quebec: the company's birthplace and where it remained still. "It became a huge distraction," Bouchard says. "And it was undermining me."

With the benefit of hindsight, Bouchard acknowledges that he could have responded differently. Even if the stores were shut down due to low profitability, he says, some of the unionized or soon to be unionized depanneurs were closed in an unusual rush, which would naturally cause suspicion. Normally, when a store has to close its doors, the employees are warned in advance, and, as much as possible, are given the opportunity to find work in the company's other establishments.

It took two years to reach an agreement with the CSN. On October 28, 2013, Couche-Tard signed a three-year work contract with the unions for six depanneurs, only one of which was owned by the company (the store in Victoriaville); the other five were managed by franchisees. It was a first for a convenience store in North America. The contract included a confidential agreement; one publicly known feature is that it included a withdrawal of all accusations that the CSN had made against the company and Bouchard.

Couche-Tard had shown that it could live with unions so long as profitability remained at acceptable levels. Indeed, the company had an interest in doing so. It had just made the biggest acquisition in its history, in Europe—in which almost all its employees were unionized.

CHAPTER 20

The European Challenge

On April 18, 2012, Couche-Tard made waves yet again by boldly presenting a friendly offer to acquire the retail activities of Statoil Fuel & Retail (SFR), headquartered in Oslo, Norway. The word "retail" doesn't quite convey all that was at stake. The company had 2,300 service stations and just as many convenience stores, 1,000 car washes, terminals, tank farms and fuel-distribution products for cars, boats and planes, a network of heating oil distribution, a factory for manufacturing lubricants and another for liquid gas, and even a car rental service, all spread out over eight Northern European countries. The acquisition alone would increase Couche-Tard's sales by 50 percent, bringing it close to USD $35 billion—and finally dethroning 7-Eleven.

As one might expect, the price tag was dizzyingly high: USD $3.8 billion, including USD $1 billion to pay off the company's debts.

* * *

SFR dates back to 1923, when the first service station was built in Norway, near the railway station in Oslo, the country's capital. First known as MIL, the chain of service stations passed into the hands of British Petroleum (BP) after World War II, and then back into Norwegian ownership in 1970. Considerable oil and gas reserves had just been discovered off the coast of Norway, and new technologies were available to extract them. In 1972, the government became actively involved in developing these resources through the creation of Statoil, a company in which it was the majority shareholder: The name, connoting "State oil," was unequivocal in this regard.

Statoil soon expanded into Northern Europe. With the fall of the Berlin Wall and the subsequent breakup of the Soviet Union, Statoil positioned itself as a leader in developing the market economy of the Eastern Bloc, by establishing itself in the Baltic countries (Estonia, Latvia and Lithuania), in Poland and in Russia. Selling oil to Russians! It took some nerves.

"World War II, for my country [Estonia], really ended in June 1991, when we got out of the Soviet Union," says Helle Kirs-Toiger, who began working for Statoil as a secretary in 1995, when the company owned only four or five stores in the country.[39] Kirs-Toiger would later become director of sales for Statoil in Estonia. She believes that investing great sums of money in this politically unstable environment was a true feat—an act of "bravery."

To open its first store in the Baltic states, Statoil needed to obtain written approval from Moscow in March of 1991. The USSR, with Mikhail Gorbachev at the helm, was engaged in a process of dissolution (which an attempted coup d'état threatened to overturn six months later). Undeterred, the first Statoil service station opened its doors in Riga in 1992. For several years, in the time it took those countries to establish a functional economic and financial system, companies had a highly unusual mode of operation: Customers could only make their purchases in foreign currency. Acceptable currencies included

---

39. 20 years later, Couche-Tard owned 55 stores in Estonia, a country with a population of one million, and held 30 percent of the Estonian convenience retail market.

American dollars, Deutschmarks, French francs or any other Western currency—but no Soviet rubles, the country's official currency.

Statoil was also the first foreign oil company to set up shop in Lithuania and Northern Russia. Their first Russian service station, built in 1993 in the Russian city of Murmansk, north of the Arctic Circle, is considered one of the most incredible successes of this wild adventure, if only because the city's inhabitants—in the largest city located that close to the North Pole—developed an infatuation for the station's... ice cream.

Throughout the 2000s, the Norwegian government benefitted from strong global markets by cashing out some of its shares in Statoil, the company having become the main oil producer outside of the OPEC[40] member countries. It was also one of the most exemplary models anywhere in terms of managing the wealth it created. The profits generated by the exploitation of the non-renewable resource were invested in a special fund that was set aside for future generations rather than being spent on social programs or lower taxes for the immediate well-being of taxpayers, as was the case for oil revenue in many countries, Canada included.

In 2001, the government sold off 17 percent of the shares of this company, with its orange logo in the shape of a drop of oil. Three years later, Statoil split into two by creating a distinct division for all of its retail operations, Statoil Fuel & Retail (SFR), led by Jacob Schram. According to Schram, the move allowed Statoil to focus all its attention on the challenges of deep-water oil drilling. "Retail sales were no longer a priority," he says. "We were no longer getting leadership attention and

---

40. OPEC: Organization of the Petroleum Exporting Countries, a cartel made up primarily of Middle Eastern and African countries that regulates nearly half of the world's oil production.

we didn't have any more money to invest. It was better to go public."

SFR therefore entered the stock market in October of 2010—but only partially, because Statoil owned a majority share. However, in the stock market, you can easily become prey. "It was just a matter of time," says Schram, "but it happened earlier than we expected."

* * *

Couche-Tard's acquisition of SFR would boost Bouchard's reputation for predicting the future—or for obstinacy. Many remembered his predictions from pre-2000, before even the company's first forays into the United States. At the end of Couche-Tard's annual shareholders meeting in 1999, he had told a journalist from Canadian Press, "Ten years from now, we should have between 2,000 and 3,000 stores in the United States." It was a done deal.

He had also proclaimed, "In 10 years, it's very likely that we'll have 1,500 or 2,000 stores in Western Europe." The predication was outlandish. Detractors said Bouchard had gotten too big for his boots—or worse, was becoming delusional. A worldwide empire of convenience stores—it was beyond imagining.

As he dreamt of expanding Couche-Tard beyond North America, Alain Bouchard expected that his first foray into Europe would have France as its target. Canadians, and particularly Quebecers, are generally positively viewed in France. Quebecers, these French-speaking "cousins" forgotten by France in North America for two centuries, came to France's defence during the two world wars. Just imagine the surprise of many French people when, during the Normandy landings in June 1944, the troops they believed to be British—with good reason, as Canada was still fighting under the Union Jack—spoke French, but with a curious accent that seemed straight out of the 17th century. A strong bond of friendship was forged between France and Quebec following those encounters. It started with the soldiers and locals, then student and cultural exchanges; later, governments and businesses joined the party. Perhaps it was Couche-Tard's turn.

However, the company's entry into the United States market demanded a great deal of time and energy. Opportunities to buy large chains at good prices were few and far between, and many attempts ended in failure, with competitors offering a higher price. Development in the United States continued, but at a slower pace than Couche-Tard would have liked. Management began looking elsewhere and naturally turned toward Asia.

Circle K was already established in Asia, with networks of licensees totalling 4,200 stores. The first network, located in Hong Kong, was called Circle K China. The company was listed on the Hong Kong stock exchange, and began to grow within the immense Chinese market. However, the Beijing government came to the defence of the local businesses by adopting new rules that prohibited foreign chains from selling the most popular kind of cigarettes, which were local; only native Chinese people were permitted to do so.

Circle K's associates were, in fact, Chinese, but from Hong Kong, a territory that had just recently been reabsorbed by China. The disparity suggested that Hong Kong citizens still did not enjoy the same rights as other Chinese. Deprived of the revenue from cigarettes, which the Chinese consume in great quantities, the Circle K stores in China had to rethink their business model and focus more on the sale of fresh produce. This model "is working well," says Alain Bouchard, "but the potential to develop thousands of stores has been compromised."

Circle K had another major licensed network in Indonesia. There were over 500 stores in this country that has a vibrant economy and a population of more than two-hundred million. Once again, the government intervened to block Couche-Tard's expansion by enacting a law that prohibits foreigners from attaining market dominance.

The Circle K franchise holder in Japan owns the brand for the region, which is home to 3,000 stores. The Circle K parent company and its owner, Couche-Tard, receive no benefits from this arrangement, apart from visibility. An international division of Circle K oversees geographic diversification initiatives in Vietnam and Malaysia, as well as in the Middle East, in Saudi Arabia, Egypt and Dubai. Other projects are in the works to penetrate new markets. However, the attempt to expand into China was a lesson on the risk of investing considerable sums of money in a foreign market, only to have the rules change under the pressure of local merchants.

"So we decided to look into Europe," says Bouchard. Earlier, Couche-Tard had made its first acquisition offer in the United Kingdom; it was rejected. It was by studying the composition of the European market that Bouchard learned of SFR and its operations in Northern Europe. SFR had already begun the process of going public when he first contacted the company. However, by then the process was too far along, and no doubt too politically sensitive, to change directions and proceed with a private sale, particularly to a foreign company.

So Bouchard moved on—until 18 months later, that is, when, during a negotiation with a large oil company in Scandinavia, a banker suggested that he get back in touch with

Statoil. A rumour had been circulating that SFR was having trouble getting off the ground now that it had left the nest of its parent company. SFR needed to make over its business model—to become a true retailer. Couche-Tard had the expertise it needed.

However, by that time, the company's shares were public, with a known value—and that value was staggering.

* * *

The founders of Couche-Tard rolled up their sleeves, as they had for all major decisions in the past. "We started travelling and visiting the stores, undercover," says Bouchard. "We visited hundreds of stores before making our offer." Although it has never been put in writing, it is part of their modus operandi that no large-scale project can be undertaken without unanimous agreement between all four Couche-Tard founders. "I had to convince them," Bouchard says, "because all of our assets are in this company."

And those assets were considerable. With their investments in Couche-Tard, the four men had more money than they could ever spend in their lifetime. If it proved unprofitable, this new acquisition had the potential to sink the company. The stakes were high; their life's work hung in the balance, and there was no margin for error. Before taking the risk, they needed to be sure they were doing it for the right reasons. "You can't make a $3.8 billion investment without being sure that you can improve things and add value," says Alain Bouchard.

By inspecting Statoil's stores and books, they were able to identify what wasn't working in the company. In order to maintain its profits and satisfy investors, SFR had decided to increase the prices of the items sold in its stores. At the same time, the Scandinavian governments were changing the rules about operating hours for grocery stores, allowing them to stay open later. The combination of these two factors represented a challenge similar to the one Couche-Tard had faced in Quebec at the end of the 1980s. The results were predictable: SFR customers went elsewhere, and the elasticity of supply and demand threatened to propel them from the business. "We decided to proceed," says Bouchard, "because we could see the potential. We were confident we could transform the network."

In January of 2012, Jacob Schram was on his way to a board of directors meeting, the subject of which was the size of dividend that would be paid to SFR shareholders, when the board president delivered the news he had been fearing: "A company has approached us and wants to buy us, so we need to start the process."

Schram was devastated. Hardly a year had passed since SFR had had its first taste of freedom. "We had just freed ourselves from the mother, started to live our own grownup life," he says. It reminded him of when he left his family home at age 20, finding himself in an empty apartment filled with hopes and dreams. The first months of SFR's adult life had been busy with planning the company's new direction and identifying acquisition opportunities. "We were looking for little fishes, but we didn't look behind us. A bigger fish was about to eat us, like Pac-Man."

The management team was summoned immediately to meet with the potential buyers, who had made the unfortunate decision to show up in the middle of the winter holiday. Thus, Jørn Madsen, director of SFR's Central & Eastern Europe division, hastily ended his vacation in Thailand and returned to Oslo to make a presentation to the Couche-Tard executives. Already feeling bitterly disappointed about the company changing hands, this didn't endear the Couche-Tard directors to him any further.

Madsen had spent his whole life building the company, first as a student working in a service station, and then in the business division, where he climbed the ladder rung by rung. He was involved in opening the first Statoil store in the Baltic countries in 1992. Twenty years later he had just 10 hours on a plane to prepare to hand over the results of all that work to a group of foreigners. "We had plans to go out and look at new markets," he says, but suddenly, it was like everything ground to a halt. "It was a big surprise. We had not seen it coming."

Hans-Olav Høidahl didn't have quite as long of a trip to make. Responsible for the Scandinavian division of SFR, he was spending his vacation week in a cabin in Norway when he was summoned to the law firm's office in Oslo for a secret meeting with the Couche-Tard management team. He was careful to hide his disappointment, however. He knew that the purpose of this meeting was not only to understand how SFR worked, but also to evaluate its management team. In short, it was a job interview. But it was also his first opportunity to size up the potential buyers. Would he want to work with the group of Canadians? All the big players were present: Alain Bouchard, Richard Fortin and Réal Plourde, accompanied by Brian Hannasch and Raymond Paré, the new chief financial officer. These people were not new to acquisitions. They were experts in the strange tango, where the two partners, one hunter and the other prey, had to delicately synchronize their personal interests.

The first impression was much better than Høidahl had anticipated: "I felt they met us with respect. They were really friendly guys," he recalls. "You felt immediately that they knew the retail business. So this first meeting was a good foundation for a better relationship later."

SFR's top leader, Jacob Schram, had the same feeling. "We were kind of negative at the start…but as we started to learn about Couche-Tard, we found out this is the best that could happen to us." The buyer could have been another oil company, or worse still, an investment fund looking for short-term returns. At least with Couche-Tard, he says, "it was someone who had the same core business as we did, and had pretty good success with it."

* * *

The friendly takeover offer presented on April 18, 2012 was negotiated with Statoil management, which agreed to relinquish its position of control over SFR—54 percent of the company. However, Couche-Tard didn't want to buy just a block of shares, even a majority block. The goal was to absorb the entire company and add it to its portfolio. But Norwegian laws dictate that approval from 90 percent of shareholders is necessary to dissolve a publicly listed company and privatize it. They needed to make an attractive offer.

At 51.20 NOK (Norwegian kroner)[41] per share, their offer represented a substantial premium of 50 percent on the latest share price at the Oslo Stock Exchange. It made sense, considering that the share price had fallen quite a bit in the previous year, because SFR had failed to deliver the results expected by shareholders.

Couche-Tard's shareholders, on the other hand, were more than happy. As soon as the offer was announced, shares of the company shot up by 15 percent, reaching a peak of $39.60 in Canadian dollars. In a single day, Couche-Tard's market capitalization had increased by over CAD $1 billion.

---

41. The equivalent of USD $9.50.

Enthusiasm was not as strong on the other side of the Atlantic, where Norwegian shareholders had until May 21 to make a decision; then the offer would expire. When it didn't reach the numbers needed, Couche-Tard had to extend the offer three times: to May 29, to June 8, and then finally, to June 20. Each time, the price remained the same, in spite of the significant general downturn in share prices that had taken place on European and international stock exchanges since the initial offer on April 18. In Oslo, the index had dropped over eight percent in the space of just over two months. The day before the final extension was set to expire, Couche-Tard put out a press release to express its worries publicly that it wouldn't be able to reach the required target of 90 percent. At that point, 81.2 percent of the company's shares had been ceded, and the other shareholders were no doubt holding out for a higher offer at the last minute. Couche-Tard announced that this was out of the question: Its offer would remain the same, and if it failed to reach the required level of approval, it could be abandoned. They could take it or leave it. Standing their ground paid off. The next day, Couche-Tard had 96 percent of the shares, and was then able to force the others shareholders to relinquish theirs. All that remained was to pay the price: USD $3.8 billion.

This had proved more difficult than expected.

The National Bank of Canada, Couche-Tard's stalwart ally, couldn't finance the operation singlehandedly. The company got support from the largest pool of capital in Quebec, Caisse de Dépôt et Placement du Québec, which agreed to invest between 860 million and one billion dollars in the transaction. The rest would come from international banks: Mitsubishi in Japan, HSBC in London and Crédit Agricole in France.

Everything was going smoothly until, two weeks before the offer was to be submitted, the Caisse demanded conditions that the other institutions had not requested. Couche-Tard couldn't accept. The Caisse threatened to pull its financing, hoping to force Couche-Tard's hand. Its piece of the pie was enormous, and little time remained to find another billion dollars. It amounted to holding a gun to Couche-Tard's head. "They were bluffing," says Bouchard. But two can play at that game. "I asked my chief financial officer, Raymond Paré, 'Can you find that money?' He was so mad. He said, 'I'll find it, Alain,' and we did."

The allocations from banks went very well, so much so that USD $200 million more was raised than planned. Now they needed to find "just" $800 million more. The Dutch bank Rabobank, which specializes in agriculture, food and distribution, joined the financial group, and HSBC increased its contribution in order to save the transaction, which promised to bring in a great deal through fees from bond issuance.

The Caisse's bluff had failed.

* * *

The takeover of SFR added 18,500 new employees to the 53,000 already working for Couche-Tard in North America— and most of these employees were unionized. Before presenting his official offer, Bouchard had taken the time to meet personally with the union representatives along with Brian Hannasch, Couche-Tard's chief operating officer. Cathrine Jørgensen, union representative since 2009, was present. "We were curious. What would they do with us?" she recalls. First, Couche-Tard's management was careful to remain reassuring. "They told us that it was going to be Norwegian leadership, so it would be almost the same as before." The plan for job cuts and operations streamlining initiated in 2009 by SFR would continue until the end of 2015,[42] allowing just enough time for the company to bounce back. "They sold us the idea by telling us that SFR would be their starting off point to expand into Europe," she said. "That gave us some positive energy—we could start thinking about growth, and that was good for morale."

More than anything, it was Couche-Tard's history that gave the union reassurance. The company was not a speculator looking for quick profits. "We told them that if they were choosing between the lesser of evils, they were better with us than with anyone else," says Bouchard. The fact that Couche-Tard is a Canadian company—Canada being a middle power with a strong international reputation and no colonial past—did the rest.

At no point during the meeting did Bouchard show any resistance to the union's presence. Nor did he refer to the battle he was currently facing with the CSN in Quebec. The SFR employees representative even seemed charmed following her meeting with the man she describes as "a cozy grandfather... a kind person."

After the official offer was made, when the acquisition project went public, the CSN directors spoke out. They organized a conference call with the SFR employee union to warn them about their future employer, accusing Couche-Tard of being hypocritical. Likely they also wanted to see how much support they could secure from the European workers for their cause in Quebec. The CSN sent the SFR union officers documentation concerning their conflict with Couche-Tard. But they received little by way of response. "There's a different way of doing things in Norway, because of the laws and agreements that we have here," says Jørgensen.

---

42. This plan anticipated cutting 500 jobs, mainly in the company's administration.

Norwegian society is indeed one of the most egalitarian in the world. It functions through ongoing dialogue between managers, the government and the unions. Important economic decisions involve all three groups, in a partnership. This collaborative relationship also exists within the company, where the unions are included in projects from the very beginning. "Sometimes they have good arguments," says Jacob Schram. "In the end, of course, management decides, but the union can say what they mean, and they want us to take consideration of that. [Bouchard] was aware of it and he, and the rest of the Couche-Tard team, respected that."

These consultations are taken for granted in Norway, and they required a good deal of patience from Bouchard. Building a relationship of trust means taking the time to explain and to listen. Schram recognizes that this was a difficult lesson for Bouchard, who would sometimes voice his frustrations: "Ah! The process in Europe takes a *long* time!"

"I didn't sleep well for the first 18 months after the acquisition," says Bouchard. It wasn't because of the time difference between Quebec and Norway; it was because of the cultural differences. He and his team had identified the problems that needed solving in order to revitalize the SFR stores, and he expected the solutions to come quickly. "In America, we have an acute sense of urgency," he says. In Europe, and particularly in Scandinavian countries, people reflect a great deal before acting, which started to drive him crazy. "Forty-six versions of a memo—that's too much for me!" he says.

The first test of blending the two approaches came very early on, and carried important symbolic value, because it concerned the decision to build the company's new main place of business in Oslo. Since it had been sold, SFR could no longer remain under the umbrella of the parent company, Statoil. But where should it go?

For Bouchard, the answer was obvious. The price of land in downtown Oslo was so steep that they needed to move out to the outskirts of the city. After all, that's what Couche-Tard had done in the beginning, settling in a wooded area of Laval. But SFR's employees and management saw things differently. Oslo is a shining example in public transportation, with its trains, subway, tramways and buses. A beautiful port city, designed well before the arrival of cars, it's at a human scale, full of parks and public spaces that encourage walking and biking. The idea of moving SFR's offices to the suburbs was met with great resistance from employees, because that would have a significant impact on their quality of life, and would no doubt force many of them to switch to a car.

SFR's management came up with a compromise. The company owned a service station near the train station, a sector with a booming real estate market, where large companies were rushing to build office buildings, each with a bolder design than the last. The service station's lot alone was evaluated at USD $30 million. In exchange for this lot, a developer was prepared to construct a new building at his own expense, and SFR would be the main tenant of the building for 12 years at a reduced price. This option also provided a symbolic advantage: The administrative office for the company would be situated where the first service station was built in Norway in 1923. The location forged a bridge between the company's past and future.

However, Bouchard was against this idea from the get-go. Hannasch had to intervene just to keep him from walking out of the project's formal presentation. Eventually, however, he agreed. He was the leader, but he also knew how to listen. It was an important signal to the management of the company's new European division, a preliminary test of the autonomy that had been promised to them, and a demonstration of the benefits of Couche-Tard's decentralized system.

After three years of construction, the new building opened its doors in the summer of 2015. With a more classic structure than the often extravagant buildings in the train station neighbourhood, it is nonetheless modern, with its vast atrium and wide-open workspaces where even the boss, Schram, does not have a walled-in office.

* * *

At that time, Hannasch was one of the top executives of Couche-Tard in the United States, and he was finding it difficult to adapt to the European ways of doing business. "I think North Americans frustrate some people and vice versa," he says. The Couche-Tard model, based on American-inspired entrepreneurial culture, had for the first time to reconcile itself to another organizational design. In America, "we simply aim and shoot sometimes," explains Brian Hannasch [with a firearms metaphor that might be considered American in spirit], "and Europeans tend to be very much 'planning, checking and then doing.' When they finally do it, they do it right." Blending the two models was going to take more work than he had anticipated.

Once the SFR acquisition deal was settled, a conference call was quickly organized between the upper directors in Europe and the vice-presidents responsible for the 10 or so divisions of the company in Canada and the United States. It was an opportunity to discuss Couche-Tard's practices, its way of operating, as well as the organization's culture and governance structure. Jørn Madsen remembers thinking, "Wow! Jesus Christ, what is this company?" Some of them sounded like they were straight out of a Western movie."

Aside from the level of English spoken, the contrast between the organizations was most visible in their approach to operational discipline. Alain Bouchard puts it bluntly: "They were heading straight for a wall when we bought them." Indeed, the Scandinavian company's business model was facing many obstacles. Inspired by North American practices, Denmark and Sweden had just lengthened grocery store opening hours, and Norway was preparing to do the same. With sales diminishing by two to three percent every year, SFR directors had increased prices in order to maintain revenue. "Not only can customers go to a larger store with more selection and lower prices, but you're also going to increase prices?" Bouchard asked with bewilderment. "We know it's not working," Schram replied. "We have to work together to find a solution."

The Couche-Tard recipe would help them find the solution. First, they had to equip all of the stores with scanners connected to a central computer system and an integrated management software system that would analyze sales sector-by-sector in real time, to better plan supply. Contracts with suppliers also had to be renegotiated to obtain more competitive prices, and marketing strategies needed to be made more dynamic. Finally, SFR needed to undergo a commercial face-lift, with an overhaul of its store designs. Some seemed better equipped to be dance floors, Bouchard says: The central areas were empty, because people didn't know what to sell. "We asked them, 'Are you really in business? What's the point of your store?'" he says.

The Couche-Tard team spent a good deal of time with SFR leader Jacob Schram visiting the Circle K stores in the United States and discussing the merits of their design, their strategic placement of products, the internal displays, their promotions and counter service. Upon his return to Norway, Schram came back to his team and said, "These guys are very good, and we have a lot to learn from them."

And they had to learn it quickly. About 40 SFR managers and employees headed to Arizona, with the task of studying as many of the group's stores as possible over a few weeks, and drawing inspiration so they could breathe new life into their stores in Europe. One month after their return to Oslo, a redesign plan for the European stores was ready; and, to the great surprise of Bouchard, who often lost patience with SFR's slow decision-making process, "they were able to develop it much faster than we could have in the United States."

The stores became brighter and more colourful. Screens were everywhere, promoting sale products, from two-for-one packs of chewing gum—an uncommon sales practice in Europe—to containers of laundry detergent sold at half price. Near the checkout area, a ready-to-eat hot dog counter was set up; hot dogs were smaller than those traditionally sold in Scandinavia, but three times less expensive. Right away, the SFR stores began selling 200 per day on average.

Conversely, Couche-Tard's management asked its American divisions to follow the example of SFR's food offerings, which were "far superior to what we have in America," said Alain Bouchard, in particular concerning ready to eat food—sandwiches and salads—and coffee. In the United States, explains Hannasch, the company had focused on the self-service concept. "SFR challenged this paradigm; that is, if we want to serve high-quality food to people, we may have to rethink that approach."

"What I really like with Couche-Tard," says Schram, "is that when they buy something, their ears are bigger than their mouth." He was explained the virtues of the decentralized structure, which provides considerable autonomy to the different divisions of Couche-Tard. Initially, he had thought it was just a slogan to sugar-coat the pill, to make it easier to swallow. Bouchard and Hannasch had also confided in him that they had never purchased a company that was as professional as SFR. "In the start, I thought it was just some polite thing to say, but they actually meant it." The clearest vote of confidence— one that Schram was absolutely not expecting—was that after investing the colossal sum of $3.8 billion to acquire SFR, Couche-Tard never tried to impose one of its trusted employees on the European management team. "Not a single one!" he says.

After the acquisition, there were no losers, no subordinates—only partners, and soon, members of a big family.

* * *

The Couche-Tard recipe proved effective once again. Rigorous internal controls, more aggressive marketing and a resolutely business-oriented shift: Once all of these measures were put in place, the European division of Couche-Tard began delivering solid performances. After several quarters of falling sales, they turned a corner and began to increase. "Since then, we've only had positive quarters," says Jacob Schram with pride. One year after the acquisition, the results from the first quarter of 2014[43] provided an indication of SFR's potential performance by showing a 50 percent higher increase in fuel sales than those in the United States, and a profit margin on each litre that was two times higher than in Canada. In-store merchandise sales increased three times more quickly than in Canadian convenience stores, which led to a higher gross profit

---

43. First quarter of 2014 (Q1), the months of May, June and July, 2013.

than the profit made in North America. In total, the entire Couche-Tard group's net profit from the first quarter of 2014 reached USD $255 million, a 21 percent increase. And that meant hopes of annual profits exceeding one billion dollars—an accomplishment that would be a first for Couche-Tard.

Cathrine Jørgensen, the union representative, notes that management is "a bit different now from before, when it was owned by Statoil." There are more controls and more procedures to follow. On one hand, the annual negotiations to determine salary increases—conducted country-by-country—are, according to Jørgensen, more difficult than before. She attributes this to the signals from Couche-Tard's executives, and their reputation for taking a hard line on saving money.

On the other hand, the union has been pleased to see that promises to reinvest in the stores have been kept, and that the employee representatives were involved in the planning from the very start, which is in line with the normal mode of operation in that region. In the end, she feels that the changes that have taken place since Couche-Tard's acquisition were less momentous than expected. Even though not all employees appreciate what they see as an Americanization of the stores, they recognize that the influence has not been one-sided, and that Couche-Tard's American stores have also learned from their European counterparts. "It's a positive to have a big company owning us," says Jørgensen, because it provides employees with professional development opportunities that were unheard-of before, such as the possibility of going to work for a few years in the United States.

The regional expansion into Europe, which is being actively pursued by the executives, is also a source of pride and an exciting challenge that has support from the union. Jørgensen's only real regret is that Couche-Tard decided to divest itself of several hydrocarbon-related sectors, such as lubricant manufacturing, gas liquefaction and kerosene distribution in airports. Many of the union directors come from the oil sector, and they fear that the next victim of the streamlining process will be the heating oil division, one of the company's sectors that has been at risk for many years.

It's clear to employees that the stores are the top priority for the new owners, even though nearly three-quarters of SFR's profits come from hydrocarbons. Regular visits from Couche-Tard's executives in Europe have reinforced that message. Each time, Bouchard has insisted on only spending a few hours in the offices meeting with the management team. More than anything, he has focused on spending time in the stores, so he can get the lay of the land from the managers and employees and measure the effectiveness of the marketing strategies, new products or updated layouts. Touching base with them is the best way to take stock of all progress and any remaining challenges. And as he had done many times in the United States, Bouchard elicited surprise by eschewing the comfortable car reserved for the executives he travelled with, and jumping into one driven by a manager he got along with for the length of his tour.

"This kind of behaviour creates a culture of respect and focus and it is very motivating for the salespeople," says Hans-Olav Høidahl, vice-president responsible for the company's Scandinavian territory. In his opinion, it's an important lesson, and an inspiration for all of leaders.

CHAPTER 21

Masters in our Own House

"Our future lies in being masters in our own house," declared Alain Bouchard, borrowing the emblematic expression from Jean Lesage. The slogan was popularized in 1962, during the Quiet Revolution in Quebec. It had been a rallying cry for the Francophone majority to take back their main levers of development—starting with the provinces great wealth of hydroelectric resources.

Half a century later, the essentially nationalist line takes on another meaning, when Bouchard applies it to Couche-Tard. He is translating the slogan into a call for commercial liberation. He believes his company isn't given enough respect from suppliers—respect it had earned by virtue of its size, its dynamism and its ambition. "We have been treated like a cash cow," he says with exasperation.

The pricing structure used by the major food poducers effectively favours large-scale distribution for companies like Costco and Walmart, and, on the other end of the spectrum, low-end shops like dollar stores. Next in their hierarchy of priorities comes supermarkets and grocery stores—then, finally, convenience stores: they are the lowest on the food chain, yet made to pay the highest prices. "Sometimes other stores would be able to sell their products for less than my cost price," fumes Bouchard.

The situation fostered a dream of freedom in Couche-Tard's leaders. The company wants to own its own brands, which would allow it to compete with the big food conglomerates and to develop unique food concepts, singular to Couche-Tard, rather than moving product for other global banners.

In short, Couche-Tard is gearing up to get in the ring with Coca-Cola, Starbucks, McDonald's, Nestlé and Red Bull—all at once.

* * *

Following the commercial success of Sloche in convenience stores throughout Canada, Couche-Tard multiplied its attempts at developing its own products. Some were more successful than others. One winner was the energy drink Joker, that's lack of brand recognition was offset by its attractive price. Sold at just half the price of competing energy drinks, it is nonetheless able to carve out a higher profit margin—a result that gives an indication of the profit margins being made by the major global brands marketing that kind of product.

In the United States, Couche-Tard's stores already serve their own version of soft drinks, in cola and lemon-lime flavours, which are sold side-by-side with the giants, Coca-Cola and 7Up. Lacking major advertising support, the generic products have little chance of developing a mass market. But they have their own role as substitutions, and with dozens of sales a day in each of the company's thousands of stores, they add a nice boost to the company's profit margins. Also, importantly, they act as a lever that allows Couche-Tard to negotiate better conditions with the major soft drink brands. In business as in politics, it all comes down to power.

"I've used that tactic all my life with major suppliers who tend to impose their magical thinking on retailers—especially on us, the small stores," says Bouchard. "They show up with their notebook and they say, 'Here are the current trends, and here's what you need to do.'" It's behaviour like that, Bouchard says, that he has fought against since the 1990s, when Couche-Tard first owned more than 200 convenience stores. Instead, he tried to reverse the equation, telling suppliers, "Here's what we want. For us," he says.

But at the time, his bargaining power wasn't quite solid enough—and in some respects, the same is true today. Most major suppliers operate by geographical sector. Couche-Tard therefore doesn't negotiate with Coca-Cola's headquarters in Atlanta on behalf of its thousands of convenience stores around the world. Instead, each division negotiates with local bottling plants. It all means that the company can't wield its true global purchasing power; its ability to attain lower prices is diminished.

"That's why we started moving toward private brands," says Bouchard. "We didn't have a choice." Thus Couche-Tard has formed a brigade in charge of developing the company's own brands, in cooperation with its North American and European units—to maximize their distribution. Some products, for which brand loyalty isn't much of a factor, are easy to substitute: chips, nuts, etc. Others require a degree of savviness. But the stakes are high, and Couche-Tard takes the challenge seriously, and invests heavily. It is a strategic bet with an eye on the long term.

"In a few years," Bouchard predicts, "when the customers are familiar with our products, we will have the possibility to reduce the number of national brands in our stores." Convenience stores that are part of the Couche-Tard family will no longer be mere distribution channels, but also flagships for a range of products created by the company for the company.

Similarly, Couche-Tard wants to become a destination for food. "The future is in fast food," says Jacques D'Amours.

Couche-Tard's acquisition of SFR gives them a strong advantage in this respect. "We learn a lot from them," says D'Amours. SFR's food selection is superior to that of the group's North American stores. There are historical reasons for the difference. Europe long avoided the onslaught of fast-food chains that North America have endured since the 1960s. Food offerings, therefore, has developed more organically, and with more respect for local eating habits. SFR's ready to eat food sales have come to represent one-third of all sales in their stores.

After gasoline, "Food is our number-one profit category, by a long shot," says Brian Hannasch. The challenge for Couche-Tard is to reproduce this model in its North American territory. Already, thousands of the chain's stores prepare food on-site. In the Southern United States, tacos and burritos; in the north, sandwiches and hot dogs; and hundreds of convenience stores offer salads and pastries. There's no single recipe, so to speak. Each division is encouraged to adapt to the preferences of local customers.

One of the spearheads of Couche-Tard's food strategy centres on a concept that its leaders hope to implement throughout its network. It involves a fully automated Swiss-manufactured coffee machine, easy to use and capable of providing high-quality coffee in different formats—espresso, latte, cappuccino—on par with the best restaurants. Couche-Tard management believes the device could help them compete against Starbucks, which popularized a taste for European-style coffee in North America.

Starbucks is not without its faults—all the more so because of its phenomenal success. Since each coffee is prepared individually by a barista, its customers are expected to endure long lines. The astonishingly high prices match this approach. Couche-Tard's offer—a high-quality coffee from a machine that the customers operate themselves—makes the experience much faster, and allows the price to be cut to a fraction of Starbucks'. A side benefit is that the offer also boosts sales for related food items.

The responsibility for extending the new offering to all Couche-Tard stores in the United States was given to Helle Kirs-Toiger, former director of SFR in Estonia. Living in North Carolina since 2014, Kirs-Toiger is supervising the U.S. rollout of these coffee machines, which have brought in a fortune in the Baltic countries. In Lithuania, says Bouchard, "each of our stores sells 330 of these coffees a day, on average." That amounts to 10,000 coffees per month per store—which brings in serious revenue.

Couche-Tard is relying on this strategy to reverse the trend that began in 2010, when the company started to lose market share in coffee sales to McDonald's, Starbucks and Tim Hortons. "We were slow to react," Bouchard acknowledges. The change came in 2012, when Couche-Tard's leaders were buying SFR. Encountering the Swiss-designed machine, they fell in love. "When we saw that machine in Europe, we knew we had found a solution."

Another offensive focusing on lower prices has been paying off for Couche-Tard: offering fountain soft drinks at a single price, regardless of the size. Marketed under the name Polar Pop, the concept rests on having a huge dispenser offering more than a dozen soft drink flavours at an incredibly low price—less than one dollar—whatever the size of the cup.

This product replaced another formula, called Thirstbuster, offering fountain drinks at a higher price that varied according to size served. As a business strategy, Polar Pop might have seemed like suicide on the surface—increasing quantities while reducing prices—but implementing the new concept in

Florida stores ended up tripling sales. And as with most successful Couche-Tard initiatives, the formula brought a greater number of customers into stores, where they would be likely to buy other products.

They would also be more likely to pay for other services. With thousands of stores spread across a vast territory and open 24 hours a day, Couche-Tard has found itself in an excellent position to expand its offer beyond gasoline, cigarettes, drinks, basic food and fast-food products. The stores have also become a haven for automated bank machines, allowing financial institutions to increase their points of service at a time when the number of traditional bank branches is being drastically reduced.

During its first incursion into the United States, Couche-Tard discovered that most convenience stores there had their own automated teller machines, affiliated with no particular bank. These cash machines finance themselves by charging transaction fees to customers for the convenience—allowing them to avoid running to the nearest branch of their own bank. Banks follow the same practice with other banks' ATMs.

Another advantage of having private cash machines, or of eventually installing them in convenience stores, is that it gives Couche-Tard an extra lever when it comes to negotiating fees with banks for their use of the space. The strategic value of these placements was proven in the middle of the summer of 2015, when Manulife Bank[44] reached an agreement with Couche-Tard for the installation of 830 ATMs in Canadian convenience stores.

---

44. Manulife Bank is an affiliate of Manulife Financial, the largest insurance company in Canada and the second largest in North America. Manulife Bank has no physical branches, but provides services online, through independent financial advisors, by telephone and through bank machines.

CHAPTER 22

Succession

O n December 18, 2014, just a week before Christmas, Couche-Tard announced that it had completed the biggest acquisition in its history in North America. The price tag: USD $1.7 billion.

The Pantry was a company that owned more than 1,500 convenience stores, concentrated in the Southeast United States, near the Gulf of Mexico, and mainly under the Kangaroo Express banner. The deal could add $7 billion to Couche-Tard's sales and lengthen its list of employees by 15,000.

With over 1,000 Circle K stores, Couche-Tard already had a strong presence in the region. The acquisition would allow it to consolidate its position in one of the most promising markets on the continent. The Pantry's kangaroo was in rough shape, however, bruised by a string of poor business decisions. It would take an experienced integrator—like Couche-Tard—to help it bounce back.

Couche-Tard had had its eye on The Pantry for more than seven years. In the summer of 2007, when competition between the big oil companies was particularly ferocious, the chain—founded 14 years earlier and headquartered in Cary, North Carolina—was struggling. That meant it was a target for acquisition.

Couche-Tard was already at the front of the pack in the American convenience store industry, with 2,636 corporate stores—more than any competitor. The Pantry followed in second place, with 1,640 corporate stores, followed closely by 7-Eleven with 1,604.[45] "We tried to make the purchase, but we couldn't pull it off," says Jacques D'Amours.

And perhaps it was just as well. Over the following years, Couche-Tard's divisions in the Southern United States developed through more modest acquisitions, especially in Florida and Louisiana, and by investing in upgrades to its stores. Feeling threatened and hoping to fend off Couche-Tard, "The Pantry spun out of control, buying anything that moved at impossible prices," says Bouchard. Worse, in his eyes, the company was run by financial specialists, rather than by retail people. Profitability eluded them; The Pantry was forced to close hundreds of stores. In a word, says Bouchard, it was broken.

Broken or not, acquiring The Pantry offered a fantastic opportunity for synergy. After the purchase of Circle K 12 years earlier, possibilities for growth were scarce in the Gulf of Mexico area. By striking this single blow, Couche-Tard could double its presence in the region. It would be particularly crucial in Florida, where Couche-Tard stores had been underperforming for several years. Bouchard had even broached the question: *Should we stay in Florida?*

Overhauling of the management team, with the nomination of Darrell Davis at its head, streamlining of the store sites and implementing a more aggressive offer for soft drinks, finally made it possible to turn the tide and make the Florida peninsula one of Couche-Tard's most profitable divisions. The purchase of The Pantry was announced on December 18, 2014; the shareholders accepted Couche-Tard's offer in March 2015. The acquisition was a done deal.

---

45. 7-Eleven's vast network of more than 4,500 affiliates helped it maintain its position as the leading convenience store chain in the United States.

* * *

One week later, Couche-Tard held its annual general assembly, for the first time in Toronto. It marked a momentous change: Alain Bouchard handed his position over to Brian Hannasch, an American and the former leader of Bigfoot, which had been the vehicle for Couche-Tard's first incursion into the United States. The news marked the turning of a page in the company's history. Bouchard was the last of the four founders to step aside from his ongoing administrative functions. When Réal Plourde, the second last founder standing, had made his departure, his position of head of operations had been given to Hannasch. Essentially, the move marked him as Bouchard's eventual successor. The three men had spent much time travelling together to the four corners of the Earth; a strong bond had formed between them. At the reception organized to honour Plourde's departure, Hannasch had surprised many present. His voice breaking with emotion, he spoke about the death of his father, not long after Bigfoot was bought by Couche-Tard.

Bouchard and Plourde, he said, had quickly become surrogate fathers for him: They were caring figures in his life. Professionally, they shared the same goals: accelerated growth for the company, territorial expansion and disciplined management, but with concern for respecting employees' autonomy through a real delegation of authority. "I feel like this is my company as much as it's Alain's, Richard's, Réal's or Jacques'," says Hannasch. Of course, he had missed its heroic beginnings. He never had to sit on a crate of soft drinks in a basement to count a day's sales; but since his arrival at the Couche-Tard group, he helped the company grow to 10 times its size, making it a global giant. "I'm having fun," he says.

"We're fortunate to be at a point where money is not such a big deal anymore. It's really about this passion you have for the business." A passion that nonetheless involves its share of stress, and can be demanding. Hannasch estimates he spends 80 percent of his time travelling beyond his two offices, one at the service centre in Laval and the other in the United States.

The four Couche-Tard founders have left their management positions, but they continue to be involved with the company. Serving on its board of directors, they still participate collegially in major decisions. According to Hannasch, that's fairly exceptional for companies that have reached that size. Not only are the founders still present after 35 years, but their egos have failed to expand along with their bank accounts, and their bonds of friendship are intact. It contributes greatly to the positive environment in the company, says Hannasch. "In the 15 years I've been with those guys, I have never seen a situation where a problem occurred and caused a break in their relationship or one of them being upset for a long period of time."

As the first founder and still the main shareholder for Couche-Tard, Bouchard's case is unusual for the active role he has been given. Along with chairing the board of directors and attending monthly accounting conferences, he retains control over the selection of new locations and store construction and renovation projects. No matter where in the world the project is, it must meet with his personal approval and respect the very strict criteria based on the model he created. Each project—and there are more than 100 each year—must be detailed in a 50-page document, containing the demographic data for the neighbourhood and studies on automobile and pedestrian traffic, road infrastructure and the presence of competing convenience stores. "He's fully focused on development," says

Hannasch, which means he's also involved in strategic acquisitions.

Some believe that this approach goes against Couche-Tard's organizational philosophy, which is to decentralize decision-making power. Despite the resistance, Bouchard holds on to the prerogative, because, he says, "there are questions that other people don't ask." For example: a manager who, having purchased land in a sector that seems promising, is determined to build a store, even though traffic doesn't justify it. "Owning land isn't a good enough reason to put another $3 million into it," says Bouchard.

Bouchard steps in as a voice of wisdom, unencumbered by the management of daily operations, wanting above all to distribute investments to areas where they will be most profitable. For Bouchard, an accumulation of poor decisions eventually causes a company to stagnate. Similarly, when changes in a sector's demographic makeup indicates that a store's existence is no longer justified, refusal to close it ends up being a drag on the company as a whole, affecting its rhythm and possibilities for growth.

But Bouchard is convinced that Couche-Tard still has considerable potential for expansion. "I want to double the size of the company before I leave it in 10 years," he said in the summer of 2015, a few months after he traded in his role of CEO for that of chairman of the board.

* * *

Doubling the size of Couche-Tard means adding 12,000 new convenience stores throughout the world, with 100,000 additional employees, and reaching business numbers in excess of USD $70 billion. At this scale, there's no sense using the word "project" to describe Bouchard's endeavour. Calling him "ambitious" seems like a ludicrous understatement. One is tempted to borrow terms from other areas—"compulsive disorder," perhaps. But then one stops short; after all, how many have pointed mocking fingers at Bouchard's dreams over the years, only to later marvel at his ability to carry them out?

Because the convenience store industry remains highly fragmented, Hannasch believes that the American market still offers tremendous growth potential for the company. There are some 140,000 convenience stores in the United States; 5,000 of them belong to Couche-Tard. That number would have to triple to reach the 10 percent target that Bouchard considers optimal. That's the degree of penetration Couche-Tard has already reached in Canada, where the company owns more than 2,000 of the country's 20,000 convenience stores.

However, number of stores isn't a sufficient indicator of success for Bouchard. His stores should also be leaders in their own market, with sales that are 50 percent to 100 percent higher than the industry average. With 10 percent of the Canada's convenience stores, Couche-Tard claims 20 percent of the sales in the sector. In Quebec, the number is 30 percent. That's the level of consolidation the company is looking for— the level that allows it to solidify its grip on success.

In Scandinavia, Couche-Tard already dominates the convenience store market, and "we're looking to neighbouring countries to expand our European platform," says Hannasch. "But we are also opportunistic. If there is an opportunity to go somewhere else, we'll take a hard look at it."

For their part, the leaders of Couche-Tard's European division see its future to the south, in the most promising markets and strongest economies: Great Britain and Germany. "If we want to be really big in Europe," says Hans-Olav Høidahl, vice-president responsible for the company's Scandinavian territory, "we need to find a solution in Germany, because Germany is the centre of Europe."

CHAPTER 23

A Unified Global Brand...
Except in Quebec

On September 22, 2015, Couche-Tard announced one of the most important strategic decisions in its history. This time, it wasn't a major acquisition or a venture into a promising new geographical territory. Instead, the convenience store empire had decided that the 15,000 stores[46] it operated around the world under a range of names would unite around a single banner. After much deliberation, the name that would remain standing was that of the group's best-known store: Circle K. Kangaroo Express, Statoil (the retail brand of SFR), and Mac's would all be set aside in order for Circle K to reign supreme. This name would attest to the strength of the world leader in convenience stores—the Circle K name would be everywhere.

Except, that is, in Quebec.

The company's birthplace and the home of its central nervous system, it was decided, would retain the Couche-Tard banner. Quebec would also hold on to two other trademarks: the Sept Jours and Provi-Soir depanneurs, reminders of the first big steps the company took in its expansion, and its smallest franchises. The four founders and principal shareholders in Couche-Tard hadn't come as far as they did to end up labelling Quebec depanneurs with an Anglicized name. The depanneur is emblematic of that unique part of North America, which has held onto its language and traditions. For the founders,

---

46. Couche-Tard later sold their 3,000 stores in Japan.

making that change would mean spending the rest of their lives defending their choice.

Even outside Quebec, the decision to unify the names of the group's stores wasn't an easy one. But the matter demanded serious consideration after the acquisition of SFR. When SFR was made public in 2010, its parent company provided that the name Statoil would have to be abandoned within 10 years. So it was only a question of time. After being acquired by Couche-Tard in 2012, SFR wanted to accelerate its expansion in Europe; therefore, it had to adopt a new identity as quickly as possible. Doing so would avoid the waste of time and money involved in promoting a banner that was doomed to change before long.

The team in charge of SFR felt the most urgency to settle the matter—a consequential one, and loaded with symbolism for the founders of Couche-Tard. Ultimately, the reasoning behind the change didn't require a lot of explaining. A unique name that's easy to pronounce for people from different cultures (certainly not the case with the name "Couche-Tard"), would strengthen the bonds within the entrepreneurial family; it would also help achieve economies of scale for producing corporate documents, advertising, and global sponsorships as well as developing in-house products.

* * *

SFR's team had already demonstrated that a name change could be implemented successfully when it rebranded one of its own businesses. JET was the brand it had on a chain of automated service stations present in Sweden and Denmark. Automated service stations are quite common in European cities, where space is at a premium. Some of the mini-stations are as small as 70 square metres (754 square feet), with just two gas pumps and not a single employee. Customers pull up, serve themselves and pay with a credit card.

The JET network of stations in Sweden and Denmark was first owned by the oil company ConocoPhillips. It later sold JET to Statoil, but held on to the rights for the JET trademark, which had a very strong reputation. Statoil had to hand over a significant sum—several million euros per year—to ConocoPhillips for continued use of the name. The only alternative would have been to rebrand the chain, but Statoil didn't dare attempt it. Changing a successful brand is a proposition that tends to be both risky and expensive.

Such was the lay of the land when Couche-Tard, a company recognized for its rigorous expenditure management, acquired SFR. The new leaders didn't mince words: They intended to save $200 million by improving efficiency. The $5 million being spent each year for the use of that three-letter word, "JET," was an ideal target for the first round of cuts.

Couche-Tard initially tried to buy the brand from ConocoPhillips to get around paying an indefinite annuity for use of the banner. The purchase would be all the more justified since the company wanted to invest in geographical expansion for its automated service stations—a move that would increase the brand's value, allowing ConocoPhillips to raise its fees. Simply buying the name therefore made the most sense, Bouchard says. "We pressured them consistently, but they refused. So finally we said, 'Then we're going to drop the name.' They didn't believe us, but we did it."

And thus Ingo was born. The name combines the words *in* and *go*, nicely evoking the simple, efficient concept of automated stations: *in*, you enter; *go*, you leave. The transformation, led by Swede Christel Nettelvik, vice-president of SFR's automats business unit, also created the opportunity to unify the banners of the other automated stations belonging to the group: SFR owned more than 100 stations under the name Statoil 1-2-3, but this trademark too was also marked for extinction, as the name Statoil had to be dropped by 2020.

The transformation represented "A huge risk," Bouchard says, and would require a vast advertising campaign in Sweden and Denmark, as well as the replacement of all the credit cards marked with the JET name. Couche-Tard expected the change to bring a loss of as much as five percent of its revenue. The results, however, were happier than expected. Sales volume swiftly increased, and surveys with clients showed a more positive perception of the new banner's price competitiveness. "I was flabbergasted," Bouchard admits. He was also reassured, at least somewhat, as to the consequences of changing Couche-Tard's principal banners. After all, he says, the name Statoil "is a religion" in Scandinavia.

* * *

Once a year, Couche-Tard's vice-presidents come together to plan the company's strategy. The gathering is also a chance to socialize, share experiences and strengthen bonds. These meetings—to which spouses are sometimes invited to foster a friendly, informal atmosphere—are also meant to transmit the corporate culture—a culture strongly inspired by the Quebec roots of the four founders. These founders try to recreate the relaxed, friendly feeling of their earlier fishing expeditions— including the sing-alongs. It is rare, to say the least, for companies the size of Couche-Tard, with sales in the tens of billions of dollars, to involve their top executives in annual events like these, asking each new recruit, at their first meeting, to show off their vocal skills... Or maybe, from another point of view, to prove their ability to handle potentially embarrassing situations with grace.

In 2013, the vice-presidents' conference was held in Norway, to mark the SFR group's arrival into the Couche-Tard family. The exact location was chosen for its exotic character. Lofoten is a small fishing port on the west coast of the country. Located on the 68th parallel, inside the Arctic Circle, it is surrounded by rocky peaks that form a spectacular archipelago shielding it from icebergs carried by the Norwegian Sea. The site—once inhabited by Vikings—is known for its views of the aurora borealis, which adds a surreal element to the landscape. It can give one the feeling of being suspended outside time. The phenomenal setting inspired long conversations, shared revelations and deep reflection. Jacob Schram, head of SFR and the meeting's host, took the opportunity to try to gain a deeper knowledge of Alain Bouchard. "I said to Alain, 'What's your dream? Is it to buy another company? What do you want to achieve?'"

The Couche-Tard founder confided in Schram, sharing his journey, the tragedy he had experienced as a child when his father was thrown into bankruptcy, and his determination that the same thing would never happen to him. That's what pushed him so intensely to build a solid, diversified, prosperous company, he told him. "So my dream," he told Schram, concluding the story, "is to have a very big company." "OK," Schram said. "How big is big?" "Much bigger than it is today," Bouchard said, and paused before adding: "The biggest."

Schram told Bouchard that the ultimate indicator of Couche-Tard's success should not be its size but its reputation as the best convenience store in the world. "And to achieve that, you have to say you want it; you have to proclaim it and decide on a path that will get you there."

"If that's what you want, you can't have all these different banners," Schram continued. "Who the hell knows that Couche-Tard owns this or that? We need a global brand that can unite all our components."

The next night, Schram was unable to sleep. After taking a long walk on the beach, he ended up at his parents-in-law's chalet on the archipelago. There he began to put down on paper his idea for a proposal, which he would submit to the other Couche-Tard leaders the following day. It was time, he told them, for the company to affirm its goal of becoming the destination of choice for customers looking for a convenience store. That meant it had to take on its main global competitor directly: 7-Eleven. But to move forward, they needed to ensure that customers would recognize the chain's stores: hence the importance of unifying the banners. They needed, Schram said, to find a common name from within Couche-Tard's existing family, to draw from its own DNA, in order to merge its multiple concepts. He had even sketched out a logo by hand during his sleepless night. With slight modifications, his creation would become the logo for the new banner: Circle K.

The next step, he said, would be to identify the things that the company would be recognized for. He proposed five elements: prepared foods, coffee, drinks, premium gasoline and car washes. Finally, to rally employees behind the common goal that would orient future decisions, he suggested they captured and articulated the philosophy rooted in the company's entrepreneurial roots. The result, *ACT with PRIDE*, turned the acronym for Alimentation Couche-Tard into both a verb, a maxim for the company to follow, and a descriptor, suggesting the satisfaction with the company's service and a sense of success felt within the group.

The project was well received by management—so much so that some started referring to Schram's proposal as the "Lofoten Declaration." With great pride, Schram describes it as "the start of a new era for the company." But it is also true, he says, that "this has been a tough journey for Alain—very tough." Bouchard was used to being in command: the conductor tirelessly steering the train, which seemed to take on an ever-growing number of cars. But Couche-Tard had gathered such momentum that it was finally propelling forward, guided by its own logic, beyond his ability to control it. The vehicle's size had grown far beyond anything that Bouchard could have envisioned 30 years prior, when he would set out on weekends, tool box in hand, to singlehandedly transform old smoke shops into small neighbourhood convenience stores.

Would any tangible trace remain from that era of pioneering? For a while, Bouchard had hoped to keep the emblem: the friendly, winking owl that watched over Couche-Tard's Quebec stores. "It's our nicest logo," he says. But the transplant would have felt forced. It also would have clashed with the new unified trademark, which would be approved by the board in the summer of 2015. The mere unveiling of that decision had such strategic importance for the company that the operation was given a code name: "Skyfall," inspired by the latest James Bond film. In Oslo, the occasion was marked by an event at Telenor Arena, a soccer stadium that can seat 25,000 spectators. With all of SFR's managers, franchisees, employees and suppliers in attendance, it had almost the quality of a spiritual ceremony to mark the abandoning of one "religion," and to announce the arrival of a new one.

The new Circle K banner, now redesigned, would begin its rollout in January 2016, first in the United States, then six months later in Europe, and the next year in Canada. But there would be no rollout in Quebec. That decision elicited a certain amount of disappointment within the company. Some saw it as a double standard on the part of management: *Do as I say, not as I do.*

Quebec is often compared to the Gallic village in the *Asterix* comics so popular in the Francophone world. The province has resisted the steamroller of Anglo-Saxon culture, just as the outrageously likeable comic book characters—from the imagination of René Goscinny and the pen of Albert Uderzo—defy domination by the Roman Empire. Couche-Tard's founders, living examples of the economic self-affirmation of Francophone Quebecers, have refused to bind their company with a name that has no connection to their own backgrounds. Not only would such a move betray their own origins, it would also have negative consequences for their business in Quebec. One of Couche-Tard's strategists puts it philosophically: "As long as the founders are still involved in the company, we understand that it would be like asking parents to change the name of their child."

CHAPTER 24

Transmitting Passion

In the months leading up to the publication of this book, Couche-Tard has continued to grow, acquiring more than 1,000 new stores.

After a year of efforts, in March 2016, the company received approval from the European Commission to complete its purchase of Shell's retail activities in Denmark, along with 300 gas stations and automated service stations. Around the same time, Couche-Tard achieved its planned conquest of a new geographical territory in Europe, with the purchase of Topaz Energy Group Limited in Ireland. Gaining 444 service stations and more than 30 gasoline terminals—a number of which had recently been acquired from Esso—the Laval-based company became in one scoop the biggest player in the Irish convenience store market.

Also in March 2016, Couche-Tard consolidated its position as the leader in the Canadian market, by announcing the signing of an agreement to acquire 279 convenience stores and service stations operating under the Esso name. Mainly located in the Toronto region—where real estate prices are prohibitive— these stores represent Couche-Tard's biggest breakthrough in Canada since the acquisition of Silcorp in 1999. The deal, for close to CAD $1.7 billion, is also the most expensive in Couche-Tard's history in terms of average price per store.

The recent slump in the price of oil didn't prevent the company from recording a 10 percent increase in net earnings over the third quarter of 2016, for a total of USD $274 million.

When the smoke clears from these transactions, the company will have 105,000 employees around the world, and its sales approaching USD $40 billion.

* * *

Surprisingly, despite his wealth and success, Alain Bouchard's life has changed relatively little over the years. He moves mainly between the office—where he chairs Couche-Tard's board of directors, attends all monthly accounting meetings and studies each project for implementing new stores—and the chalet he owns in the Laurentians, north of Montreal, where he has friends and hobbies. There's no castle in Spain, no apartment in New York or Paris, no yachts or helicopters. He continues to have a passion for great wine from France or Italy, and for fishing trips that take him all over the world, from New Zealand to Patagonia, from Northern Quebec to the Antarctic. "We're a little obsessed," says his fishing buddy, Réal Raymond. The first real luxury Bouchard acquired came in 2016: a floating condo on a cruise ship that constantly travels the world. As for his house in Laval—posh, but with no extravagance that would make it stand out from neighbouring properties—Bouchard says it's a little bigger than he needs now that the kids have left the nest.

His son Jonathan lives in an adapted home, a dozen apartments, built, with financial support from Bouchard, to house people suffering from cerebral palsy or intellectual disability. This way, Jonathan enjoys a healthy amount of autonomy and a social network suited to his condition. A sports lover, Jonathan cycles thousands of kilometres a year—his main means of transportation. Neither his condition nor his father's fortune prevents him from making a contribution by working.

That's why he spends one day a week at Couche-Tard's mail service and two days housekeeping.

For Bouchard, the adapted home project sprang out of his growing awareness of the lack of resources for people with disabilities; it was also a point of entry for his increasing engagement in philanthropic activities. Having dreamed in his twenties of devoting his life to social work, only to throw himself into the all-consuming project of developing his own company, Bouchard ended up accumulating a considerable fortune. His wealth would allow him to make up for lost time. You might say the ant was ready to discover the joys of living like a grasshopper.

Already, in the 1990s, Bouchard had invested in fundraising campaigns for various organizations, like United Way, which funds myriad services for the less fortunate. His son's illness had required Bouchard to visit one hospital after another so he started handing out millions of dollars of donations: for stem cell research at Maisonneuve-Rosemont Hospital in Montreal; for the establishment of a research program for developmental disabilities at the Montreal Neurological Institute and Hospital; and for the creation of the Jonathan-Bouchard Intellectual Disability Research Chair at Sainte-Justine Hospital, the principal children's hospital centre in Quebec, which brings together the province's top cerebral palsy specialists.

These funds come from the Sandra and Alain Bouchard Foundation, which has vast resources at its disposal—close to $100 million. Donating millions of dollars each year, the foundation is dedicated to two causes: developmental disabilities and the arts. Its projects have included the expansion of the Musée National des Beaux-Arts du Québec (Quebec Fine Arts Museum); and providing funding for the Peter Hall School, which specializes in education for youth with developmental disabilities. Bouchard has powerful memories of his first visit to the Peter Hall School, where he was moved to tears by the dedication of employees working with children with conditions so severe they were unable to even feed themselves.

The three other founders of Couche-Tard have their own foundations as well, through which they share their good fortune with the communities they grew up in. The founders sometimes coordinate their philanthropic activities to carry out projects. One such project was a home for palliative care in Laval. Réal Plourde's wife, Ariane was responsible for bringing that project to the founders. As she neared the end of her career in community health care, Ariane found it harder and harder to accept that citizens of Laval, the second biggest city in Quebec, lacked a peaceful place for people to die surrounded by their loved ones. The only real alternative was dying in a sterile, anonymous hospital room. Approaching the end of one's life, she believes, should not be treated the same as suffering from a disease. After looking at various sites on the immense island of Laval, Ariane and her team found a large plot of land near the river. It belonged to a religious community that was ready to part with it for such a good cause—a cause that would also give them a cash infusion, which they would use for their aging members who needed more care as time went on.

It took only a few minutes to settle the matter during a dinner with the four founders of Couche-Tard. Each of them would take on an equal share of the cost for the land along the Rivière-des-Prairies. Bouchard also took the role of chair of the fundraising campaign, which raised the money for construction of the building. Today, 250 people each year spend their final days in the establishment; Bouchard's own mother passed away peacefully under its roof. He believes he couldn't have asked for a better environment, so much more intimate and peaceful than a hospital, especially for a woman who had suffered the trauma of spending two years in a psychiatric institution.

Réal Plourde has long held the position of chair of the palliative care centre's board of administration, and has spent 20 years with the Centre de Bénévolat et Moisson Laval, first as an administrator and later as president. This organization was originally created to provide food to those in need by taking donations from food chains, distributors and farmers (of which there are still many in Laval, despite the extensive impact of real estate development on the island). The centre has diversified its operations over the years: for instance, by helping students with learning disabilities with their homework after school, and recruiting volunteers to assist the elderly in preparing their tax returns.

* * *

Alain Bouchard is at the age where one starts to focus on the next generation. The future of his own company isn't his sole concern: He has made a number of public comments on the woeful state of basic economic education in Quebec public schools. The education system, he believes, should properly prepare young people, the workers and consumers of the future, to prosper in their society. What tools are students being given to help them escape the traps of overconsumption and debt? What role models will they look to as they make their career choices?

Although economics courses have disappeared from Quebec's curriculum in secondary school, the neighbouring province of Ontario offers introductory business courses to high school students. The Future Entrepreneurs program focuses on exploring the fundamentals of economics—demographics and natural resources, for instance—but also promotes entrepreneurship, ensuring that young people can envision a career in business.

The concern has almost become an obsession for Bouchard: that of introducing young people to the field of entrepreneurship, and convincing them that they too can be the inventors of their own lives. Through mentoring and talking to budding entrepreneurs and delivering university lectures, Bouchard has sought to share the flame that has inspired him since the age of 10: the desire to build, the hunger to win and the pride in achievement. For Bouchard, it's tragic that this feeling is weaker and less urgently felt in Quebec today than in the time when he grew up, during the Quiet Revolution, when the desire for economic liberation was blended with the passion for national affirmation.

At the start of 2015, the disappearance of a number of well-established head offices in Quebec led to a debate on the importance of keeping decision-making centres within the province and thus maintaining the expertise that goes hand in hand with them. Formally, Couche-Tard may claim that their operation in Laval is not a headquarters, rather a mere service centre; but there's no denying that this centre is more *central* than most. That's also where the company's corporate taxes to the Quebec and Canadian governments are paid. At a time when governments around the world are worried about eroding revenue caused by the virtual economy, Couche-Tard and its founders still remember where the ground under their feet is from.

The debate on the preservation of Quebec's headquarters gave Bouchard the opportunity to defend preferred shares with multiple voting rights. A number of leading Quebec and Canadian multinationals own these kinds of shares, called Class A shares. Normally reserved for founders and their families, it allows them to keep a majority of votes while holding only a minority of shares in the company. Each preferred share can count for five, 10 or even 25 votes, while a common share, called a Class B subordinate voting share, only grants one vote to its holder.

In the case of Couche-Tard, the four founders share 113 million preferred shares, each of them counting for 10 votes, and 16 million subordinate voting shares. While possessing "only" 22.7 percent of Couche-Tard's capital, they hold 60 percent of the votes.

CGI, a Quebec technology giant that employs more than 65,000 workers around the world; Bombardier, third largest civil aircraft manufacturer in the world and second largest manufacturer of rail equipment; and even Quebecor, the media empire: All of these companies benefit from this type of share ownership, which helps ensure the companies' stability. With a controlling interest, the founders or their heirs can run a company based on its long-term growth, rather than letting it be governed by the desire to please the markets quarter after quarter, with the risk of being the target of a hostile takeover at the slightest misstep.

The Couche-Tard shareholders would probably be the first to acknowledge that they haven't suffered much hardship as a result of the control of the four founders. One hundred dollars invested in 1986, when Couche-Tard went public, was worth $60,000 30 years later, in the spring of 2016. In just six years, from April 2010 to 2016, the share price rose by more than 800 percent, while the average index value rose by 25 percent over the same period.

The preferred shares formula does have its critics. They see a risk that the companies will become locked into incompetent management with no regard for the interests of "common" shareholders. They also worry that management's position of control would discourage any attempt from an outside firm to acquire the company, depriving shareholders of an attractive premium meant to incite them to sell their shares. But who's to say whether Couche-Tard or CGI wouldn't have been swallowed by a competitor, or worse, by a speculative fund, that would have split it up and sold it in pieces to make a quick profit?

Yet the dual categories for Couche-Tard shares will come to an end when the youngest of the company's four founders, Jacques D'Amours, reaches the age of 65, in 2021. The group will then hold just less than 25 percent of the votes. "The company will become vulnerable to acquisitions," says Bouchard with regret. Bouchard tried unsuccessfully to have a postponement of this sunset clause approved by Couche-Tard's shareholders during the annual shareholder's meeting in 2015. "It's not attractive to leave our children a company that they won't have any control over," says the Couche-Tard founder. His displeasure was so great he went so far as to publicly[47] entertain the idea of selling the company—even if "it would break my heart."

* * *

The exceptional history of Couche-Tard is no doubt a textbook case of a business success, one that could be taught in universities to spark the wildest dreams of young entrepre-

---

47. *La Presse +*, April 20, 2016 edition.

neurs. Starting with nothing, lacking a diploma, fired by Perrette, expelled from his first two first Provi-Soir depanneurs, Bouchard went on to conquer Canada, then the United States, then Europe, to become a world leader in convenience stores. But it would be a mistake to grant Bouchard sole credit for the accomplishment. Moreover, by his own admission, it would betray everything that made the company succeed. Bouchard's formula is based precisely on recognizing his own limits and surrounding himself with people he considers better than himself. "It starts," he says, "with my three partners."

Jacques D'Amours, the meticulous operator; Richard Fortin, the ingenious financier; Réal Plourde, the logistician of human resources: All three supported Bouchard in his passionate, sometimes impetuous approach to developing their shared project. They were even obliged, at times, to protect him from himself. This complementary relationship between the four partners grew organically, becoming stronger with each of Couche-Tard's conquests, and even more so with every crisis they had to make it through. "Every obstacle helped each of us learn about our strengths and weaknesses," says Bouchard. They discovered how to find their own place, to develop their area of expertise, which meant that the CEO didn't have to try to play every role himself. "A bank would call me and I would tell them, 'Talk to Richard,'" Bouchard explains. "That's the secret," says D'Amours. "We never looked over each others' shoulders. We trusted each other completely. And we've always respected each other."

Like a powerful engine, constantly pushing forward to lead the development of the company of which he is the founder and main shareholder, Bouchard is the public face of the company. Internally, however, he has not dominated like some all-powerful father figure, with authoritative reign over his family. Instead, he always played the role of a big brother, focusing on unifying and inspiring. "It has never been a one-man-show," says Plourde. "Alain knew how to give us room to develop."

The philosophy that pervaded the very top of the company ended up seeping into the entire corporate culture. "These guys, they have their feet on the ground," says Hans-Olav Høidahl, the vice-president of Couche-Tard's Scandinavian business area. "After all these years, despite the fact that they have an immense fortune, you still feel that they are ordinary people." And in his view, that, almost paradoxically, is what makes them extraordinary leaders. "They listen. When he [Alain] is visiting stores, he isn't talking to us. He's talking to the store managers, the store employees and the market manager. He has strong interpersonal relationships skills. He connects and he gives them attention." Høidahl even compares Bouchard to Bill Clinton, with his ability to energize the people he meets.

Humility and lack of ego as a business model and mode of operation: It's an unusual proposition. But that's the inspiration for the highly decentralized structure of Couche-Tard; and according to its founders, it's the reason for its international success. Bouchard summarizes this philosophy in one word: empowerment. The concept doesn't merely weaken the notion of top-down authority—it establishes a whole new category of leadership, one based on trust.

"Empowerment" has a constellation of meanings: emancipation, autonomy, accountability. All of these follow from the Couche-Tard model. But above all, it's about a single belief: that human beings will find fulfillment in their work so long as they face the right challenges, and have the freedom they need to meet those challenges and to prove themselves. Giving them room to manoeuvre encourages initiative and rewards creativity. The corollary of empowerment—an indispensable corollary—is tolerance for error. Without that, creative impulses end up being repressed, and new ideas quashed as soon as they appear, or, worse, punished if they fail to bring about the desired results. Ultimately, empowerment for Couche-Tard means fostering, throughout the entire organization, a state of mind that makes the company a network of entrepreneurs.

That's Alain Bouchard's fundamental belief, a notion embedded in his life since childhood: that being an entrepreneur means having the power to invent one's own life, and there's no greater feeling than being able to achieve that dream.

Epilogue

As this book was going to press at the end of August 2016, printing had to be delayed in order that an epilogue could be added. The timing was remarkable: Once again, Couche-Tard had just made "the largest acquisition in its history," this time by purchasing CST Brands, the fourth largest network of convenience stores and service stations in North America. The addition of almost 2,000 stores would allow Couche-Tard to surpass 7-Eleven as the biggest player in the convenience store industry in the United States and Canada. When the process of converting the additional thousand-odd stores acquired by its affiliate in Mexico to the Circle K banner is completed, Couche-Tard will be in first place in terms of number of stores in North America.

The company has also risen to the top in terms of gasoline sales. "Now, with CST, we are certainly one of the largest fuel retailers in the world," says Brian Hannasch, president of Couche-Tard. "We retail almost 17 billion gallons. That's starting to be in the same league as the BPs and Essos of the world."

The story of CST Brands is similar to that of SFR, Couche-Tard's last multibillion dollar acquisition, in Scandinavia. SFR was an outgrowth of Statoil. CST Brands was an outgrowth of oil company Valero. After taking a beating on the stock market and failing to produce results that satisfied shareholders,

CST Brands had been forced (unlike SFR) to publicly announce its intention to sell to the highest bidder. Its fate would be decided by auction, and Couche-Tard took home the prize. It was an outcome that Alain Bouchard had dreamed of for 20 years.

CST Brands, based in San Antonio, was something of a strange creature; a two-headed beast, in effect. It had more than 600 stores in Texas, one of the largest American states and one in which Couche-Tard had hardly any presence. But it also owned more than 800 stores in Canada, mainly in Quebec, directed by its headquarters in Montreal. The company had also recently bought several hundred stores in Georgia and the New York region, going heavily into debt to do so, which put it in a vulnerable position. Its service stations in Canada operated under the Ultramar brand, with gasoline provided by the refinery of the same name in Lévis, on the other side of the St. Lawrence River, from Quebec City—a refinery owned by Valero. The refinery was thought to be one of the most profitable in North America. It is certainly the one with the nicest view, looking out onto the fortifications of Old Quebec, with its ramparts and the crown of the magnificent Château Frontenac hotel.

In the mid-1990s, a few years before embarking on the expansion into the United States, Bouchard had set his sights on Ultramar's service stations—indeed, he had practically moved heaven and earth to acquire them. The refinery had just launched a network of convenience stores operating under the "Dépanneur du coin" (meaning "Corner Store") banner, after having bought a number of Sunoco stations in the Quebec City region, but the company was struggling. The head of Couche-Tard thus began a search for a partner to take over the refinery, leaving Couche-Tard with the service stations and convenience stores.

Bouchard knocked on the door of Robert Dutil, owner of Canam Group, a firm specializing in steel processing. The argument Bouchard pressed on Dutil was that the latter's reputation as a formidable entrepreneur would help him diversify in the oil sector. "He told me, 'It's too big, we aren't going to do it,'" says Bouchard. But the refusal did nothing to discourage the founder of Couche-Tard.

Bouchard turned instead to the energy giant Hydro-Québec, which had a virtual monopoly on production, distribution and retail sale of hydro-electric energy in Quebec. The company had recently acquired a 42 percent stake in Noverco, the holding company for Gaz Métro, the main distributor of natural gas in Quebec and Vermont. The new president of Hydro-Québec, André Caillé, the former head of Gaz Métro, declared that he wanted to transform Quebec into an "energy hub in northeast North America." Bouchard took him at his word. Along with Richard Fortin, he approached Caillé to propose that he add oil refining to his energy portfolio, by adding the Ultramar refinery, leaving Couche-Tard in charge of retail distribution. The discussion was short. Thierry Vandal, the Hydro-Québec president's right hand man (and his successor-to-be), was firm: The refinery didn't fit with Hydro-Québec's mandate.

A third attempt was necessary. Bouchard approached Jean Gaulin, head of the Ultramar refinery—which, a few years later, in 2001,[48] would take Gaulin's name after it was acquired by Valero Energy. It took a certain amount of boldness to propose that the loyal leader take advantage of his group's temporary weakness to purchase it. Gaulin's response was that,

---

48 The Jean Gaulin Refinery has a production capacity of 265,000 barrels a day, making it the 19th-largest in North America and the second largest owned by Valero.

unlike Bouchard, he didn't have the entrepreneurial drive; the project didn't interest him.

Bouchard's hopes would be in limbo until almost a decade later. In the meantime, Couche-Tard became the biggest network of convenience stores in Canada, and the company was about to expand across North America. Then, Bouchard, along with Hannasch, visited Valero headquarters in San Antonio to make an offer: Couche-Tard would buy all of Valero's retail operations in the United States and Canada. It was right after the economic crisis of 2008, and the Couche-Tard owl had caught the scent of vulnerable prey. But the two men were refused once again. A few years later, in 2013, Valero chose to create a new company listed on the New York Stock Exchange—CST Brands—which would take over its entire retail sector, just as Statoil had recently done in Scandinavia with SFR.

The same recipe, the same disappointing results for shareholders. Bouchard believes it's hard for administrators from the oil industry, a world in which heavy management infrastructure is common, to make the transition to retail. Founded in 2013, CST Brands launched itself too quickly into costly expansion projects, says Hannasch. "They had a cost structure that grew too fast. The costs seemed to rise at a faster rate than the sales and the profit margin did," he says. Share value stagnated.

At the end of 2015, two activist investors, the speculative fund Engine Capital, L.P., and JCP Investment Management, started demanding a change of direction. In a letter to the CST Brands' board of directors made public in December 2015, they attacked the administration's inability to perform as well as their leading competitors: "CST has consistently lagged the better operators on the key relevant metrics," they charged.

Four months later, the board moved into action, announcing that it would be "exploring strategic alternatives to enhance stockholder value." The result: The company was put up for sale to the highest bidder. Engine Capital, L.P., publicly expressed the desire to see shares go higher than USD $50. In August 2016, Couche-Tard finally pushed the price to USD $48.53 per share, a 42 percent premium on the last share price of March 3, 2016, before the intention to sell the company had been revealed. The friendly offer was signed on Sunday, August 21, after being unanimously approved by the two companies' respective boards. It was, Bouchard says, "the end result of an epic six-month battle." With the U.S. economy having rebounded after some difficult years, a number of other players had been in the running.

Once the deal was approved by shareholders and regulators, the acquisition of CST Brands brought an additional USD $10 billion to Couche-Tard's annual sales: The total rose to USD $50 billion. According to analysts, the company's pre-tax profits were set to rise from USD $2.2 billion to USD $3.3 billion in two years—an increase of more than 40 percent.

It goes without saying that the news made a splash on the markets. Couche-Tard shares, being traded around $58 during the summer, leapt to $68—a historic increase. Couche-Tard's management team was universally applauded for its exceptional ability to successfully transform each of their acquisitions and create value for shareholders. It was true that, despite its liquidity and lines of credit, buying CST Brands for USD $4.4 billion in cash would significantly increase Couche-Tard's debt level; but the company had always been able to regain equilibrium in a very short time. "We take it seriously," says Hannasch, "and we will be focusing on deleveraging as quickly as we can in order to be ready for other opportunities."

Press coverage of the deal reflected Couche-Tard's reputation as a sharp and disciplined decision-maker, and there was little in the way of skepticism. The company's exceptional performance has provoked widespread admiration, if not outright envy: $1,000 invested in 2003, the year of the Circle K acquisition, gained enough value to be worth $25,000 13 years later.

The acquisition of CST Brands was also a strategic coup, since its main assets in the United States are perfect complements to the territories already served by Couche-Tard. This is especially true in Texas and, to a lesser extent, Georgia and the U.S. Northeast. Kim Lubel, president and CEO of CST Brands, says that the two companies's respective geographical footprints "fit together like a jigsaw puzzle." But while this may be true in the United States, the reality is different in Canada, and especially in Quebec.

While Bouchard was achieving the dream he had cherished for 20 years—to acquire the Ultramar network—he also found himself facing a dilemma. Couche-Tard had become too big; its share of the retail oil market in Quebec was too dominant. The company had become a target of suspicion for the Competition Bureau.

Thus the announcement of the purchase of CST Brands was accompanied by news of another deal: The Alberta company Parkland Fuel would buy the majority of the Canadian shares of CST Brands. For approximately USD $750 million, Parkland would take over 490 dealer-owned Ultramar stations, 72 automated supply sites for trucks, the heating oil distribution network, the company's headquarters in Montreal, and close to half the corporate stores owned by CST Brands, operating under the "Depanneur du coin" and "Corner Store" banner. The Competition Bureau would determine how much needed to be shed to maintain healthy competition in Quebec's gas market.

Couche-Tard's administration had other dealings with regulatory authorities in the recent past, when it purchased several hundred Esso stations. One of the lawyers advising the company during the CST Brands deal had worked for the Competition Bureau several years earlier. "When you go past 35 percent of market share in a sector," Bouchard says, "the Bureau asks you to dispose of some assets. We agreed."

In Bouchard's assessment, Couche-Tard could keep around 160 of CST Brand's corporate stores in Canada, most of which are in Quebec, which would allow it reach optimal market penetration. Its future expansion will take place in other territories. With the company having surpassed 7-Eleven to become the leader in terms of number of stores—an achievement that feels really good, Bouchard admits—the United States market offers much more opportunity for an integrator like Couche-Tard.

It's clear that the incredible size Couche-Tard has reached today makes the company a growing target for a hostile takeover. While such a possibility is not beyond imagining, it would be almost impossible in practice, under current market conditions in which investors, trusting in the performance of Couche-Tard's administrators, grant it a high premium. In another era, not so long ago, when Couche-Tard shares were unpopular, the company could certainly have been seized by speculative funds, had it not been for the four founders' ability to block these attempts. It's impossible to say whether a similar situation could happen in the future; but some analysts believe that the best guarantee of Couche-Tard's longevity remains its discipline and its culture, which make the company truly unique, and which are the reason six million customers return to its outlets, day after day.

Acknowledgements

I would like to thank everyone who contributed to the creation of this book: first and foremost, Alain Bouchard, who took the risk of telling his story to a journalist he barely knew, and who could not be certain how it would all turn out. Many thanks as well to his three loyal partners, Jacques D'Amours, Richard Fortin and Réal Plourde, for having generously shared their time. I would like to mention the contribution of Martine Coutu, assistant to Alain Bouchard, who provided constant support as I dug my way through the company's archives. Dozens more people generously gave me their valuable time, some by offering their thoughts and memories for this book, others by helping me come to a fuller understanding of the company and its history. I would like to offer my deepest gratitude to all of these individuals, and I hope that they see this book as a true reflection of the things they shared with me.

I would especially like to thank Pauline Normand for her invaluable advice, and Monique Leroux for having agreed to write the preface.

Finally, this book would not have been possible without the support of my beloved spouse, Brigitte, who had to endure my absence for much of the last year or so. I thank her for her limitless patience.

Table of Contents

RECYCLED
Paper made from
recycled material
FSC® C103567

Printed by Marquis Imprimeur inc.
Printed on Rolland Enviro, which contains 100% postconsumer
fiber, is ECOLOGO, Processed Chlorine Free,
Ancient Forest Friendly and FSC® certified
and is manufactured using renewable biogas energy.

PERMANENT

100%

Ancient
Forest
Friendly™